Women Can Find Shipwrecks Too

a true story by

MARGARET L. BRANDEIS

for Comet Shipping Corp. Ltd.

Le Gesse Stevens Publishing

WOMEN CAN FIND SHIPWRECKS TOO

Le Gesse Stevens Publishing
3333 Midway Dr.
Dept. 102
San Diego, CA 92110

Cover Photo by Terry VanderHeiden

First Edition

Manufactured in the United States of America

ISBN: 1-893181-28-6
Library of Congress Card Catalog Number: 99-65662

This is a true story however some of the names have been changed so the real people may remain anonymous

This book is dedicated to Kevin

Author's Note

Of all the soul-gripping, risk-taking, spine-quivering adventures available in this world, I chose treasure hunting. The kind of hunt that puts you out on the high seas searching for a sunken Spanish galleon. The kind that infests you with gold fever and taunts you with old treasure maps. The kind that twists your guts with…... anticipation.

In the beginning, I couldn't wait to get my hands on that treasure. Every ounce of me tingled with the excitement of the hunt, the thrill of fortune within my grasp. Every sensation I experienced was magnified, because I wasn't just living, I was living an adventure.

But adventures have a way of turning into journeys that take us deep within ourselves. Journeys that test our fortitude and challenge our belief systems.

On this particular adventure, as I craved for riches, I was forced to examine my inner thought processes in such fine detail that by the end of the journey, I had discovered the very nature of our world and how it is intrinsically linked to the contents of our thoughts.

So I started out searching for sunken treasure and ended up finding the secret to the physical universe: That as you believe, so it is with you.

Mount of Christo at SE
apeares thus

is the fault point
is the ancre

Zecula   Manta

C. S. Luini
End of Larene

End of Larene

Rand   Flagat

End of Manilt

End of Cement

In this ship was 30 million royals
and 37 pieces of ordnance. And on the
same rocks hath been lost many more ships.

PART ONE

... your imaginative people swing farther in any direction, as if given a longer scope of cable in the uneasy anchorage of life.

Joseph Conrad
Lord Jim

Chapter One

Did you ever wonder what might happen if you suddenly got the notion to run off in search of sunken treasure? I never really had the notion, but Kevin did. In fact, I never wondered about treasure at all,until the night of the big celebration party at our ranch. The night Kevin and Jake and I were lounging in the hot tub drinking a bottle of tequila someone from the party had left behind.

It was 1977, the beginning of the yuppie era, and my husband Kevin and I were at the head of the yuppie pack. We swore we would escape the monotonous, predictable, sitcom life by concentrating on money and the accumulation of material wealth. We were DINKS (double-income-no-kids) before the word was ever invented. I was a real estate broker and Kevin owned a scuba diving school and retail dive shop. We had a gray BMW, a hairy sheepdog named Brandy, and two Arabian horses with a third on the way. As soon as we bought the ranch, which my real estate guide had called a "genuine fixer-upper," I decided to retire from the commission-check world and start devoting my days to fixing up the property.

Mornings began with a country breakfast and Kevin driving off to his dive store. As his van rumbled away down the dirt driveway,

Brandy would meet me on the porch, wait for me to pull on my cowboy boots, then race me to the barn door. I would feed the goat, the chickens, the sheep, the horses, and shoot at the neighbor's ducks with my BB gun to keep them from shitting all over our yard. By noon the garden was watered, all the chicken eggs were found, the horses were turned out to graze, and I was headed back to the house to find Brandy sprawled on the porch, flinching through her afternoon nap. It was great. I could hear nature. The breeze that rustled the birch leaves mingled with the sounds of stomping hooves and chirping birds. The nearest human noise was on the other side of the hill. My hands were always dirty. I spent afternoons just walking the fence line smelling the hay or picking apples in the orchard. I knew the time of day by the position of the sun and had dinner ready when Kevin's van came rumbling back up the driveway. The ranch had been *my* lifelong dream.

Jake came to live with us just after we moved to the ranch. We met him at somebody's wedding reception and he followed us home in the faded, sky blue, '56 Chevy pickup truck he called *La Bamba*. Boredom and the lack of good-paying jobs had brought Jake to the bustling San Francisco Bay Area from the pine-tree-covered hills of north central California. He was a real mountain boy, with rugged hands and a natural way with animals. He had twinkling eyes, and jolly, round Santa Claus cheeks that rested on top of his mustache and beard like two rosy golf balls. An unruly mop of curly brown hair covered his head. We gave him the spare bedroom in exchange for helping us renovate the ranch and he soon became family.

With a beer in hand and his carpenter's belt half falling off his narrow hips, Jake helped me finish building the twenty horse stalls that had been started by the previous owner. It was a filthy job. The cobwebs in the lumber stack were so thick we found

2

dead mice inside them. There were mounds of horse manure so big it took a bulldozer to move them. And behind the barn, we sorted through a pile of scrap building materials so high, we found a two-ton dump truck buried underneath. We sold the truck to buy eighty gallons of paint and when we were finished, the barn was pale yellow with white doors and brown trim to match the house. The grounds were planted with pine trees and roses, juniper bushes, and lawn. We even put planter boxes, bursting with yellow daisies, at the stable entrance.

Now it was two years later, the stalls were all rented and the work was done. We had transformed a run-down, half-finished, manure-smelling barn into a picturesque horse boarding stable, nestled in the rolling hills east of San Francisco. My dream had come true.

To celebrate we threw a party nobody would forget, a real boot-stomping humdinger with a live band playing for three hundred of our friends and neighbors. The orchard was lined with hay bales and brightly colored plastic flags. Under a blazing noon-day sun we barbecued a hundred chickens smothered in hickory-smoke sauce and served 'em up with beans, potato salad and thirty homemade apple pies.

The redwood deck and hot tub we'd built behind the house were the main attractions at the party. All day long pretty, blond cowgirls in denim hot-pants just seemed to fall into that hot tub as the aroma of beer and barbeque sauce swirled through the air.

At sunset, when the band finally packed up and the partygoers staggered home, the place looked like a cyclone had hit it. The orchard was carpeted in paper plates and loose straw. Cowboy hats dangled from tree branches. Beer cans were scattered everywhere. As the stars came out, only Kevin, Jake and I were left, sitting in the hot tub, drinking tequila shooters.

3

The night was warm and we were glowing with self-satisfaction, remembering the highlights of the afternoon. Then silence overtook us for awhile, each of us lost in our own private replay of the day, until Jake broke the stillness with a seemingly innocent question.

"So, you guys have finished the ranch," he said, tugging at his beard hairs. "Now what are you going to do?"

"I don't know," I confessed, frowning a bit. "I thought the ranch was my dream come true. But I'm getting tired of all the chores, the constant repairs, and the griping horse owners. I guess my dream was a still-life photograph. I never thought about dream maintenance."

We pondered Jake's question for a long while, like you tend to do when you're inebriated. Silence and the night were drifting in on us again as we tried to think of something worth doing. Suddenly, Kevin sat bolt upright, splashing water over the edge of the hot tub. "I know," he shouted as if some equation in his head had finally flashed the correct answer, "Let's go treasure hunting!"

That's how this whole adventure started.

❦

When a scuba diver says treasure hunting, there's only one thing on his mind - sunken ships. As for me, sunken treasure was never on my mind until I saw the far-off look in Kevin's eyes that night in the hot tub. It was the same look I'd had whenever I'd thought about the ranch. It's the unblinking stare one has while in the grips of raw desire uninhibited by obligations, or rationality, or cost. It's a fixation on a single idea that has clawed its way into conscious thought, holding you spellbound. It's the look of someone dreaming.

Okay, I thought. Why not? I'm up for an adventure. If I had a crack at my dream, Kevin should have a crack at his. I had had my fill of ranch life for awhile, and we were only talking a year or so, right? Might be fun. We might even find a bunch of treasure and be rich. The idea was sounding better all the time.

We discussed sunken treasure every night that week after the party. On Friday it was my turn to be the dive master on Kevin's monthly dive trip to the Channel Islands, off the coast of southern California. The trip consisted of bussing thirty fun-loving divers from the Bay Area down to Santa Barbara, where an eighty-five-foot boat would take them diving all weekend. Kevin and I usually went on the trip together, but a backlog of office work made him beg me to go alone this time.

The bus ride was the usual drunken mayhem - people falling into the center aisle, or trying to squeeze themselves into the overhead luggage racks. The sport of scuba diving had come to attract a different crowd since I had taken my first plunge more than a decade before. These weren't burly, spear gun toting divers in black rubber wet suits anymore. No, they were young couples trying the hot new sport everyone was talking about. They carried underwater cameras and wore neon colored dive gear. For them, the bus ride was a five-hour party.

The charter dive boats had changed with the diving clientele. No longer did the boats smell like rotten seaweed or bear the scars of previous lives as fishing tugs. They were now sleek and clean, with air conditioning and stereo music. The thing that hadn't changed was the ritual of carrying your dive gear down the dock and stowing it on board before drifting off to sleep on a vinyl-covered mattress.

Kevin's dive store always chartered the same Santa Barbara boat. She was a beauty, a steel-hull trawler design with parallelogram-shaped windows down both sides of the galley. She

5

had a fifty-foot-high crow's nest, a flying bridge, and a helicopter landing pad. On the bow, painted in large white block letters, was her name, *Coral Sea.*

The vessel had been built in an empty lot close to the harbor. A thousand people showed up at the dock the day she was launched. The local newspaper had described her as the Rolls Royce of the charter diving fleet, complete with three hot-water showers, five staterooms, and a microwave oven. Her impressive wheelhouse was trimmed in polished brass and had a carpeted floor. Electronic display monitors were mounted on the walls next to several different types of radios and radar screens. It was said that the captain's stateroom was bigger than the one on the famous ocean liner, the Queen Mary. She was the pride and joy of her designer, builder, and owner, the infamous Captain Glenn Miller.

Glenn was a mixture of Will Rogers and Ebenezer Scrooge. He was medium height, stout, and slightly bow-legged, a leftover from his rodeo days, he would say. He could be folksy and good-natured or stubborn as a mule. Most of all, he was a kid in a fifty-year-old body who had spent the better part of his life on the ocean, living as he pleased, hauling divers around to pay the bills.

Glenn and his springer spaniel dog, Mac, were minor legends around the Santa Barbara harbor. Every morning Glenn pulled his backfiring Volkswagen van into the marina parking lot, then he and Mac strode down the dock leaving a trail of smoke from Glenn's pipe as they headed for the *Coral Sea* berthed at the end of Marina #4. Diving was becoming popular enough to fill up a weekend charter, and Glenn, though not offering smiling service, knew all the best dive sites in the Channel Islands, just a two-hour ride from the harbor.

"Mac the Diving Dog" was also famous for setting world records. Wearing a pair of swim goggles, the dog could dive to the bottom of a twelve-foot-deep swimming pool and retrieve an abalone shell. On the *Coral Sea*, when Glenn shouted "shark!" Mac would race to the stern of the boat and jump into the ocean, barking all the way. When he came back out of the water, Mac usually went down into the bunk room and coiled up on someone's sleeping bag to dry off.

The escapades of Glenn and Mac were written up in a diving magazine, which gave them instant notoriety and nurtured Glenn's growing attitude of self-importance.

Glenn's circle of friends included pioneers in the diving industry, photographers, engineers, and Hollywood directors. Diving had a way of cutting across career boundaries, and Glenn had a way of attracting unusual charters. If you paid the price, you could come on Glenn's boat, unless he didn't like you - or Mac didn't like you. And once on board, you'd better not complain about anything or you would never be allowed on board again. Glenn had a pleasant way of treating you like shit, and the customers kept coming.

The crew aboard the *Coral Sea* consisted of Glenn's son, Zachary, and an endless succession of young, tanned girls with sun-bleached, blond hair and tiny bikinis. They came for the adventure and left when they were fed up with Glenn and with cooking for thirty divers. There was even a succession of Macs. When one Mac died, Glenn would buy another brown and white springer spaniel puppy and name it Mac. Glenn liked consistency.

It was Mac #3, barking at the sunrise, that woke me up that morning of the weekend dive trip, just before the engines roared to life and the *Coral Sea* motored out of the harbor towards the islands. As usual, I stayed in my bunk for the two-hour trip. Glenn once told me that crossing the Santa Barbara Channel was as dangerous as crossing the treacherous Straits of Magellan, but then everything Glenn said was exaggerated for effect. He also told me he never let the truth get in the way of a good story.

When we finally anchored in the calmer waters surrounding the islands, I went out on deck with my clipboard to compare the passenger list with the actual bodies on board. My main job was to make sure I came home with the same number of people with which I had left.

The uninhabited island shore, covered with tall grass bending in the breeze, lay a few hundred feet off the stern. Strands of tan-colored kelp floated peacefully on the gently surging water. Seagulls screeched high overhead. Playful sea otters popped their sleek heads above the surface to see who had invaded their marine playground, then they twitched their whiskers and dove underwater again to hide in the kelp. I sat at the stern on the wide metal railing checking off divers as they jumped overboard and sank out of site while Glenn's son, Zachary, filled scuba tanks nearby.

Zachary was the perfect example of Southern California youth; slim, tan, and muscular, with a smiling face and sun-streaked sandy brown hair. His job as first mate of the *Coral Sea* consisted of driving the boat and keeping the customers happy. Zach felt that life was for having a good time, and no matter what you did or promised, it was all over Sunday night when the charter ended.

When all the divers were in the water, I hung up the clipboard and passed through the galley on my way to the wheelhouse. I didn't really feel like diving that weekend. I could talk over the choice of dive sites with Glenn and then head for my beach towel. When I got to the top of the stairs I found Glenn, pipe in hand, laughing out loud as he stared out the back wheelhouse window. I peered out myself to see Mac, hind leg raised, pissing all over some poor customer's yellow dive bag.

"Damn dog's got a great sense of humor, ya know what I mean?" laughed Glenn. I tried to ignore the scene.

"What's the order of dive sites for the weekend?" I asked him, all businesslike.

"What's the matter with this place?" he snapped.

"Nothing," I said, a little defensively, "but people like a little variety."

"Aw, people don't know what they like," he grumbled. "They got clear water here. We'd probably go through all the hassle of pulling up anchor and motoring around, and all the other places would have wind chop and bad visibility and they'd just want to come back here, ya know what I mean?"

"It sounds like you're getting bored with these diving charters," I surmised as I gazed around the wheelhouse at the memorabilia. The ceiling was covered in framed photographs of Glenn and Mac and the *Coral Sea* in all phases of construction. On the walls, along with the vessel licenses and radio permits, were a commendation from the FBI for special service, autographed pictures, Coast Guard citations, and a dead frog carcass nailed through the belly.

"Yeah, well, I've been doin' these damn charters for twenty years," Glenn stated emphatically as he lit his pipe.

"Where did this come from?" I asked, nudging a coral encrusted cannonball with the tip of my sandal.

"That's a cannonball off the *Maravilla*," he said, leaning back in his chair. "The second richest ship ever to sink in the Western Hemisphere. Bob Marx gave me that after treasure huntin' in the Bahamas. Beauty, ain't it?"

"Yeah. But why don't you ever take *your* boat treasure hunting?" I asked, wondering where the conversation would lead.

"Hell, I *built* this boat to go treasure hunting!" he shouted, as if I were an idiot for not knowing. "Marx and I were going down to Panama until the whole thing fell apart. What do you think those stern capstans are for? Half the shit on this boat is just for treasure hunting. I'd go in a second if someone could put the right deal together. Takes a lot of money, ya know what I mean?"

"And if you had the right deal, where would you go?" I egged him on.

"Shit, I'd grab my buddy Dick Anderson and head right back to the Bahamas. They never got all the treasure off the *Maravilla*, and Anderson knows exactly where the rest of it's at!"

I kept Glenn talking all morning. He told me that Dick Anderson had been chief of diving operations when Bob Marx started excavating the shipwreck of the *Nuestra Señora de Las Maravillas*, a Spanish galleon that had sunk in 1656. They had only been working on the bow section of the wreck when the business dealings with the Bahamian officials went sour. "Marx got mad and called them a bunch of dirty names so they canceled his salvage lease," was the way Glenn put it. The main point was, there were still tons of gold and silver lying on the ocean floor. Glenn convinced me that he and Anderson were the best of buddies, and that the *Coral Sea* was the best boat for a treasure hunting job. If I really thought I could put a deal together, he said, I should go see Anderson in Santa Monica. It was that simple.

The only thing I remember about the next day was confusion - last-minute dives, counting noses and securing loose gear for the channel crossing back to Santa Barbara. I busied myself with dive master duties and had no time to think clearly until we were all back on the bus heading north to San Francisco.

Whew, what a weekend! Had I really discussed sunken treasure with Glenn? Was he really telling me the truth about the *Maravilla*? Maybe it was all just part of the charter, another scheme for keeping the customers happy. Maybe I was just another gullible diver sucked in by Glenn's treasure stories. Boy, he was slick.

I was smiling to myself at the whole silly weekend until I put my hand in my pocket and pulled out the napkin on which Glenn had scribbled Dick Anderson's address and phone number.

❦

I don't really know what I was expecting to find the morning I parked in front of a pea-green apartment building with 1940's style architecture. I couldn't quite believe that a real treasure hunter would live on the lower residential side of Santa Monica, two blocks off the main drag. I climbed the cement steps and knocked on the door marked 2B. Perhaps this was just a meeting place and the guy lived somewhere else. Smart thinking. He's probably very cagey. He's probably been watching me through a telescope from the moment I arrived. The palms of my hands started to sweat. What was I getting into here? I actually started to back down the steps when the door squeaked open slowly to reveal a tall, anorexic-looking man in a blue work shirt and jeans. His abundant silver gray hair was flying out in every direction from under an Australian bush hat.

"Are you Margee Brandeis?" he asked in a monotone voice as if my name were some kind of a password.

"Yes, Glenn Miller sent me," I answered innocently.

"I'm Dick Anderson," he said gallantly as he swung the door wide open. "C'mon in and have a seat. Don't mind all the junk. I spend a lotta time at flea markets. Can't pass up a good deal no matter how much I don't need it."

I stepped into a room that looked like a flea market itself; piles of boxes and magazines, bent and tarnished brass trumpets, a dirty leather-covered trunk, glass balls covered in fish netting, a wooden chair with a broken leg, tilted pictures on the wall to hide

11

the cracks. I sat on the well-worn sofa and Anderson sat at his desk, on the other side of the room, on an old, gray, office chair that had no back. The top of the desk was buried in disorganized stacks of paper a foot high with one lonely typewriter sitting stubbornly in the center. The Venetian blinds on the front window were casting a horizontal line pattern across the room as Anderson and I stared at each other for a few seconds, exchanging wary smiles.

"Glenn says you're interested in going after the *Maravilla*," Anderson said finally, getting straight to the point. "Let me tell you right off that I won't go into any deal for less than twenty-two percent."

"I suppose that's fair if you can take us right to the treasure," I replied. "Do you really know exactly where it's at?"

"Lady, I can smell gold underwater," he answered intently. "I found more treasure on that damn wreck than all the rest of Bob Marx's divers put together. And another thing. You'll have to agree to give me complete control of the salvage operation. If you or Glenn are gonna start interfering, it'll be all over. Glenn's my buddy, but he doesn't know shit about treasure salvage."

After I had agreed to his demands, Anderson loosened up. He swiveled around on the chair, searching through drawers and the mountain of papers to find me several magazine articles written about himself and ones he had written about Glenn and Mac. He gave me a blue business card with a caricature of a hard hat diver on it that read,

DICK ANDERSON Limited
(but not very)
Commercial Diver, Underwater Photography

He told me he'd been around diving all his life. Said he invented the single hose regulator but somebody else got the credit for it. He knew everybody in the diving business worth knowing, and by the end of the afternoon he had me believing he was the best salvage master I would ever find to recover the treasure of the *Maravilla*.

"We'll anchor right over that son-of-a-bitch and pull it all up in one 'swell foop,'" was the last thing he said to me, deliberately switching the first letters of the words. He'd say anything for a laugh.

It would be a year and a half before I realized he had never really answered my question about knowing the exact location of the treasure.

Chapter Two

The next thing I had to do was find the money. After Glenn and Dick helped me total all the costs, I realized I'd have to convince at least twenty people to give me ten thousand dollars each to finance the expedition. I had no idea of how to do that, but finally decided it was a question of appealing to instinct. Primeval hunters searched for food first, and then for wealth. Treasure hunting, I reasoned, is in our blood. It's one of the things people dream about. It's fortune and glory!

"It's also the Securities and Exchange Commission, angry partners, a waste of money, and dangerous!" my pessimistic lawyer friend told me the day I walked into his office, laid a thousand dollar check as a deposit on his desk, and told him I wanted to hunt for sunken treasure.

"You can't be serious," Ed said. "Treasure hunting is one of the riskiest ventures around. It probably has the highest failure rate of any endeavor on the planet. Margee, you're a smart girl. You've got a future in business. Why do you want to go flying off to never-never land?"

Ed was Harvard Law School from the tip of his neatly combed hair to the cuffs of his pin-striped suit. He was tenacious, sarcastic, and ambitious, and he always made me feel like I was on the witness stand whenever we talked. I was the kind of client he kept around for amusement, not for income, and I was definitely amusing him this time.

"Ed, I know this sounds a little crazy," I admitted, "but it's a great deal. I've got the wreck, a fantastic boat, and a professional who will teach me everything about treasure salvage. I can handle the administrative end. Just help me put it all on paper."

Ed was upset now. He was a man with a short temper and no patience for frivolous pursuits. When common sense failed to dissuade me, he started pacing the room.

"Have you considered for one single moment the liabilities and contractual obligations of such a risky enterprise?" he huffed.

"No, but I'm sure you're gonna tell me about them," I answered curtly.

"Well, a thousand dollars isn't going to get you anywhere," he scoffed, waving my check in the air.

"I've got lots more," I lied, not wanting to lose the argument.

He stopped pacing and squinted at me.

"In that case, pull up a chair."

I didn't lose the argument, but over the next two months I did lose eight thousand dollars to legal fees. This prompted some very serious discussions around the dinner table at the ranch. This wasn't hot tub fantasy anymore. This was our savings we were spending. It was major decision time.

In the end it was the idea of adventure that made us decide to sell everything we owned and commit ourselves to looking for treasure. Tom Robbins once wrote, "The principal difference between an adventurer and a suicide is that the adventurer leaves himself a margin of escape. The narrower the margin, the greater the adventure." Considering that the only things we would have left after we sold the ranch would be our furniture and clothes, this was going to be one hell of an adventure.

We rarely recognize it when the most pivotal moments in our lives are occurring. Usually because, they occur so innocently, when nobody else is watching. Also because it takes the clarity of hindsight to pinpoint the exact pivotal moment when your life was irretrievably altered.

I realize now that my pivotal moment occurred the day before the sale of the ranch. The day I found myself sitting alone on the front seat of Jake's truck, *La Bamba,* staring blankly through the windshield. It was then, in that manure-scented moment of solitude, that I convinced myself I had the guts and persistence to find a shipwreck.

I was twenty-seven years old. If I wanted to see the world, this was a glamorous opportunity. If I wanted to lose weight, being stuck on a boat would make it easier. If I needed a challenge in my business career, this would suffice. And if I didn't do it now, I probably never would. So I squinted my eyes like a cunning outlaw, clenched my fists in defiance of the ordinary and made up my mind to lead a treasure hunt, no matter what it takes!

❈

In order to raise money it was mandatory that I became acquainted with the Securities Act of 1933 and exemptions thereof. The words *whereas, therein, heretofore,* and *hereinafter* entered my vocabulary. My briefcase was filled with Private Placement Memorandums, Diver Applications, Prospective Purchaser Questionnaires, Subscription Agreements, and Photography Releases. I learned that my primary job while soliciting funds for our expedition was to tell people why they should *not* invest, summing it all up in one neat legal phrase: *the overwhelming statistical likelihood of failure.*

More lawyers got involved and the phone bill skyrocketed. I put 45,000 miles on our BMW in five months. I gave 216 presentations of the project to family, friends, friends of friends, business partners and innocent bystanders. In a stroke of inspiration I had named the partnership the **Caribbean Gold Company**, and my parents became my first investors.

There is no common denominator among people who invest in treasure hunts, no way to tell by looking at someone if they would even be interested. I told my story to anybody who would listen. I was shocked by those who turned me down, and more shocked by those who invested. I found out that as many as three hundred treasure expeditions get funded every year, although we never hear about most of them. Mine was the only one lead by a woman.

One sure way of attracting investors was to allow them to participate in the expedition. That way they think of the expedition as a vacation instead of a risky investment. The problem is that a bunch of vacation hunters does not constitute a professional diving crew. But you rationalize that by admitting there would be no need for a crew without the investors. Balancing the pros and cons of each potential investor is very frustrating, until the moment when one of them hands you a check.

By the time I had raised $350,000 for the expedition, my crew of participating investors consisted of a paint salesman, a fisherman, a ranch hand, a paramedic, three businessmen, and a one-legged Vietnam vet. Add to that Captain Glenn Miller, his son

Zach, Katie the cook, Dick Anderson, Kevin, and me, and you end up with fourteen people who had absolutely nothing in common. The oldest was sixty-two and the youngest was twenty-four. All of us had different backgrounds, different income levels, and different ideas about treasure hunting. Fourteen other investors wisely chose to stay at home and enjoy the expedition vicariously through my monthly letters.

I now had a considerable fiduciary responsibility. I had promised twenty-eight people I would take their money and, according to the prospectus, "engage in the search for sunken shipwrecks with the intent to salvage". I had a salvage boat, a known wreck and working capital. The only thing missing was the permission from the Bahamian government to excavate a shipwreck located in their waters. To get that, I had to turn my back completely on the relatively normal life I had known since birth.

We moved out of the ranch in July of 1980. Jake had gotten married and sold *La Bamba* to Kevin, who had hitched a trailer to it and driven off into the mountains with Brandy to pan for gold. Kevin and I had decided we needed some time apart if we were going to spend the next year living on a boat together, twenty-four hours a day. We agreed to meet at the Biltmore Hotel in Santa Barbara at 6 p.m. on Christmas Day. That would give me five months to finalize all the paper work for the expedition, get the permission from the Bahamian government, and put the ranch completely out of my thoughts.

It was just after sunrise when I walked through the barn for the last time, smelling the hay dust as it swirled into the pale light of morning. The horses were munching grain and swishing their tails, unaware that this day was different from any other. My tears didn't distract them from their breakfast. They wouldn't miss me. The new owners would fill their feed troughs. I climbed into the loaded U-Haul truck and blotted them out with a cloud of dust as I drove down the dirt driveway, leaving a dream behind me.

❈

Nine hours later I parked the U-Haul in front of a two-story house I had rented in the hills behind the Santa Barbara Mission. I had just enough time to unload the truck and change before I had to meet Glenn and Dick Anderson at Joe's Cafe on State Street.

Joe's Cafe was a smoke-filled Santa Barbara landmark where sailors, businessmen, university students, and vagabonds gathered to chat. Martinis were the house specialty and Italian seafood dinners were served in the back room, scenting the air with garlic and tomato. Glenn, Dick, and I sat at a small table close to the massive bar lined with the boisterous bodies for which Joe's was famous. We had to shout to hear each other above the noise.

"Glenn says you got all the money," yelled Dick, always the one to get right to the point.

"That's right!" I yelled back. "Will you guys be ready to leave in January?"

"Hell, I'm ready right now," Glenn shouted out of the side of his mouth. He was paying more attention to the smooth, tan, female legs at the bar than to our conversation.

"Now listen, Margee Brandeis," said Dick, leaning on the table for emphasis. "How the hell did a novice like you come up with the dough? I've been trying for five years. What did you do, sell off part of my 22 percent?"

20

"How come he gets 22 percent and I only get 10 percent?" Glenn interrupted, suddenly giving his full attention to the conversation.

"Because you're also getting a charter fee!" I yelled at Glenn. "Don't worry about your 22 percent, Dick. Just tell me how we get the salvage lease from the Bahamians."

"Well, what we'll actually have is a sublease," shouted Dick. "And tell this skinflint captain to my left here that he'll have to do what I say when we're on the site."

"What do you mean sublease?" I yelled.

"I'm the captain and it's my boat." roared Glenn. "The captain always gives the orders. That's the law of the sea."

"Glenn, you've never had that damn boat out of California," Dick shouted. "You don't know what you're doing in Caribbean waters."

"What do you mean, sublease?" I hollered again.

"I know a damn sight more than you! You never even *owned* a boat," screamed Glenn.

"That's because my head isn't swelled up enough," yelled Dick. "You gotta have a big head to fit those captain hats."

"Tell me what you mean by sublease!" I shouted louder than both of them. "Who's got the real lease?"

Anderson was smirking and Glenn was looking at legs again. I sat contemplating the chilling possibility that the two of them were not the great buddies they had led me to believe they were. But I was determined not to let it ruin the expedition.

"Rodney Baron's got the lease," Dick told me, lowering his voice a little. "He's a swimming pool contractor in Daytona Beach, Florida. Bob Marx has already talked to him, and he'll let us work the site for 10 percent."

"Why didn't you tell me this before?" I yelled, suddenly furious. "I've got to talk to him!"

"You can't," Dick hollered.

"Why not?" I demanded.

"Rodney doesn't talk to women. You'd only blow the deal."

"He sounds like a good ole boy to me," Glenn interrupted again. "You better listen to Dick here, Margee. He knows what he's talking about."

Glenn ordered another round of martinis and the conversation got sillier. By the end of round three, we were slapping each other on the back and crowing that we'd all be swimming in treasure by this time next year. I decided not to worry too much about Glenn and Dick's differences. I figured they were grown men who would cooperate with each other, since we were all after the same goal. I did worry about this sublease situation though, and decided there and then to go to Florida and sort things out for myself.

❦

In August, Anderson and I flew to Florida. It was my first trip to that flat, sun-bleached state, where every third person is a treasure hunter, or related to one. Anderson remained adamant about keeping me away from the lease holder, Rodney Baron. Instead he had arranged to introduce me to Robert Marx, the man who has found more sunken treasure than anybody in the world.

As we pulled up in front of Marx's white, brick, suburban house, Bob came running out of the front door. He jumped into our rental car and told us excitedly that according to a marine radio report a boat was coming back from the Bahamas. He was sure there was stolen treasure aboard.

"Damn pirates," grumbled Bob, as he impatiently pointed Dick toward the waterfront. "I *know* those guys have been working my wreck. I saw them outfitting that boat a month ago. Just because I'm not here all the time, they think I don't know what's going on. Hell, I know the movements of every damn treasure-hunting boat on this coast. Oh, excuse me," he said, looking at me for the first time. "How do you do? I'm Bob Marx."

He was an historian, but with his thick shoulders and rugged features he looked more like a football player. It was hard to imagine him sitting in archives studying books. I pictured him commanding a fleet of ships going into battle. He was an impatient person, always moving, acting as though he had one foot out the door even though he'd just arrived. I soon learned that he was a walking encyclopedia of maritime history and a worldwide authority on shipwrecks.

"So you're the young lady who's going to recover the rest of my *Maravilla*," Bob said to me, clearly amused. "Nice legs."

"Thank you," I said adjusting my skirt. "That's what I intend to do, with Anderson's help."

We cruised several marinas without finding the boat Bob was looking for, then we returned to the house. Inside, Dick and Bob disappeared into Bob's office, and I was left to wander around the living room and admire the shipwreck artifacts, old books, and amphora lying on their sides on the floor. When the two men emerged from the office, Dick had a roll of charts in his hands and a satisfied smile on his face.

"Have you got those blasters mounted to Glenn's boat yet?" asked Bob as we sat down in the living room.

"The blasters are in a yard in Ventura," answered Dick. "We'll put 'em on when the boat gets drydocked in December. Glenn had them designed by some oil company engineer. They probably won't work."

"There's one more thing I'd like to discuss," I said, reminding the two of them I was still in the room. "I'd like to have a backup site."

They both looked at me as if I'd taken a glove off and smacked them both across the face.

"You didn't tell me she was the greedy type," Bob smiled at Dick, obviously amused again.

"What the hell do you need a backup site for?" Dick asked indignantly, watching to see how Bob would react.

"I've gone to a lot of trouble to raise all the money and get everything ready for this project. Just in case there's a problem with this sub-lease situation, I want to have somewhere else to go," I answered.

"No problem," said Bob as he pulled out a slide projector. He set it up on one of the end tables and, with his back to me, he asked, "Did you bring your checkbook?"

During the next fifteen minutes we watched a series of photographed archive documents flash across the screen. Some were old book pages, others were yellowed sheets of parchment scrawled with blotchy script and columns of numbers. Each image stayed on the screen just long enough for us to figure out what we were looking at, but not long enough for us to memorize any particular data. The last slides were crudely drawn charts with writing across the tops of the pages, some in Spanish and some in English.

"These are my top ten wrecks," Bob said in a voice mixed with pride and exasperation. I had the feeling he was accommodating me while considering my demand a big waste of time, and the waste of a good wrecksite. "All of them are of the same caliber as the *Maravilla*."

"Which one's got the most treasure?" blurted Dick, before I could say a word.

"The one in Ecuador," answered Bob.

"We'll take it," said Dick.

I paid five thousand dollars for the slide and four typed sheets of data about the Ecuador wreck. The data included names of people on the ship, its owner and captain, sailing dates, totals in ducats of the amount of gold and silver carried as cargo, and the circumstances surrounding its sinking. The slide was a nautical chart with the word MANTA written above a coastline with several bays and one darkened spot. Beside the dark spot were written these words:

Amongst which rocks was cast away
a ship in which was a prodigious treasure.

I was feeling quite proud of myself as Dick and I were driving back to the airport, racing a tangerine, Florida sun setting behind tall thin pine trees. I was also wondering how Bob Marx had found all the information and books he'd photographed and how he planned to find all those shipwrecks.

"Bob Marx has already found enough treasure to last him the rest of his life," Dick said smugly. "But some places he can never return to...... never mind why. The point is, the *Maravilla* site is one of those places. That's why Bob gave me all that information." Then Dick got conspiratorial. "There's something else you should know, Margee."

Hunching over the wheel, Dick told me that Marx had given him additional information on two more shipwrecks sitting side by side in international waters. "We'll be passing right over them on our way to the Bahamas and we don't need permits from anybody." Dick said hastily. I could feel my eyes widen and pulse quicken. "But you've gotta swear." Dick said, glancing at me with narrowed eyes. "Swear you won't breathe a word about these two wrecks to anybody on the *Coral Sea*, especially Captain Glenn."

❦

Back in Santa Barbara, the excitement about our expedition started to take hold of me. It was really happening now. We were really going on a treasure hunt for millions of dollars in gold and silver. Adrenaline was mounting like the magma rising inside a volcano. What a blast! I was charged like a lightning bolt. Couldn't get that shit-eating grin off my face. We were actually going for it!

I put the information about the Ecuador wreck in a safe deposit box thinking I would never need it. I had all the pieces now for a successful recovery of the *Maravilla* shipwreck, and that would be enough treasure hunting for one lifetime.

Anderson and I began planning every detail of the expedition. In the days and weeks that passed I came to trust not only his ability to direct the salvage work but also his honesty. On the other hand, he didn't trust me as far as he could spit. He'd been on too many treasure hunts to be fooled into thinking everything would turn out fine. "Gold turns people to shit," he told me. "It doesn't matter how well you know somebody, gold will bring out the worst."

I'd been living in Santa Barbara for more than two months when Glenn suddenly asked me to be a guest on one of his weekend charter trips. I soon discovered that his friendly invitation was actually a ploy for getting me away from Anderson so he could give me his list of demands for the forthcoming voyage. It seemed that Glenn had considered the whole thing just a pipe-dream until Anderson and I had come back from Florida and actually started buying things for the expedition.

Glenn presented me with his terms: a two-month supply of all filters, seals, and gaskets for his engines; Katie, his current cook, to be kept on as cook; the right to bring his girlfriends out to the boat when we were working on the site; a supply of Tia Maria liquor on board - even though I had already specified no liquor allowed - and fuel money to be put in an escrow account for the return trip to Santa Barbara when the expedition was over. Besides all that, he wanted firepower.

"Those thieving pirates in the Caribbean will ram your boat in the middle of the night, kill everybody on board, and use the boat for a dope smuggling run to Florida," Glenn warned me. "I want something that'll blow them out of the water before they get near us, ya know what I mean? I want some missiles on board or this boat's not going anywhere!"

I agreed to everything except the girlfriends.

When December arrived and the last charter was over, Glenn and Zach took the *Coral Sea* down to Los Angeles and drydocked it, as they did every year, at Al Larson's Boatyard. The place had a carved wooden sign over the door that said

'SERVICE WITH A SNARL.'

Buzz saws, hammers pounding on metal, welding sparks, and air compressors filled the boatyard with noise, while a raspy female voice on a PA speaker constantly paged someone to the office. Men in greasy coveralls and thick leather gloves worked feverishly on the barnacle-covered hulls of several vessels propped up with wooden scaffolding. Diesel fumes hung in the air like a fog. I had arrived in the middle of all the bustle, just in time to see the *Coral Sea* being slowly pulled out of the water at high tide. For the next two weeks Glenn, Zach, and I would live on the boat and supervise the work.

First the hull was sandblasted and painted with red bottom paint, then measurements were taken for tubular metal frames to be attached to the stern of the boat to hold the propeller blasters. Blasters are the one unique tool of a treasure hunter. They are giant elbow-shaped tubes that hang behind a vessel's propellers and channel the water flow down to the ocean floor. The force of the water excavates a cone-shaped hole in the bottom sediment revealing any objects resting on the harder layer underneath.

It took fifteen days and thirty thousand dollars to prepare the *Coral Sea* for the task for which she had been built. A few days before all the work was finished the owner of the boatyard came over for a visit. He had seen the blasters being mounted and knew exactly what we were planning to do. Having a keen interest in treasure hunting himself, he had brought with him two small, yellow books that he had found in Europe. "Authentic pirate stories," he told me, snickering, as he handed them to me to read. Actually, they were a scribe's account of four voyages of a pirate ship captain, a Captain Sharpe, in the years 1681 to 1684. The books had been printed in London by special request in the year 1762. The pages were thin and brittle, the type was old style script, and antiquated British phrases dotted the text. But what the scribe had to say was astonishing.

He described voyages that covered the entire west coast of South America, in what was then called the South Sea. Sharpe's pirates overtook vessels, stole the cargoes, and then set the boats adrift on fire. Or they anchored in front of small coastal villages, tortured the townspeople, and stole their food. Discipline was enforced on board the pirate vessels by starvation and the slicing off of fingers.

Three quarters through the second book, I sat up so fast I smacked my head on the bunk above me. The author described how Captain Sharpe held a knife to the throat of a town mayor and demanded all the town's grain, pigs, and chickens. To save his life and the lives of the villagers, the mayor offered to show the captain where one of the Spaniards' richest ships had gone down, in Manta Bay. Sharpe was unconvinced. He slit the mayor's throat, took the grain, pigs, and chickens, and sailed northward.

Manta Bay - the name had jumped off the page like fireworks. It was the same name written on the Ecuador chart I had purchased from Bob Marx. I was suddenly giddy, grinning from ear to ear, feeling the thrill of discovery. I read the account over and over, then copied the publishing information for future reference. Any doubts I might have had about the validity of Marx's research, had just been erased.

Like a seasoned treasure hunter, I kept the discovered information to myself and the next day I simply returned the old books to the owner of the boatyard, squirmishly remarking on the barbarity that was rampant in the seventeenth century.

The *Coral Sea* was scheduled to be launched at high tide late that afternoon. I packed my things and walked through Al Larson's Boatyard for the last time. I would be driving Glenn's truck back up to Santa Barbara to meet the boat at the marina.

"Before you head back to Santa Barbara," said Glenn as he handed me his truck keys, "I want you to give this guy a call. I wasn't joking about those missiles. We don't leave till they're on board!"

Glenn handed me the business card of a horseshoer. When I called the man, he knew exactly who I was and gave me strict instructions to meet him at a certain restaurant, at a certain time, in a tourist establishment on the San Pedro waterfront. I was to bring $2,800 in cash.

At exactly eight p.m. I was seated on the third stool from the left at the bar inside the designated restaurant. The lights were low and ships passing slowly up the harbor channel were visible through the windows. I ordered a drink and eyed the bartender, wondering if he had anything to do with this clandestine meeting. After an anxious wait of twenty-five minutes, a balding middle-aged man sat down on the stool beside me.

"Good evening, Margaret," he said openly. "Sorry I'm late. Do you mind if we take that table in the corner? I'm starved."

"Not at all," I said and carried my drink to the table. He was the last man in the room I would have guessed was an arms dealer. "Do you have them with you?" I asked when we were seated and alone.

"A few things first," he said intently. "Are you an agent of the federal government or a member of any police organization?"

"No," I answered, a bit startled.

"Do you have any voice recording devices or transmitters attached to yourself or in your purse?"

"No," I repeated.

"I've been watching you for the last half hour and there doesn't seem to be anyone following you. Why don't we order some dinner?"

"Sure," I said cautiously. "How do I know you're not an agent or a policeman?" I asked, trying not to sound naive.

"Because I'm telling you I'm not," he said emphatically. "Listen, Glenn and I have been friends for a long time. Don't worry about anything."

We had a nice fish dinner and talked about Glenn, the ocean, expeditions, and shipwrecks. He pretended to be fascinated and I pretended not to be nervous. After dinner, as we walked through a darkened section of the parking lot on our way to the truck, I passed him the envelope with the money.

"What am I buying, anyway?" I asked, thinking it was finally safe to talk.

"LAWS missiles," he answered.

"And what are LAWS missiles?"

"Light anti-artillery weapons. You bought two."

He stopped behind a well-used Ford Fairlane, opened the trunk, and took out an ordinary looking canvas beach bag with something heavy in it. He escorted me by the arm to Glenn's truck, asked for the keys, and placed the bag inside on the floor. It was all very smooth and a bit surreal. When I got behind the wheel of the truck, he rolled down the window and closed the door for me.

"Drive out of the parking lot and turn right at the first light. The freeway entrance is three blocks up. Get on the freeway, don't speed, and don't stop for anything until you get to Santa Barbara. Good luck on your expedition," he said sounding a little worried.

"Thank you," I replied. "I'll be all right. Why do you sound so worried?"

"Because you've just committed a felony," he said flatly, waving goodbye. "Drive safely now."

Chapter Three

January was cold and rainy. We spent the whole month packing things aboard the *Coral Sea* for our two-month voyage south to Panama, through the canal, and across the Caribbean Sea to Florida. We planned to be working on the site in the Bahamas by the first of April. Actually, the trip would only take one month, but we packed for two to cover the unexpected. For a long trip, people tend to pack what they think they'll miss the most. I myself packed seventeen boxes of Cheez-its™.

I felt like Christopher Columbus preparing to leave for the New World. But unlike Columbus, I knew nothing about provisioning boats. Besides paying for food and fuel, I found I had to buy an extra refrigerator, mooring lines, outboard motor oil, shackles, turnbuckles, bungee cord, welding rod, light bulbs, Never-Seeze™, Never-Dull™, navigational charts, quarantine flag, hand tools, marine binoculars, marine radios, fish gaffs, come-alongs, waterproof flashlights, goodie bags, silicone sealer, high-pressure 0 rings, toilet paper, extra Dement Coat™, electric winches, stainless steel cable, and rat guards.

Rat guards are round thin pieces of sheet metal about two feet in diameter with a long slit and a hole in the center. They are supposed to hang on the mooring lines to prevent rats from crawling up the rope and onto your boat. I thought that was a great idea until we tied up in Panama, where a three-foot-wide plank connected the boat to the dock at all times. The rats didn't have to risk their lives on the rope; they could just walk on board.

For the salvage work I had to purchase a magnetometer, which locates deposits of iron on the sea bed, underwater metal detectors, for short range detection of gold and silver, Norwegian buoys, underwater work gloves, a hundred cement blocks to use as underwater markers, polypropylene line, chart recorder paper, batteries, a radar reflector, fifty-five-gallon drums for outboard gasoline, and a seventeen-foot ski boat to be used for the magnetometer surveys.

Then I met Katie the cook. She wasn't one of Glenn's usual young, tan blondes. She was a beanpole with wild, curly black hair and a wiry disposition. She was in her late thirties trying to pretend she was still twenty-two. She was divorced from an older man who had taken her sailing all over the world, stopping to anchor in foreign ports for months at a time and then moving on with the wind. She told me that for her resume she'd need at least a page and half just to list all the countries she'd been to.

"I'm a gourmet cook," Katie insisted. After a month on the boat with her, though, I thought she could have made more money as a gossip columnist. It was impossible to walk through the galley without Katie asking you what was going on or telling you what she'd just heard. And the one thing she made sure I knew right from the start, was that the cook had the hardest job on the boat.

Since we were the only two women on the expedition, I thought Katie and I would stick together, be pals, help each other out. Instead, she would become the sole reason why I have never, ever, hired another female crew member. Katie would bitch about the crew, the work, the weather, the fact that we were using ketchup, the mess we left in the bathrooms, the pain in her knees, the bread not rising, the lack of days off, and my handling of the entire expedition. She would even keep a running total of the number of meals she had cooked since the day we left Santa Barbara, and the current number would be on the tip of her tongue whenever we had an argument.

Kevin and I were happily back together now, sizzling with the prospect of finding treasure. Visions of gold doubloons and jewel-encrusted goblets consumed us. We were willing to do anything for the sake of the expedition, even sleep in separate bunks, because on boats, walls have ears. We knew our deep friendship and commitment to each other would hold us together, but by mutual agreement, we decided I would play the role of expedition leader and he the role of crew member until the whole expedition was over. Actually, it worked out well. Kevin just blended in with the crew and became my secret spy, letting me know immediately if there was any dissent or mutiny brewing.

Toward the end of that drizzly January, the participating investors/crew moved on board. First there was Duane, an avid sport diver, who was taking some time off from the hectic wholesale paint business to buy himself some real adventure. He had been on the *Coral Sea* many times for the weekend charters and saw this as his chance to be part of the crew instead of a visiting guest. Duane was the type of person who was always on the outside trying to get in. He wore an old white sailor's hat to cover his oily black hair and kept a wooden match stick between his lips, to look the part of an old salt. He had an irritating personality and a nauseating nasal laugh, but he was the second one to put up his money.

Next came Bill, an old friend who hoped to find his fortune and get out of the fishing business. He sold his dory fishing boat and took out a second mortgage on his one-bedroom house to come up with the minimum $10,000 investment, telling his wife that "this is the big one." What you noticed first about Bill was his bright, yellow-blond hair and his two hundred-pound belly. He once told me he had to stay fat, because when he lost weight, he looked like Robert Redford and the girls wouldn't leave him alone. We called him Bubby, or just plain Bub. He was a great carpenter, so we put him to work building a workbench for the back deck and permanent shelving for all our dive gear. Bub was a fun-loving extrovert but if you got him mad he could crush you as if you were a gnat. Life was serious to Bub, and as a fisherman, he had respect for the sea and a fierce loyalty to fellow crew mates. It was crew loyalty that Bub taught to Duane the night he pulled Duane out of his sleeping bag by his hair and rapped his head several times against the steel bulkhead for running off down the dock without unlocking the marina gate for the rest of the crew. You didn't mess with Bub.

Long, lanky, blue-eyed Marc was the only crew member besides Anderson who had had any commercial diving experience. When he wasn't being lowered a thousand feet into the ocean, Marc was a paramedic for the county of Santa Barbara. He liked being proficient at things and he loved emergencies. On my first visit to his house to discuss his possible involvement in the expedition, he had shown me his worksheet of pros and cons for making his decision. There were four items under pros and nineteen items under cons, but he invested anyway. He made it clear to me that he was coming on the trip because he believed in Glenn's abilities as a captain and Anderson's honesty about knowing where the treasure was.

36

Next were Old Joe, Little Joe, and Billy. They were all related and all put their money in because they knew Dick Anderson and his knack for finding gold. They also knew every detail about the *Maravilla*, including the fact that it was ripe for picking. Billy owned a large manufacturing business and retail store that specialized in ocean sports. He liked to keep his business transactions short, sweet, and profitable. Old Joe was retired and Little Joe, his nephew, was in electronics. Both were coming along mostly as observers, thinking of all the great stories they would have to tell when they got home.

Steve was another old friend who had told Bub about the expedition. Steve was a bit of a wanderer who left his cabin in Oregon every year when the weather got cold and drifted south with whatever female would take him along. He got $400 a month from the government for having lost his lower right leg in a helicopter crash in Vietnam. That was enough to keep him in food and gas money. He was a real charmer with wavy blond hair and a big strong chest, but beneath his cuddly nature and easy-going lifestyle, Steve was a pirate. He wore a small gold-loop earring in his left ear, and figured that sailing off with us on a treasure hunt was his true calling in life. It was only a minor detail that his grandmother had to put up the investment money. He would pay her back triple when we divided up the treasure.

Our ranch hand, Jake, was the last crew member. Although he'd only been married a few months, Jake had made it a part of his prenuptial agreement that he would be on the *Coral Sea* when she sailed. The day he and his wife arrived on the dock, I went out to greet them and ran smack dab into a screaming, crying she-cat who threatened to kill me for stealing her husband away. "She gets a little emotional," Jake told me. He shared a bunk room with Kevin and I, along with a hundred pounds of buckwheat, a hundred pounds of dried garbanzo beans, and twenty-seven sacks of flour.

When a break came in the gusting winter weather, after weeks of back-breaking preparation and anxious anticipation, we all thought it would be the historic day we set sail on the adventure of a lifetime. That's when Glenn announced that we couldn't go because the toilets were backed up.

"You've put so damn much stuff on this boat that the shitter hole is below the water line!" Glenn roared at me, making sure everybody knew the delay in departure was my fault. We spent another week cutting a new hole, and rerouting the plumbing.

Finally we were ready. At 6 a.m. on January 27, 1981, the engines roared to life and we all gathered along the starboard railing to watch the propellers churn up the harbor water as we eased away from the dock. The day was cold and foggy, but the weather didn't dampen our spirits any. We had just cast off our ties to the everyday world to make reality out of a dream that many talk about, but few have the guts to undertake.

The only ones who saw us off that morning were the screeching seagulls and a pathetic trio standing in the mist on the dock - Glenn's latest girlfriend, Mac the dog, and our salvage master, Dick Anderson. I probably should have recognized it as a bad omen that Anderson was on the dock instead of the boat, but I was too elated at being underway to care. He had promised to meet us in San Pedro, where we would take on ten thousand gallons of diesel fuel for the voyage.

Anderson showed up just as the fuel tanks were filled and decided we should make a short trip to Catalina Island to try out the propeller blasters before leaving the country. I was agreeable to anything.

Like everyone else on board, I was completely happy. I figured the hardest part was over for me now that we had actually left the mainland. It was up to Glenn to get us safely to our destination and Anderson to show us where and how to dig up sunken treasure. I gave myself an imaginary pat on the back and went down to my bunk to keep from getting seasick.

We anchored in the Santa Catalina harbor for the night, and in the morning motored down the coast, away from the town. Anderson took charge, and the crew practiced putting the ski boat on and off the deck without banging it into the *Coral Sea* too much. When they could launch it with a minimum of yelling and swearing, they connected all the cables and winches and safety lines to lower one of the propeller blasters into position.

The blaster was sitting vertical in its tubular frame, bolted to the stern of the helicopter pad. A steel cable ran from a hook at the top of the frame to a boom mounted on the top sun deck. A five-ton electric winch slowly unreeled the cable, and the blaster was lowered into the water. Once the blaster was horizontal, lying on the water's surface, a diver had to swim to the top of the frame and unhook it, letting it roll back on small steel wheels to its position behind the ship's propeller. Then the diver had to go under the boat and bolt the blaster securely to a welded plate. On paper the plan had looked great. Out on the ocean, with the *Coral Sea* bobbing up and down in the swells, executing it was a nightmare. The blaster was fifteen hundred pounds of dead weight completely at the mercy of ocean currents, passing waves, and the rise and fall of the stern. In two seconds everything went wrong. The boom arm bent under the strain, Anderson starting screaming his fool head off, and people were running everywhere grabbing ropes or getting out of the way. Suddenly there was a gigantic snap. The blaster fell into the water and drifted out of sight.

The next scene I saw was nine men together at the edge of the helicopter platform, staring down into the water looking dumbfounded.

"I *knew* it wouldn't work!" was all Dick said to me. His attitude had changed from cautious optimism to unabashed defeatism - in one 'swell foop.'"

Actually, the blaster hadn't fallen off. It was just hanging upside down under the boat. The crew managed to get it back to its upright position and Dick got out a pencil and paper to start redesigning it. The atmosphere was tense when we pulled up anchor and headed for San Diego to clear customs before leaving the United States.

By the time we docked in San Diego in mid-afternoon, doubts and second thoughts were permeating the crew. Anderson was pacing back and forth across the stern deck, glancing up occasionally at the blaster mountings and shaking his head in disgust. Bub was sanding a piece of wood absentmindedly, looking like he'd just lost ten thousand dollars at the roulette wheel. Steve and Marc were reading books at the galley table, tapping their fingernails on the Formica tabletop. The businessmen were huddled in their bunk room, reevaluating their investment. And Kevin and Jake were busying themselves with marking dive gear, camouflaging a nagging frustration and knowing there was little they could do to improve the situation.

Only Duane was bouncing around the boat like a well-fed parakeet, oblivious to any lurking negativity. Glenn had told him he could drive the boat on the way to Panama, and that was all he cared about. It was some invisible magnet that drew us all to the galley just as Glenn came down from the wheelhouse all dressed up for a date.

"Well, I'll see you all in the morning," mused Glenn as he drew a comb through his hair.

The air, which had been thick with pent-up aggression all day, exploded in a verbal conflagration.

"What do you mean, in the morning?" I snapped, leading the attack. "All the papers are ready. We can leave in an hour."

"Margee, you don't know *anything* about boats!" Glenn hollered back, instantly in fighting mode and more than ready to put me in my place in front of the crew. "It's bad luck to leave at night."

"That's a bunch of crap," shouted Billy, determined to get his two cents in. "We've got three hours before sunset."

"What's the matter, Glenn?" taunted Steve. "Can't you get your boat out of the harbor at night?"

"I can do my job just fine," hollered Glenn like an angry cat with back arched and fur pointing straight out. "You guys are the incompetents who can't get a blaster up and down!"

That was it! The whole galley burst into wild shouts and accusations. Fingers pointed like pistols. Foreheads wrinkled and eyebrows drew together. Mouths stretched wide open to let out extra loud judgments or to gasp in horror at the implications of an overheard rebuttal. In short, male egos raged in all their wrath and fury.

"You've been smug about this whole operation since the start," Anderson yelled at Glenn. "It's your own fault those blasters don't work. Your asshole friend designed them."

"They're outright dangerous, Glenn," added Marc. "You get in the water with them if you think they're so great."

I looked around at all the red faces. We weren't even out of the country yet and we were at each other's throats. I had to end it before it broke into a fist fight.

"All right, Glenn," I shouted, putting my hands up in the air to call a momentary truce. "Just when are we going to leave?"

"Twelve hours from now." Glenn answered. The thought that he was going to win this argument seemed to be calming him down.

Then Bubby spoke up in his powerful, threatening voice. "Listen, Glenn, we've been busting our asses for four weeks. We want to get this show on the road."

"Twelve hours is four o'clock tomorrow morning, Glenn," I stated, trying to keep control of the conversation. "Is that when we're leaving?"

"Sure, four o'clock in the morning," Glenn agreed. "Now, can I please get through here? I have an appointment."

And Glenn walked out, leaving us all staring blankly at each other, exhausted after venting off four weeks' worth of anxiety. Someone mentioned that the whole reason we weren't leaving until morning was so Glenn could have dinner with his daughter. We chewed over that for a while.

"At a time like this there's only one thing to do," smiled Marc. He reached into a bag and slowly laid out thirteen Groucho Marx plastic noses with black rim glasses and furry black eyebrows. All of us put them on and instantly broke out laughing at each other, partly for looking like goofballs and partly for surviving our first raging battle aboard the *Coral Sea*. Then we all went to our bunks to sleep off the tension.

I didn't sleep well at all. I knew there had been more going on during that verbal boxing match than just a letting off of steam. Glenn had let me run around raising all the money like a naive little dupe and now he was going to take over the operation to show me how insignificant I was. He was going to have it his own stubborn way, just as he had on the diving charters he'd been running for the last twenty years. Well, Captain Glenn Miller, I thought, you'd better think twice. I'm not going to let you bully me, or this project, around. I can't gain control by force, but I *can* do it by holding you to every single verbal and written commitment you've made. I command this ship, I realized in a flash of legal insight, and *you* work for *me*. That settled, I drifted off to sleep. I woke up without an alarm clock at ten minutes to four in the morning.

"Go wake up your dad," I told Zach, who was sleeping in the wheelhouse when I went up to turn on the lights. "It's four a.m."

"Margee, you don't really want to wake him up," pleaded Zach, yawning and stretching. "You're really going to piss him off."

"He's going to keep his word as long as this boat's chartered to me," I insisted, "Now, go wake him up, or I will."

Five minutes later Glenn came grumbling up the stairs in his pajamas, with Zach trailing behind him.

"It's pitch black outside," Glenn roared. "What the hell's the matter with you."

"You told us all 4 a.m. Glenn," I said, standing my ground, "So start the engines and let's get going."

"You're out of your damn mind," mumbled Glenn as he turned to go back down the stairs.

"I guess you really *can't* get your boat out of the harbor at night," I said, knowing I was looking for trouble.

"Of course I can!" He swung around to face me, glaring. "I'm also smart enough to know it's a stupid thing to do when it's not necessary."

"Then I'll have to wake up the rest of the crew and tell them you lied to us last night. You had no intention of leaving at 4 a.m."

"You're a real bitch, you know that? Zach, go start the engines." Glenn switched on the radar and running lights to get underway. "You know, Margee, you may be a financial wizard, but as a person, you're nothin'."

43

A little voice deep down inside me yelled, "I won!" and there was nothing Glenn could say that would diminish the moment. From that point on, the crew secretly referred to Glenn, Dick, and me as the Holy Trinity, and Anderson took to calling me General Brandeis.

By sunrise we were twenty miles south of San Diego heading into Mexican waters. Stubbornly, to prove my victory, I remained in the wheelhouse until Glenn went back to his cabin to change, leaving Zach to captain the boat. The incident marked the end of my naive phase in the treasure hunting game.

It took us seventeen days to reach Panama. The weather was calm and I got accustomed to the moving vessel to the point where I stopped getting seasick. Glenn recovered from his defeat in a couple of days and went back to doing as he pleased.

We gradually adapted to sea life, growing accustomed to the constant vibration and hum of the engines. Mornings were the prettiest. We glided across a lavender-colored ocean and watched a yellow-orange sun crawl above a distant strip of land.

Sometimes the surface of the water looked like millions of tiny pockets filled with peach colored liquid, jostled by the wind. The bow cut through the water like a butter knife, bringing up curls of white water. Dolphins appeared to outrace the curls and ride the wake like surfers. If you leaned over the bow railing and clapped your hands hard, the dolphins would jump out of the water, arch in the air, and then splash back down and sink below their playmates to get back into line. We rarely saw other ships. Solid land was a thin strip of gray that never ended and never left our port side. Notebooks and journals started appearing on board as people became introspective.

After eight days at sea, Duane finally got his chance to drive the boat. From then on he was a permanent fixture in the wheelhouse, standing in a military at-ease position behind the wheel, hands clasped behind his back, match stick protruding from his lips. Everyone found a special place on the boat. The smell of suntan lotion hung over the top sun deck and glowing red bodies appeared every night at dinnertime. Beards started sprouting on half the crew.

As for Kevin and me, shipboard life meant pretending we weren't married. We showed no affection for each other in front of the crew, saving it all for the rare moments when we would sneak into each other's bunk to snuggle.

Just when everything was going smoothly, a bell suddenly went off and a red light started flashing on the warning panel in the wheelhouse. Even Anderson, who had been spending all his time in a hammock doing crossword puzzles, came dashing into the galley to see what had happened. Sweating profusely, Glenn emerged from the engine room to announce that one of the generators had burnt out and we would have to conserve energy.

First the air conditioners had to be turned off. The bunk rooms became stifling sweat pits. Then the engine room temperature rose to 150 degrees, and since the water tanks were next to the engine room, the water had heated up to 150 degrees as well. We couldn't touch any of the water coming out of the faucets, so there were no more showers, and some people really began to stink. As we traveled south into increasingly warmer weather, more and more people began to stink.

Then another bell and flashing red light went off and Glenn stomped into the galley with bits of turds clinging to his ankles and covering his feet. The sewage lines had backed up again and deposited four inches of shit on Glenn's bathroom floor and he had stepped right into it.

On our tenth day at sea, with the sky a glorious cobalt blue, I took my beach towel up to the helicopter pad to soak up some sun. I was soon joined by several crew members.

"Hey, General, how's it going?" Steve said as he spread his towel next to mine. "You look like you're deep in thought."

"Oh, I was just mesmerized by our wake," I said, still daydreaming a bit, "It makes you feel so temporary when you watch the white water trail off and disappear."

"Yeah, and did you notice that we're not going in a straight line?" asked Steve, tracing the wake in the air forming an 'S' shape.

"So what does that mean?" I asked, hoping it wasn't serious.

"It means the captain doesn't know how to navigate very well," interjected Marc as he sat down on his towel to join our conversation.

"Check out the chart sometime," suggested Steve. "It's a nice straight line when Zach's driving, but we're all over the fucking ocean when Glenn's driving." he chuckled.

"Is this a crew meeting?" came Kevin's voice from behind us as he and Jake scrambled up onto the helicopter pad and sat down.

"We were just giving the General some insight into a few minor details of our illustrious voyage," said Steve.

"Well, did you tell her about Glenn's stash of marijuana? We found it hidden in the water heater," said Jake, looking around to see if anybody else heard.

"Are you kidding?" I gasped, getting my answer when Jake shook his head from side to side and grinned.

"And did you know that half the electronics in the wheelhouse don't work?" asked Kevin very seriously. "The armature on the generator burned up because there are no vents in the engine room. There's no place for the hot air to go."

"But how did he make all those trips to the Channel Islands and back?" Marc asked. He was becoming visibly disturbed at the possibility that Glenn's reputation as a great captain might not be accurate.

"Anderson says the engines don't get hot enough in a two-hour trip to make a difference," said Kevin. "He says Glenn wore a rut in the ocean from the Santa Barbara harbor to the islands and has never been anywhere else."

"That's nothing!" remarked Steve "I heard Glenn talking on the radio this morning to some tuna boat asking him directions, and the tuna guy told him he'd better be prepared for the eighteen-foot waves they call the Tehuantepecers [Too-ah-na-peckers]. Glenn was shittin' a brick."

"Can this boat make it through eighteen-foot waves?" I winced.

"When are we going to hit 'em?" grinned Jake, bouncing up and down with excitement.

"Tomorrow," answered Steve, raising his eyebrows up and down.

At that point Bubby heaved himself up onto the helicopter pad. He was breathing deeply, visibly upset, and he looked me right in the eye.

"I'm gonna kill Glenn Miller," Bubby snarled. "He lied to us and I'm gonna kill him."

"Now, that's not going to solve anything, Bub," I said, trying to placate the beast in Bubby. "There are just a few wrinkles to work out, that's all."

They drowned me out with their laughter.

Later that afternoon Glenn called us all to the back deck for a practice fire drill. He explained that we would be passing through the Bay of Tehuantepec, where strong winds sometimes come down from the mountains and create giant waves in the bay. So just to be prepared for any emergency, he was going to show us how to connect up the four-foot fire extinguisher that was secured to the pole in the middle of the back deck.

The sun was beating down on the rubber mats covering the wide steel deck as we all gathered round. As with every other detail on the *Coral Sea*, the fire extinguisher displayed Glenn's hot-air-balloon-size pride in his vessel. Keeping assets looking new was just as important as having them in the first place, according to Glenn. That's why, in the three years since he had purchased this Coast Guard-approved, top of the line, heavy duty fire extinguisher, he had never taken it out of the bag.

With the gesture of an artist unveiling a masterpiece, Glenn pulled off the canvas covering. Then, to allow us time to appreciate his shiny new apparatus, Glenn sat on one of the fifty-five-gallon drums full of gasoline and in a moment of absentmindedness, whipped out his antisque Dunhill lighter and lit a cigarette.

"Now, this is a complicated piece of equipment here and I don't want anyone playing with the knobs," began Glenn, holding the cigarette between the first two fingers of his left hand and pointing it at the fire extinguisher.

"Shouldn't we have the thing all connected and ready to use?" came a question from the audience.

"Aw, it only takes a few seconds to put it together," Glenn assured us as he jumped down off the gasoline drum and walked over to the device. "It's simple." He put the cigarette between his lips and grabbed two of the flex hoses. Smoke curled up into his face as he tried several different connections and none seemed to work. Then he threw his cigarette on the deck, crushing it with his shoe, and bent down to inspect the underside of the extinguisher. After a long moment, he straightened up, handed the hoses to

Dick, and walked back into the galley bellowing, "You figure it out!"

Dick stood motionless in the middle of the deck, with his arms hanging limp at his sides and hoses dangling from one hand. He was wearing nothing but his bathing suit and bush hat. After a dramatic pause, he raised one bent index finger in the air, the one that had a huge round knob on its knuckle from an old sea urchin spine injury, and said, "I have one more thing to add before we adjourn this drill... if this boat's going down, the first thing you do is lash Glenn to the wheel! Then, it's every man for himself!" He set the hoses on top of the fire extinguisher and went back to his crossword puzzles.

On the twelfth day at sea, when the discussion at the supper table had turned to pirates, someone asked if anybody really knew how to use the submachine gun Glenn kept in the wheelhouse.

"Of course I know how to use it!" Glenn hollered from his usual spot at the end of the table. "I don't keep it on board just for looks, ya know what I mean?"

To squelch any further doubts, Glenn marched up to the wheelhouse and brought down the gun in pieces, which he had hidden in different places. Automatic weapons like this one were technically illegal, so Glenn figured he'd outsmarted everybody by dismantling the thing. He could put it together in two seconds if he had to, he assured us. This time he really did know what he was doing, and the gun was together in a flash. The excitement came when he pulled back the spring-loaded lever and headed out the galley door to the side of the ship to let off a burst of machine gun fire - rat-tat-tat-tat-tat-tat-tat-tat. We could see him through the galley windows, and it only took a few tat-tats to make us realize that the gun was out of control and Glenn was being thrust back against the side of the ship by the force of the blasts. The gun aimed itself here and there and everywhere - into the air, into the water, into the air again. Bright staccato flashes of yellow and orange lit up the night sky. All of us in the galley dove under the table and covered our heads. Rat-tat-tat-tat-tat-tat-tat-tat. "Goddamnit! Son of a bitch!" Glenn yelled. Rat-tat-tat-tat-tat-tat-tat-tat.

"We don't have to worry about pirates," someone mumbled under the table. "Our own captain's going to kill us."

When the firing finally stopped and we felt safe enough to come out from under the table, Glenn re-entered the galley with the machine gun pointed at the ceiling.

"That should take care of any doubts you all had," Glenn said in a haughty tone. Then he turned stoically and went back up the stairs to the wheelhouse. Nobody else said a word.

On the fourteenth day at sea we were off the coast of Costa Rica. The thin gray strip that was the mainland had turned to green and grown bumps. It was so hot now that everyone wore a bathing suit all day long and no one could remember what it felt like to stand on a floor that wasn't moving. We had all developed a ducklike, wide-apart gait to compensate for the constant roll of the vessel.

I convinced Dick that he should start giving some instruction to the crew so we would be ready to work when we got to the Bahamas. That night he put a notice on the blackboard that treasure hunting lessons would begin next morning on the bow at 0800 hours.

Dick started everybody off with remedial knot tying. We learned the clove hitch, the half hitch, the bowlin, the rolling bowlin, the Spanish bowlin, the trucker's hitch, the three-strand eye splice, and the seaman's whip. We were also taught to forget that the square knot ever existed.

50

On the sixteenth day at sea, with Nicaragua off our port side, Anderson came down the stairs and sat down on the bottom bunk opposite me.

"It's completely hopeless, Margee Brandeis," he told me, resting a hand on each knee. "I don't know why I got on this fucking boat in the first place."

"For 22 percent" I reminded him, sitting up to look him square in the eye.

"The only way this nightmare has any chance of succeeding is if we throw the whole crew off in Panama and start over," he said, looking sincere. "And that includes the lunatic we've got for a captain."

"You know we can't do that," I said, trying to sound firm and consoling at the same time, "They all paid to be here and you agreed to be their salvage master."

"At least let me throw Duane overboard before we get to Panama," Dick pleaded, clasping his hands together like he was praying. "You'd be doing the whole crew an immense favor."

I couldn't help smiling at the idea but I quickly put on a stern face and ignored the suggestion.

On the seventeenth day at sea, the other generator burned up and we had no electricity at all. We also discovered that the water gauge, which had indicated half full for the last two weeks, was broken, and the tank was now empty. At dinner that night, adding the final blow to our desperate situation, Billy announced that we were out of ketchup.

We kept the running lights on that night with a tiny portable generator. When we dropped anchor in Panama Bay the following afternoon, there was no fanfare, just a mad scramble among the crew to be first on the tiny ferryboat that had come by to take us ashore.

Chapter Four

We were anchored in a small side harbor waiting for the customs officials and canal inspection officers to board our vessel. The entrance lock to the Pacific side of the Panama Canal lay before us. Anchored on either side of us were yachts and boats of all sizes, some polished white and new, others battered and rusted with age. On shore, low cement buildings lined the water's edge, competing for space with tall green palms and leafy bushes. Behind the treetops, four miles in the distance, stood the hazy skyline of Panama City, with skyscrapers poking their square flat faces above the green countryside. Narrow, canopy-covered ferryboats scurried from vessel to vessel loading and unloading passengers and parcels. A heavy, light-gray cloud layer hung in the air, as if about to descend and smother all life. I had the feeling that this wasn't a happy place, just a necessary way point for people going elsewhere and a catch-all for those who had no place else to go.

Glenn used his persuasive charm to convince the canal officers that our desperate need for water and repairs entitled us to tie up at the pier, which in normal circumstances was prohibited. By sunset we were docked alongside a slime-covered concrete pier. A clanking yellow forklift drove up to the edge with a heavy wooden boarding plank. The driver gently lowered the plank to us and secured his end to the pier with thick ropes. Three hours later, when all of us were asleep in our bunks, a horrible crash - bang - clunk vibrated through the ship, sending us all scrambling to the back deck to see what happened. We found the twelve-foot boarding plank hanging vertical by its pier ropes, and our vessel, like an elephant dangling on a kite string, was hanging by our bow and stern lines. It didn't take long to figure out that while we slept the tide had fallen eighteen feet inside the harbor and that the lines we were hanging by were going to snap.

It was Marc, ever ready for an emergency, who whipped out his jungle survival knife and ordered everybody back into the galley. He crouched down below the railing for protection, and slowly cut the ropes. Anderson tossed another rope up and over the pier bollard just as the stern line zinged up into the air like a slingshot and the boat splashed down into the water like an overripe watermelon.

"Ever heard of spring lines?" Dick screamed at Glenn.

"Course I have!" Glenn defended himself. "How was I supposed to know there's an eighteen foot tide here?"

"It's the captain's job to know that shit!" bellowed Dick.

"Never mind the spring lines," barked Billy. He was waving his hands in the air signaling the end of one argument and the start of another. "How soon before we get this turd of a boat going again?"

"Well, we're gonna have to cut holes in the deck and send those generators out to be rewound," said Glenn. "And while we're at it, we'll have to weld in some pipes for ventilation and mount fans over the engines. I hope you brought plenty of cash, Margee."

"Wait a minute!" I snapped, suddenly realizing I was going to get the bill. "You guaranteed that your boat was seaworthy when you signed the charter agreement, and it hasn't even lasted seventeen days."

"We got here, didn't we?" yelled Glenn, sounding defiant and relieved in the same breath. "Anyway, you agreed to pay for repairs and maintenance."

"Reconstructing your boat to ventilate the engine room is not normal repairs, Glenn," I pointed out, barely suppressing the urge to scream. "That falls under the category of latent defects. And the vessel owner pays for those."

The rest of the crew slithered out of the galley one by one, knowing that Glenn and I would be yelling at each other for awhile. During these confrontations of Charteror versus Charteree, the crew waited to see whether Glenn walked out of the galley or stomped out, to determine who won the bout. This time I ended up paying for the repairs and Glenn promised to reimburse me when we reached Florida.

The construction work started the next day. Holes were torched in the steel deck and pulley systems rigged to raise the thousand-pound generators out of the engine room. Trucks came and went all day, delivering men and materials to measure, weld, and hammer. Anderson used the opportunity to rework the blasters, welding extensions in the frame and cutting air escape holes in the tubes. I consoled myself for the loss of time and money with the idea that every expedition had kinks to work out in the beginning. It would all be worth it when we got to the wreck and found the treasure. We'd be rich. We'd forget these minor problems ever existed. The treasure became a gleaming light at the end of the voyage that kept me titillated with excitement.

When one generator was finally working, we received clearance to transit the canal, expecting the repairman to deliver the second generator when we arrived at the other end. A slender, clean-shaven man in a sailor's hat and khaki bermuda shorts was assigned to our boat as a pilot who guided us through the locks that spit us out into the Atlantic Ocean.

When the second generator was finally installed we were ready to continue our voyage to Florida. That's when Anderson took Glenn and me aside to make secret plans to stop at the island where, according to Bob Marx, the two treasure wrecks were sitting side by side.

By the dim glow of a bedside lamp in the captain's cabin, Anderson unrolled a nautical chart of a long, thin island that curved into a shallow reef running east and west. Fathom markings dotted the whole page and a tiny square was drawn at the north end of the island. Glenn puffed smoke swirls out of his pipe as he studied the chart. He spread it out on the glass-covered, antique, wooden ship's door that served as a coffee table between his king-size water bed and his built-in couch.

I sat on the edge of the bed studying the two men studying the chart. This piece of paper was all they needed to put aside their petty grievances, I thought. The stuff treasure hunting is made of - paper charts and golden dreams.

"Now, we don't want the rest of the crew knowing the name of this place or exactly where it is," explained Anderson. "This is going to be a hit and run."

"Why do we have to play all this stupid secrecy stuff?" questioned Glenn, as if this were a kid's game that he had outgrown. "And why do we have to run? Don't you guys have permits for this place?"

"We don't need permits. These are international waters," said Dick. "And we have to keep it a secret because if we hit it big, we might want to come back here without the rest of the world following right behind us."

"The closest land to this place is Jamaica, 150 miles to the northeast," I said, not wanting to be forgotten. "I checked with the consulate in San Francisco and they said they have nothing to do with this area."

"Okay, but how are you going to keep the crew from knowing where we are? asked Glenn. "And I'm telling you right now that Zach has to know or we ain't stopping there, ya know what I mean?"

"Of course Zach will be told," agreed Dick, as if it had been a foregone conclusion all along. "You two are the captains. You have to get us there. We'll just cover the compass and the satellite navigation screen. Either Margee or I will be with you in the wheelhouse all the time."

That last statement startled me, but when I tried to get Dick's attention, he ignored me. Not wanting to appear at odds with Dick's plan, I offered no objection and the three of us shook hands to seal the deal.

At dawn the next morning, everybody was awake to celebrate our departure from Panama. As we traveled north into the Caribbean Sea, Glenn reluctantly taught me to read the navigational chart, check the compass, and adjust the auto pilot control. The satellite navigation system was covered with a brown potato sack, and covered again by a yellow mesh goodie bag closed with a padlock. An upside-down bowl covered the compass.

For a while the crew went along with the idea of secrecy, accepting it as part of the business of treasure hunting. Only Duane, with his adolescent need to defy authority, kept trying to peek through the wheelhouse window at the compass while he pretended to be merely enjoying the view.

At 6 p.m., Glenn and I were relieved by Zach and Dick, who had slept all day in preparation for their nighttime duties as captain and mate. We followed this routine for three days and nights, until Zach noticed a vessel following us on the radar screen. We stopped the engines and drifted for four hours, watching the blip on the screen come directly towards us. Suddenly, ten miles behind us, it abruptly changed course. We motored ahead for another two hours and the blip corrected its course to follow us again. A second time we stopped the engines and drifted, waiting only an hour this time before the blip realized what we were doing and altered its course. The cat-and-mouse game continued for half of the next day, until whoever was following us gave up and the blip on the screen disappeared completely.

The crew actually made a contest out of guessing our destination. Maps, rulers and scratch pads filled with mathematical calculations were scattered all over the galley tables. Hefty bets were placed as to when and where we would anchor. It was generally agreed that we were going north, but at what angle? Anderson outsmarted everybody by pointing us toward a different island, only changing course toward the right one in the middle of the night, twelve hours before our arrival.

On the chart, the island we came upon was a black dot the size of a pencil point. Through the binoculars as we approached, it was a strip of aquamarine blue floating on the horizon. On the fathometer, it was a mound that rose up out of nowhere from a depth of two thousand feet to bask in the sunshine two feet above sea level. On Dick's face, the island was a long-awaited chance of recovering treasure.

On our approach, we stayed well away from the brilliant turquoise-colored water that rose up as white waves to tumble over the submerged reef that stretched a mile to the east. Only the color of the water and the wave, like a ripple on the ocean's surface, indicated the presence of the island. It was a flat crescent-shaped patch of eggshell-colored sand a hundred yards long. There were no trees, no rocks, no hills, no animals, and the only indication that humans had ever set foot there was a square cement tower that had once been a radio beacon.

I was tingling with excitement again, grinning at the thought of diving into that aquamarine water and finding gold coins scattered all over the sandy ocean floor. We were really here, surveying an uninhabited island as if we were the first to discover it in the vastness of an uncharted sea. We could pretend we were roving pirates of the sixteenth century and there was no one and nothing as far as the eye could see, to remind us otherwise. The only task before us was to find a sunken ship in the warm Caribbean waters surrounding a deserted, coral-reefed island. What a dream! What an adventure!

We motored completely around the island and reef and anchored on the south side. The Velveeta boat (the name the crew had given to the ski boat for its creamy orange color), was lowered into the water and Anderson, Billy, and I drove off in the direction of a narrow inlet between the reef and the tip of the island. The hot sun stung our heads and necks. It reflected off the water with blinding brilliance as we carefully navigated the shallow passage and entered the lagoon-like bay inside the reef. The water was so clear, we could have been looking through glass at the round coral heads blossoming up off the ocean bottom. Rainbow-colored parrotfish darted among the coral heads, stopping to break off hunks of the rock-hard substance and munch on it as they sprinted away. We gently ran aground on the beach of that pancake-flat island, and set foot on a mass of broken, sun-bleached seashells and coarse sand.

"Gee, we're just like the Spanish explorers discovering the New World," I exclaimed, surveying the puny little island. "This is neat!"

"Nothin' neat about the day this place was found," remarked Dick. He was crouched down and running his hand through the sand, searching for solid objects. "They probably never even saw anything when they hit that reef. It sure as hell wasn't on the chart they had. The ship probably came clean over the reef and settled on the inside here. The only report Marx was able to find said the wreck was east of the island out the distance of a cannon shot. The survivors who swam to this sand trap had the privilege of baking to death instead of being eaten by the sharks."

"But if everybody died, how did any information get out at all?" asked Billy, eyeing the dilapidated cement structure at the north point of the island.

"Seven guys did manage to find a lifeboat. They drifted for a month before they hit Jamaica," Dick answered. "Marx couldn't find any record of a salvage attempt. They probably didn't know how to get back here."

Dick inspected the cement tower while he talked. The thing was hollow and just big enough to contain some electrical connectors and batteries, all corroded and useless. A weathered brass plaque said something about radio aficionados of Colombia. Dick ran his hand over the plaque and turned to Billy and me. "I don't want the crew snooping around this place. The island is off limits. Got that?"

Billy and I nodded silently. If Dick wanted the island declared off limits, we weren't going to argue. Dick was the expert treasure hunter. We assumed he had a good reason.

Some time during the first night we spent anchored outside the reef, I started thinking about pirates. I remembered Glenn telling me that they would ram a boat and shoot everybody on board. When I suggested that somebody should be staying up all night to keep watch, I was elected. But when I suggested the radar be used at night to warn us of approaching vessels, Glenn ruffled his feathers and shouted, "No way! There's only so many revolutions on that radar, Margee, and when you use them all up, that's it!" I credited this idiotic excuse to Glenn's fanaticism about keeping everything looking new. I used the radar anyway.

In the morning, Dick divided the crew into diving teams. He volunteered Duane to be the first diver to be dragged underwater behind the rubber Zodiac boat to scout for evidence of a shipwreck. "Tell-tale signs of man-made symmetry," was what Dick directed him to look for. "Square corners, flat surfaces, any shape that doesn't normally occur in nature. Anything that looks vaguely familiar, pick it up and bring it to me."

The only drawback to being towed underwater is that you are perfect bait for sharks.

Old Joe, Little Joe, and Billy were assigned to the Velveeta boat with the magnetometer. Their job was to survey the inside of the reef for large concentrations of metal. Dick stood on top of the *Coral Sea's* wheelhouse, supervising the whole affair through binoculars, while Glenn walked around below in his yellowish-green paisley swim trunks with street shoes and brown socks.

By the end of the day, Bubby and Jake had found eleven giant lobsters, Steve had found an old bottle, Marc had found some round steel rings, and Duane, beaming with pride, had spotted a giant galleon anchor hooked into the reef. Treasure fever took hold of the crew instantly. Eyes popped wide open, faces grinned, and hands rubbed together hungrily. Everybody buzzed around the boat grabbing dive gear and jumping into the water to see the anchor.

The way the anchor was situated near the top of the reef clearly suggested that the vessel had tried to save itself on its way over the top. We decided to move the *Coral Sea* around to the inside of the reef to facilitate the search.

Dick started holding crew meetings in the galley after breakfast each morning and for the next four days we were the model treasure hunting expedition. Unfortunately, the only wreck we managed to find was a rusting, modern, steel cargo ship that was partially sticking out of the water.

We continued the search until our solitude was interrupted by the appearance of two fishing trawlers. They anchored some distance from us and three men rowed over in a dugout canoe. In broken English, they explained they were from Honduras, looking for lobster, and had bent one of their propellers on a coral head. We used our diving gear to take off the bent propeller and used the acetylene torch on board the *Coral Sea* to heat and straighten it. Within two hours we had the propeller bolted back in place, receiving a dozen grand-daddy size lobsters for our efforts. After launching twenty long narrow canoes and fishing all day, the two ships left in the middle of the night, leaving us alone again, anchored on a peaceful turquoise sea.

The next day, a small twin-engine plane appeared out of nowhere and flew a couple circles around us. We all waved at it before it disappeared out of sight. Then we started wondering. What was it doing over the middle of the ocean so far from any land? What was it looking for? What nationality was it? By morning all our questions were answered.

The brass ship's clock rang four bells, six a.m., signaling the end of my night watch. I scanned the horizon one more time with the binoculars, bracing against the roll of the vessel with my back against the bulkhead. Nothing but tranquil blue ocean. Okay, time for bed, I thought, as I replaced the binoculars in the wall holder and headed down the stairs to the galley. The smell of warm oatmeal filled the room.

"Good morning, Katie," I said cheerfully, as I watched her put out the bowls and spoons. "Are you the only one up?"

"Of course I'm the only one up," Katie grumbled. "I have to ring that damn bell before anybody else gets up. Could you please get me a box of raisins from downstairs?"

"You bet," I answered quickly. "Anything else before I disappear?"

"No, I can manage with what's here," Katie grinned. "If I need something else I'll just give Kevin a shopping list and he can take the Bentley into town."

"Right!" I grinned back.

We were 150 miles from the nearest land with a road, but I knew the Bentley was one of Katie's standing jokes with the crew. She had little jokes with everybody. It made them talk more freely so she could stay abreast of the latest gossip. I delivered the raisins, saying "I'll see you at dinner," and then groped my way downstairs into a dark bunk room. Within five minutes I was asleep.

After breakfast Kevin thought he would sneak up to the top sun deck for a little snooze. Propped up against the smokestack, he was watching the sun reflect off the water, when he saw something moving. He gazed out between the metal rails at the horizon, squinting his eyes to focus on a distant speck. The speck, he soon realized, was definitely a large vessel, but that didn't bother him as much as the fact that it was painted gray and coming toward us. Oh, shit, only navys paint their vessels gray, he was thinking, as he rushed down the ladder to the main deck and bolted for the galley door.

"Hey, bucko, you missed the crew meeting this morning," Bubby greeted him, blocking the doorway momentarily.

"Yeah, I know, I was brushing my teeth before the rush," Kevin replied, obviously in a hurry. "Is Dick still in there?"

"Yeah, he's in there arguing with Duane again. Duane doesn't wanna be towed behind the boat anymore. He saw a shark yesterday."

63

"Well that's nothing compared to what he's gonna see today," Kevin predicted as he squeezed passed Bubby into the galley.

"Listen, Duane," Dick was shouting.

"It's the fifth time I've had to do it," protested Duane, standing defiantly in front of Dick with his arms crossed. "How come you don't make Steve do it five times?"

"Because we'd miss Steve if he got eaten!" Dick said smugly.

"Have you seen the big gray boat off our starboard side yet?" Kevin interrupted breathlessly.

"No! Show me where," Dick shouted, ignoring Duane and following Kevin out to the back deck.

"It's right out there. Can you see it?" Kevin pointed over the railing.

"Shit! It's a gunboat!" Dick said after staring at it for a long time. "Better go down and wake up General Brandeis. She'll want to see this." Then he turned to the crew. "Okay, I want everything put back! Steve, take the metal detectors downstairs and put 'em under the bunks. Marc, hide the magnetometer. Duane, stack all the tanks back in place and everybody stow your diving gear in your boxes. Don't ask questions, just put stuff away fast!"

A state of alarm spread over the boat like wildfire. Bodies and equipment scurried all over the deck as nervous glances were cast over the starboard railing. Noticing the unusual flurry of activity, Katie sprinted for the captain's cabin to wake up Glenn. By the time I got on deck, the alarm had turned to panic and Glenn was heading for the wheelhouse.

"What are you going to do?" I questioned Glenn as I followed him up the steps to the wheelhouse with Zach close behind me.

"I'm gonna outrun 'em," Glenn said, starting up the engines with a fierce look on his face.

"Don't be ridiculous!" I laughed. "This boat only does eight knots - they'd start shooting!"

"Then I'll blow 'em out of the water! Zach, go get the missiles."

"Zach! Don't you dare!"

"Get outta my way!" Glenn growled as he jerked at the controls and we almost backed into the reef.

Then a man's voice came over the VHF radio talking in Spanish, and Katie was called up to the wheelhouse to translate.

"They want us to come out into deeper water," she said, listening to the same message several times. "They say we're under arrest."

"Can't we call somebody on the long-distance radio?" I asked.

"Zach, get Miami Coast Guard on the radio," Glenn yelled "And get somebody up on the bow to man the anchor."

"It's a Colombian boat," Katie reported, still listening to the radio. "They're demanding we come out to them."

"Colombian!" Glenn shouted, "They take your boat first and ask questions later. You'd better pray we're not in Colombian waters, Margee. Now, go get everybody up on the bow looking over the edge, like we're picking our way through the coral heads," Glenn ordered me. "We need time to talk to Miami!"

Within minutes I had people on both sides of the bow looking down into the water. At a snail's pace, we motored toward the darker blue water where the gray vessel, with its big cannon, was waiting. Zach had gotten through to Miami and was giving them our passport numbers and navigational position. After explaining our situation to them, they told us to stand by while they analyzed our transmission. Three whole agonizing minutes ticked by in silence before a voice came back on the radio.

"Whiskey Yankee Victor 6106. This is Miami Coast Guard. Over."

"This is Whiskey Yankee Victor 6106. Go ahead. Over." Zach spoke into the radio microphone.

"Gentlemen, you are in Colombian waters and completely under Colombian jurisdiction. We will maintain radio contact with you every four hours. There's nothing else we can do. Good luck. Miami Coast Guard clear."

Chapter Five

"It's the beginning of the end, Margee Brandeis, the beginning of the end!" Dick said it over and over as he paced nervously back and forth. "It's the beginning of the end, I'm telling you. First they'll confiscate all our gear, then you'll have to pay an enormous fine, and we'll be damn lucky if they don't impound this boat."

"But I thought we were in international waters," I moaned.

"So we were wrong," Dick shrugged.

The Colombian navy vessel had sent six soldiers in a rubber boat armed with semi-automatic rifles to keep us under guard during the trip to the island of San Andres, the closest Colombian port authority. They collected all our passports and stationed themselves throughout the *Coral Sea*. In a futile attempt to convince them we had stopped at their island because of mechanical problems, Glenn had spread broken generator parts all over the wheelhouse. To prove that the Bahamas was our final destination, that we were only passing through this area, I had shown them copies of our agreements with the Bahamian government. Nothing worked. After searching our vessel twice and talking by radio with Bogota, they accused us of smuggling guns to Nicaragua. Then Katie offered them lunch.

It was decided that our vessel would lead, since the navigation system on the Colombian gunboat was acting up. So the *Coral Sea's* engines were started up and she motored away from the tiny sand spit of an island, leading the procession to her own funeral.

Glenn was a walking atom bomb looking for a place to explode. He carefully plotted the course four hundred miles back toward Panama, wincing slightly every time he glanced up to see the armed guard in the wheelhouse doorway. When we had to be together in the same room and he thought the guards weren't watching, he sliced me into a thousand pieces with his razor sharp glare of hatred. He made it unmistakably known that *I* was the idiot who had gotten us into this mess and *he* would have to get us out of it. Anderson had somehow disappeared from sight.

The feelings of the crew ranged from disbelief to a morbid fear of being thrown into a Colombian prison for the rest of their lives. Tension was everywhere. Talk was minimal. Desperate, inquisitive glances met me every time I came down the stairs from the wheelhouse, and changed to expressions of hopeless despair when I reported the situation was the same.

Of course, Duane was still bebopping around the boat with his Walkman earphones on, as if the whole thing was just a planned gag to amuse the guests. He thought it would be a great time to go on a diet and began a three-day fast. Katie, the only one on board who knew any Spanish at all, had to act as interpreter. As one possessing inside information, she conclusively convinced the crew that the whole thing was definitely my fault.

I lay on my bunk staring up at the pictures of the ranch I had taped to the underside of the bunk above me and wondered why I had ever left. What had made me think I was so smart that I could lead an expedition of crazies on a treasure hunt? And why had I been so dumb that I failed to check on Dick's information about international waters? Yes, the whole thing was my fault, and I was really scared of what might happen. I'd never been in jail before.

By the next day the tension had eased a bit. The soldiers had stacked their guns in a corner of the galley and were watching James Bond movies on the wheelhouse television. Glenn had given up on his idea of trying to outrun the navy vessel, and Zach was keeping radio contact with Miami Coast Guard every four hours. After intense discussions with Anderson, he and I decided to sneak two crew members at a time down to Glenn's cabin so we could make sure everybody told the same story when we reached San Andres.

We started with Glenn and Zach. Glenn controlled his bulldog anger long enough to agree to stick to the story about generator trouble. The crew, we would say, had been diving and calibrating equipment during the six boring days it took to repair the motor. Glenn made *us* agree that he would do all the talking when we arrived in port. Zach just gave me a sympathetic look and nodded.

Dick and I took the crew downstairs two by two and instructed them to tell the same story about the broken generator. The only thing they had to do immediately, and Anderson insisted on this, was throw all their notebooks and journals overboard before we got to San Andres. The Colombians could use anything we had written, against us.

Bubby tied hunks of pipe and diving weights to the journals so they would sink when they hit the water. Forlorn faces watched weeks of patient journal entries get tossed over the side, hoping the painful sacrifice would save our meager lives. Even Glenn's porthole swung open releasing a barrage of items that went flying out into the water - rolls of paper, books, plastic bags of marijuana, a pipe, and the two green LAWS missiles I had bought in San Pedro.

Three full days after leaving the sand-spit island under armed escort, we pulled up to a dock on the military base side of San Andres Island. The place was a lovely tropical cove with aqua blue water meeting a dense line of coconut palms along the shore. I peered out a porthole window to see five more soldiers with machine guns waiting for us on the dock. This doesn't look good, I thought to myself. As I paced the narrow walkway in my bunk room, I was constantly rubbing my hands trying not to think the worst.

In the galley, Katie was telling everybody that we would be kept there that night and brought around to the other side of the island in the morning to face the port captain and plead our case.

The other side of the island turned out to be a commercial dock just outside the city. We were forced to tie up to an old, worn-out fishing boat, because there were so many impounded vessels there was no dock space. On our way around the island, Glenn had been talking on the radio with the captain of an American vessel that was just leaving port. "Call Mr. Thomas Livingston," the captain had said. "If anyone can get you out, he can."

When the engines were shut down and most of the crew was gathered on the back deck to get a better look at our new surroundings, a sickly looking, weather-beaten man with a sunken face and torn, dirty clothes cautiously poked his head out the door of the barren fishing boat tied next to us.

"I've been here for forty days," he managed to say in a raspy, weak voice. He shuffled his bare feet, making his way to the railing. "They took the rest of the crew and threw them in jail. Do you have any water?" He raised a bony arm listlessly in the hope of receiving a glass.

70

"What happened to you?" asked Jake as we all crowded the railing to hear what he had to say. Katie ran off to get some water and whatever was leftover from lunch.

"We were drifting because the fuel line was clogged up. All of a sudden there was this navy boat. They accused us of illegal fishing and towed us here." He coughed and hacked a few times and then gulped down the water Katie had brought him. "We ain't got enough money to pay the fine. We'll probably be here forever. I ran outta food and water two days ago and they won't even let me off to get more." Then he sat down on the deck with the plate of food Katie had given him and began eating with his hands.

"Uh-oh. We're in some deep shit now," was Steve's summary remark. The rest of us just stared.

"Wait 'til Glenn hears this, Margee," Katie threatened in her tattletale voice. "If it wasn't for you, we wouldn't be here."

"You're absolutely right!" I shouted back at her with a glare of self-righteousness. "If it wasn't for me, you wouldn't be here! Just go ahead and squeal to Glenn."

I was scared but I wasn't spineless. The crew was looking to me for support. Katie and I were just getting ready for a fight when the Port Authority truck pulled up to a dusty stop on the dock across from our boat. A short, fat man with a bushy mustache and an impeccably white, gold-braided uniform walked stiffly to the fishing boat and carefully climbed over it to board our vessel.

"You are here under investigation of your documents" was the practiced statement the port captain delivered, once inside the wheelhouse. "We would like the captains to make a statement, yes?" He gestured toward the door and smiled curtly at Glenn and Zach.

For three tortuous hours we waited for our captains to return. Glenn came back with a tight chin and a protruding lower lip as he stomped directly to his cabin without saying a word.

"What happened?" We asked in unison when Zach entered the galley.

"What did you tell 'em?" somebody insisted.

"That it was too dangerous to stay outside the reef because of the currents." said Zach, eager to tell his tale. "We thought we would end up on the reef. Then they showed me the photograph of us with that Honduran fishing boat and four guys rowing in a canoe between the big boats. And they asked me what we were exchanging with the fishing boat."

"What did you tell 'em?"

"About the propeller and how we fixed it, and they didn't believe a word I said. They had pictures of us every day we were out there. That plane only came down low enough for us to see it on the last day. It was incredible."

"So, then what did you tell 'em?"

"The part about the broken generator and that we were just on our way to the Bahamas. And then they asked me if we ate any of the fish we caught there. And I told them just the lobsters that one time. And then one of those guys in a white uniform said we were accused of smuggling refugees to Costa Rica."

"Oh, shit," someone groaned. "It's getting worse."

"Then they put me back in the same room with my dad and told us there would be a thirty-day investigation of our activities. And we're not to leave the boat. I'm telling you, my dad is really pissed off."

The crew sauntered off to their bunks and I was left standing alone. There was no way I could put off my confrontation with Glenn forever. We were forced to face each other a few hours later when Mr. Thomas Livingston V, Maritime Agent, arrived in his beat-up red Volkswagen van truck with bright white lettering on the door.

Mr. Livingston was a plump, jovial man, a native of the island who, owing to the fact that he knew several languages and most of the people who worked for the port captain, was noted for his success with foreign vessels. He had dark skin, greased-down hair and good British manners. He was an instant hit with Glenn when he told him he could order whiskey and cigarettes and have them delivered. Glenn had very little to say to me except that I would get the bill for everything, and if I knew what was good for me I'd keep my trap shut and let him get us out of this mess.

Mr. Livingston initiated a rash of correspondence directed to the port captain and several government agencies protesting the abduction of our vessel. It was all very proper and judicious and completely ineffective. Every day he showed up in the morning with a package for Glenn and patiently told us the newest developments that were delaying the release of our vessel.

For five long, tedious, slow, sun-baked days we sat tied to the fishing boat, trapped like rats in our own floating cage. Hopeless hour after hopeless hour dragged on until it was time to sleep through the hours of darkness and start another day of waiting. Bubby passed the time carving a miniature fishing boat out of a hunk of wood. Duane lost ten pounds. Old Joe, Little Joe, and Billy set up their plastic lawn chairs on the helicopter pad and sun-bathed the afternoons away reading books and magazines. The rest of us paced.

The days themselves were quite beautiful. Puffy white clouds drifted through an azure sky looking as if their bottoms were flattened by an invisible sheet of glass. Tall green coconut palms with slender gray trunks and bunches of young, mustard-yellow coconuts swayed just beyond the dock. From the starboard side of the ship we could look across the blue, harbor water to the outskirts of the city. San Andres was Colombia's "Hawaii". The city was crawling with young women in bikinis, but the crew could only lean against the railing and fantasize.

I avoided everybody as much as I could. Guilt weighed on my shoulders like hundred pound dumbbells. My stomach felt like someone was twisting my intestines in opposite directions. The fear of a Colombian jail sentence made me despondent and inactive like a wild bird being caged for the first time in its life. I had nightmares of being thrown in the same cell as Glenn, who spent the rest of his life trying to strangle me.

On the fifth night Glenn couldn't take the stress anymore and retired to his cabin with a full bottle of Tia Maria. A little while later he stormed belligerently through the galley, climbed the stairs to the wheelhouse and locked the door behind him. He sat down at his desk with the microphone of the long-distance radio and called his congressman in Santa Barbara to say we had been hijacked at gun point. Then he called the editor of the *Santa Barbara News Press* and told him it was the Iranian hostage deal all over again. From that point on, it was out of control.

The *New York Times* got hold of the story and put it on the wire service. Then the *San Francisco Chronicle* called Glenn on the radio. Next, the U.S. State Department got wind of the situation and by morning the whole world knew that Glenn and thirteen other Americans were being held captive on a vessel at gun point, somewhere in Colombian waters. The Colombian consulate in Washington, D.C., was asked what the charges were against us, and they were told we were poaching lobsters.

By the evening of our sixth grueling day of captivity, we were notified that we would be released in the morning without charges. I had never been so relieved in my life. The knots in my muscles were just starting to relax when Glenn announced that we were heading back to Santa Barbara.

"What do you mean, Santa Barbara?" I demanded with renewed energy. "This boat is under charter to go to the Bahamas."

The Holy Trinity had gathered in the captain's cabin to discuss the future, now that we were free again.

"You almost got this boat confiscated and I'm not taking any more chances," said Glenn.

"Glenn, where's your sense of adventure?" I teased. "They weren't going to take your boat away. They never even formally charged us with anything."

"Yeah, thanks to me." Glenn barked. "I got friends in the right places."

"Well, I couldn't do too much with you locked in the wheelhouse. You wouldn't even let me use the radio."

"I don't trust either one of you guys." Glenn said eyeing both Dick and I severely. "You lied about that island being in international waters and you're probably lying about having a lease in the Bahamas. I'm taking this boat back to Santa Barbara."

"Listen, we were misinformed about that island," I admitted. "But that was never the point of this expedition in the first place."

I was starting to get perturbed at Glenn's childish attitude. It's amazing how fast your wits return when a gun is no longer pointed at your head. "We've spent a lot of money to get your boat ready and to get this far," I reminded him. "And we're not turning back now. This boat goes to the Bahamas!"

It was another standoff. Glenn was fuming as he paced back and forth across his cabin. I sat on the couch clasping my hands together tightly to maintain my composure. Dick sat beside me, silent as a rock. I could see the situation from Glenn's point of view, but I was utterly determined to see the expedition through. The argument heated up.

"I don't give a damn about the treasure," Glenn went on, narrowing his eyes, assuming a defiant stance. "It's not worth losing this boat over, and there's no way you've got three million dollars to replace it with. So it's settled. I'm going back to my charter business in Santa Barbara."

"No, it's *not* settled," I shouted, my cool melting like an ice cube in the tropics. "If you go back to Santa Barbara now, I'll use the investors' money to sue your ass. And I won't just sue you for the amount of the charter. I'll sue you for the amount we lost by not recovering the *Maravilla*. You don't have to worry about the *Colombians* taking your boat, Glenn. *I'm gonna take your boat!* I can run that damn charter business just as well as you can... probably better!"

I was on my feet now ranting and raving, sounding just like Glenn. I was jabbing my finger in the air at him and swearing up a storm.

"I was right the *first* time I called you a bitch!" yelled Glenn, and he stomped up the stairs to the main deck.

"Well," I said sweetly, brushing my hair back and straightening my blouse. "It looks like this boat is going to the Bahamas."

"General Brandeis," said Dick. "You never cease to amaze me," and he too climbed up the stairs and out of sight.

I had the rosy smile of victory the next morning as Glenn and I waited in the wheelhouse for Mr. Livingston to deliver our release paper. The *New York Times* woke my parents up in California at 6 a.m. to ask them if they knew I'd been arrested. In Santa Barbara, there were news flashes on the radio every fifteen minutes reporting the latest development in the capture of the *Coral Sea*. Front-page headlines from coast to coast announced our imminent departure from San Andres Island.

When Mr. Livingston rumbled up in his red, van truck with the release document and our passports, he also had his bill for $690 and a stack of flyers soliciting help for his civic movement against the repressive Colombian government.

When Mr. Livingston left the boat to return to town, he had Jake, Billy, Old Joe, Little Joe, and Dick Anderson with him. They'd had enough of treasure hunting. They wanted to return to the real world. I grabbed Anderson fiercely by his lapels and made him promise out loud that he would meet us in Florida. I made him cross his heart and hope to die if he didn't show up. Once he nodded agreement and I released him, the diesel engines started up, the lines were cast off and the *Coral Sea* slowly drifted away from the dilapidated fishing boat, leaving the coconut palms, white sand, and captivity behind us.

During the seven-day trip north to Florida, Katie was still blaming me for the whole ordeal and managed to divide the remaining crew into two factions: Them (me, Kevin, Steve, Marc, and Bubby) and Us (Glenn, Zach, and Katie). Neither side claimed Duane. There was orderly calm with little communication between the two factions, and Glenn didn't say one word to me the entire seven days. I slowly regained my confidence, taking a little credit for the fact that we were still headed towards a shipwreck full of treasure. It just didn't seem so glorious at the moment.

We passed Providencia, the Cayman Islands, and curved around the west side of Cuba, just as the galleons themselves had done centuries before us. We passed a place called Misterioso Bank, where, Anderson had told me, hundreds of ships had been lost in hurricanes. The weather and water got colder and rougher. In the Gulf of Mexico we had to put on our foul-weather gear when huge waves started breaking over the bow and swamping the deck with gray sea water. At the Florida Keys, we entered the Gulf Stream, picking up speed from the northerly six-knot current that carried us back into U.S. waters. We finally dropped anchor just outside West Palm Beach and waited for the sunrise before clearing customs.

Chapter Six

Sunrise over the smog layer of West Palm Beach wasn't as colorful as the sundance of light that heralds a Caribbean morning, but the relief of being back in the United States more than compensated for the lack. It was the end of March, two months since we had left Santa Barbara, enough time to make any person hunger for the familiarity of home. Of course, I expected there to be some behavioral differences between Californians and the inhabitants of this southern, sun-belt state. What I wasn't prepared for was treasure hunting, Florida style.

We motored slowly and cautiously into the Palm Beach Inlet, one of several narrow passages connecting the Atlantic Ocean with the strip of water running the length of Florida known as the Intercoastal Waterway. In the wide turning basin bordered by the northern tip of the Palm Beach Peninsula, the *Coral Sea* gently turned on its axis and sidled up to the rubber-cushioned pier of the U.S. Customs Dock.

Two uniformed customs officers came aboard to check our passports and record all the information about our vessel. There were no reporters or cameramen, none of the hoopla I expected to welcome home a boatload of escaped hostages. By the time we had reached Florida, our ordeal in San Andres was yesterday's news and nobody cared. We were just another boat with those weird tube things on the stern, and we were duly given an entry number and recorded in the customs logbook. The officers took a quick look through the vessel, then directed us south, down the Intercoastal Waterway, to the yacht harbors of West Palm Beach.

Glenn was particularly careful in navigating the swirling, eddy-filled channel. The waterway was bordered by wealthy estates on the port side and commercial storage yards on the starboard side. Brightly colored, canvas-topped, sport fishing boats and sleek, pointy-nosed speedboats zipped passed us in both direction. Twice we ran aground on sandbars, hurled forward by the abrupt stop both times and embarrassed when the engines revved loudly in reverse to dislodge us before we could move on downstream. Glenn finally set his chair right down in front of the depth recorder and stared at it as if in a trance. We passed underneath arched, cement bridges inundated with automobile traffic and tied up on the end berth of a moderate-sized marina. Our port side faced across the water to the palm-tree-lined entrance to the rich people's winter-time resort, Palm Beach.

After the engines were shut down, the shore power cord connected, and mooring lines fastened, Glenn hopped off the boat and briskly walked down the long dock to meet a flaming red Jaguar that was waiting in the parking lot. He got in and the car sped into the stream of traffic paralleling the waterfront. While everybody else was arguing over who was next in the bathroom, I checked in at the marina office and paid for one week's use of the dock facilities.

A week should be sufficient, I thought. It couldn't take more than a week for Dick to get here and confirm our agreement with Rodney Baron, the sublease holder. Even though it had taken us two months to get to Florida, the worst was over. Now we could get down to the real business of treasure hunting. That pleasant, reassuring thought lasted the length of time it took me to walk back to the boat. Glenn had returned from his mysterious car ride and was waiting for me in the wheelhouse.

"I'm not paying you the seven thousand dollars for the repairs in Panama," he said, standing beside the wheel with his arms crossed.

"But you promised me you would when we got to Florida," I reminded him timidly, hoping to avoid another battle.

"Yeah, but that was before I talked to my lawyer back in California. He says I don't have to pay you. You accepted the condition of the vessel when we left Santa Barbara. I ain't paying."

"Then I'll just stop payment on the check for this month's charter fee and deduct the seven thousand dollars from it," I countered.

"You go ahead and do that," Glenn snapped. "This charter's through anyway. I got you to Florida. That's as far as I go. Besides, I can get more money chartering this boat here than the measly amount you're paying me."

"Glenn, don't do this," I pleaded. "A lot of your friends put their money into this deal because of you. Anderson's going to be here and we're heading for the *Maravilla*."

"Anderson's an idiot," Glenn bellowed. "And you're a bigger idiot if you believe anything he says. I see it all now. He's just jealous of my boat. He wants to have it confiscated. He ain't no friend of mine, ya know what I mean?"

"Glenn, *you're* the one who introduced him to me, remember? You said you'd been best friends for years."

"That was before I found out what a lying sneak he really is. It don't matter now anyhow. You got yourself a bigger problem. This charter is canceled!"

Glenn sauntered down the stairs to the galley, leaving me stunned by the idea of having to look for another vessel. I mulled the idea over a few times, weighing the freedom from Glenn versus the costly search to find a comparable vessel. Deep in thought, I got off the boat again and walked towards the parking lot to begin what would be a long-standing relationship with the phone booth at the end of the dock.

I was just hanging up the phone when Anderson, bush hat and all, came walking towards the phone booth with an apprehensive smile on his face.

"Welcome to Florida, Margee Brandeis," he said as he extended his bulbous-knuckled hand. He wore his familiar blue work shirt and blue jeans, carried a dog-eared leather briefcase, and looked ready to get right down to business.

"Thank you for coming back. I knew you'd show up," I sighed.

"Don't thank me yet," he cautioned. "I only came back to tell you I quit."

"What? *Why?* Tell me you're just joking."

"I thought a lot about it back in California. I was a fool to think I could stomach Glenn for longer than three hours. Sorry, Margee, but I'm not going to show you where that treasure is because I could never live with myself if Glenn got 10 percent of it."

"You can't quit," I panicked. "Don't get fickle on me now. We're right across the Gulf Stream from the wrecksite. You agreed in a written contract to take me to the *Maravilla*."

"So sue me. It won't be the first time I've been sued over a fucking treasure deal. You'd think I'd learn by now. Listen,

Rodney Baron will be here in a few minutes. I'll put the two of you together and then I'm outta here."

He really meant it. I could tell by the complete lack of humor in his words. He usually ended every sentence with some wisecrack remark, but now there was none. Gold really does turn people to shit, was the only thing that came to mind as I stood there in the Florida afternoon sunshine. As I stared down at my feet, trying to invent another tactic for convincing Dick to stay, I caught a glimpse of two gigantic, black cockroaches at least four inches long, scurrying up between two wood slats of the dock. They disappeared over the edge before I could let out a piercing female scream. I jumped back two feet, frantically inspecting the dock for more of the obnoxious, unpredictable, fast-moving creatures. When I finally looked up again, Dick was shaking his head unsympathetically and using his thumb to draw my attention down the dock.

Walking casually towards us in gray coveralls, with a bulging pocket protector full of pencils and pens, was a studious looking man in his late forties, wearing round-rimmed glasses. His black slicked-down hair was parted on the side in an unsuccessful attempt at covering his very large ears. He carried a worn briefcase that suggested his visit was other than social, in fact, he seemed like a man who seldom made social calls. He was interested in straight business talk or nothing. Giving off a distinct air of southern pride and prejudice, he introduced himself and the three of us continued down the dock to the *Coral Sea*, which had been abandoned hours ago by our entire adventure-seeking, travel-weary crew.

"Heard you had some excitement down in San Andres," was Rodney's opening line. "Never trust those damn Colombians."

"We lost a couple of weeks and learned a lot about international waters," I told him snidely. I was struggling to soften my tone, hoping desperately for some good news that might change Dick's mind about quitting.

"There's no such thing as international waters," laughed Rodney, pounding the table top decisively. "Take the *Maravilla*, for instance. Technically, she's sitting in international waters too, but if you don't cut a deal with the Bahamians you're a sitting duck out there for every machine-gun-toting pirate who wants to take your treasure. It's worth the 25 percent the government takes just to get the protection. There'd be chaos out there otherwise."

"Rodney, Margee Brandeis here is the head of this operation," said Dick, cutting to the heart of the issue. "The boat is chartered to her and she controls the investors' funds."

"Ah," said Rodney with a slight air of incredulity. "He who has the gold makes the rules."

Rodney opened his briefcase and tossed a manila folder full of jumbled, legal size papers onto the galley table.

"We have a little snag in the paperwork that you should be aware of," he continued, pulling off his glasses and using them to point at the folder. "While you were dallying around in San Andres, the Bahamian government mistakenly issued another lease on the exact same four square miles covered by my lease. I flew over there last week to straighten it out but they're too embarrassed to admit they blew it, so it'll be thirty days or so before they decide which lease to honor."

"Are you serious?" I moaned, as I saw another piece of my expedition pie break off and fall on the floor.

"I never joke about treasure, darlin'," came Rodney's pointed reply. "My buddy, the Minister of Transport, says he signed the lease thinking it was for another area. When he found out, the sly bastard who tricked him had already left the country with the lease. It's just as valid as mine right now."

"Well, if the minister knows he screwed up, why doesn't he cancel the second lease?" I demanded desperately.

"You gotta understand Bahamian mentality, darlin'. They have to kick a thing around awhile until they think that everybody's forgotten whose fault it was in the first place. But they'll cancel the second lease, don't worry. I'd say about thirty days ought to do it. The weather's still a little rough anyway."

"So we have to just sit here and wait?" was my next dumb question.

"You got that right," Rodney said as he replaced the folder in his briefcase and snapped the locks shut. He complimented us on the boat and our timely arrival and said he'd be back in touch with us when the lease situation was cleared up. Just before he disembarked he warned us not to fall for any schemes concocted by any of the many treasure hunting kooks in Florida. Then he was gone.

Dick and I sat in silence for several long, soul-searching minutes. Then I told him that Glenn wanted out of the charter agreement and had gone off to look for a local attorney here in Florida to defend him. "He's probably in cahoots with the other lease holder," was Dick's cynical remark. My mind flashed to the red Jaguar that had whisked Glenn off that very morning. Then Dick headed down to his bunk to collect his belongings. He had made up his mind to quit and there was no changing it. "Margee, if you ever manage to get another boat and actually get out to the site, give me a call." Those were Dick's last words to me before he walked off down the dock, duffel bag over his shoulder, on his way back to California.

If my first fight with Glenn two months ago in San Diego had marked the end of my naive stage, my current loss of the boat, lease, and salvage master all in one day marked the end of my trusting faith in humanity. "Everyone's out for himself" was the cruel lesson being taught here. Only dogs are loyal, and then only if they're fed regularly. And written contracts are only as good as the lawsuits that enforce them. As for a person's promise, it's as changeable as the weather.

Glenn, Zach, and Katie returned an hour later accompanied by a dumpy looking lawyer with sagging pants, twisted eyeglasses, and a business card that proclaimed him a specialist in divorce, injury, and maritime law. He had a thick mustache, bulging jowls, and a body shaped like a bowling pin with a beer belly. He squeezed himself in at the galley table and proceeded to dictate to me his client's terms for canceling the charter agreement. There was to be no communication between the parties except through their respective attorneys, and the cook was relieved of all duties with respect to the charteree, meaning me and the dive crew. I pointed out that the terms were a little ridiculous, since we were all living together on the same vessel. Besides, I needed some time to find a local attorney too. He gave me one week. Then he squeezed himself out from behind the table and waddled out to the back deck to confer in private with his three clients before they all left the boat to have dinner on Glenn's tab.

By nightfall the dive crew had found their way back to the boat with stories of sun-tanned beauties, the best cheesecake in town, and the shortest route across the Intercoastal Waterway to Palm Beach. Kevin had stuck with the crew to make sure no one got into any trouble. He was one of them now and I felt totally alone.

I imparted the news that Dick had left and that it would be at least thirty days before the *Coral Sea* would move, if at all. Their mild disappointment was overshadowed by wide-eyed thoughts of thirty days of freedom on a Florida beach decorated with rich women. After they all went to bed, I walked out to the end of the pier, sat down, and cried.

I had a canceled boat charter, a contested lease site, no salvage master, and a crew that would rather chase women than anything else. So ends my career as a treasure hunter, I sobbed to myself, letting all the anxiety, guilt, hatred, frustration, and disbelief come pouring out under a starry sky, sixty miles away from the wreck I was supposed to recover. I guess it wasn't meant to be, I consoled myself.

I wiped my nose on the sleeve of my tee shirt, and leaned back until I was lying on the dock with my arms outstretched. Suddenly I felt cockroaches racing all over my hands in the darkness and I screamed. Jeez, I hate these bugs. And I don't really like boats either. Maybe it's a blessing that I failed. I guess I'll go back to real estate and leave this treasure hunting stuff to men. I'm through. Washed up. End of story.

The next day I went exploring with Kevin and the boys to get my mind off my troubles. We walked down Worth Avenue, mingling with the wealthy snowbirds from New York who invade Palm Beach from December to May to soak up the sun and throw lavish parties at their winter mansions. Mercedes convertibles cruised along landscaped streets. Blooming flowers and hanging bougainvillaea splashed color and perfume everywhere. Ornate hotels with shiny brass handrails lining their front steps radiated the presence of excessive money. Store windows offered designer clothes, exotic jewelry, one-of-a-kind knickknacks, imported shoes, polo accessories, and silk underwear. The cheapest ice cream cone was five dollars and carpets covered the sidewalks in front of banks.

We were clearly out of our element, but it didn't seem to matter to the firm-bodied females strolling the sidewalks in their gauzy dresses. They eyed my crew, flashing coquettish little smiles that invited the boys to follow. And that's exactly what the crew did. Only Kevin, Bubby, and I were left when it came time to explore the other side of the Intercoastal Waterway.

West Palm Beach was a whole other world. Flat concrete buildings lined wide boulevards full of low-income cars and service trucks. Instead of signs offering French cuisine there were billboards advertising Blue Front Barbecue Sauce: "Put some South in your Mouth." Instead of tennis and polo you could find a backgammon game atop a conga drum in a place called Conchy Joe's. Instead of caviar there were conch fritters. And huddled in doorways were unemployed black men waiting for something to come along and make things better.

This was where Bubby had grown up, and it was the first time he'd been back in fifteen years. To celebrate, we ate a huge order of the local specialty; catfish and hush puppies. After dinner we headed back towards the marina, stopping in souvenir shops along the way. Among the Florida saltwater taffy and alligator statues, I found a small wooden plaque with these words carved into it:

FOUR THINGS EVERY SUCCESSFUL WOMAN KNOWS
How to look like a girl
How to act like a lady
How to think like a man
How to work like a dog

The saying haunted me all night. I could do those four things. I could be successful. Why was I giving up? Why was I letting Glenn weasel out of the charter agreement? Who needed Dick Anderson anyway? I'd show them I could find a shipwreck! It couldn't be that hard, I reasoned. Other people have done it. First thing I had to do was find another salvage vessel.

For the next seven days Kevin and I rented a car and embarked on a quest through every coastal city in the state of Florida. We looked at tugboats in St. Petersburg, shrimp boats in Vero Beach, converted supply boats in Fort Pierce and surplus war-vessels in Fort Lauderdale. Then we headed south through Miami all the way to Key West to look at already equipped salvage boats. None of them compared to the *Coral Sea*, and no monthly charter fee was as low as the one I was paying Glenn. What I did find was a high-priced law firm in Miami that stalled Glenn's plan to evict me until I could solve the Bahamian lease problem.

Actually, the lease problem solved itself on the evening Zach and Katie returned to the *Coral Sea* with a rather large man dressed in a captain's hat and a double-breasted blue blazer with brass buttons. He introduced himself as a Greek sponge diver from Tarpon Springs. He had a massive salt-and-pepper beard and eyebrows that were so bushy they curled down into his eyes. He was hardy and big-bellied with a deep voice that boomed off the walls, as if Pavarotti were singing in a kitchen. I was standing at the opposite end of the galley when he entered behind Zach and Katie, and the instant he saw me he spread his arms wide, smiled broadly, and bellowed, "God sent you to me!"

"You must be Margee Brandeis," he continued as he approached me, his smile growing bigger with each step. "I was on the bridge the day you and this marvelous vessel arrived and I knew, God had sent you to me."

Then he grabbed me by the waist and danced me around in circles. I couldn't help laughing at this good-natured fool. He was either drunk or the happiest person I'd ever met.

"My prayers have been answered," he sighed, releasing my waist to grab both my hands and place them against his chest. He closed his eyes and grinned toward the ceiling. "I know this seems crazy right now, but you and I have a tremendous task in front of us. I have much to tell you. May I come by tomorrow to explain everything? Is nine o'clock too early?"

"Nine is fine," I heard myself say, somewhat overwhelmed.

"Excellent! Isn't this a fabulous world we live in?" he remarked. He said goodnight to Zach and Katie and left through the galley door, leaving me staring in astonishment at the ridiculous encounter.

"What was that?" I finally asked Zach and Katie.

"Milo Zorbas," answered Zach apologetically. "He kind of joined us for dinner at the restaurant. He knew all about us. He knew your name and begged us to introduce him to you. He says he has some very important information for you. What else could we do?"

"You could have warned me first," I suggested, figuring Katie had more to do with the impromptu meeting than Zach. Katie was a conniver who excelled in cajoling people into doing things her way. What I didn't realize then was that Milo Zorbas could teach even Katie a thing or two about cajoling.

Promptly at nine the next morning, Milo Zorbas returned to the boat, this time dressed in yellow plaid pants and a safari-style shirt with the buttons stretched tight at the waistline. He escorted me down the dock to the parking lot and directed me toward a strange looking El Dorado Cadillac with its back half cut down to make a cargo space, like a truck. The whole thing was spray painted black. The inside of the car was completely lined in black fur. Note papers were scattered all over the dashboard. Milo opened the passenger door for me, maintaining his jovial smile and gentlemanly manners. My mother would have screamed if she had seen me get into that bizarre looking automobile, but then she never was the adventurous type.

Milo drove south through town, gabbing all the way about the ocean and how he and I had been brought together by the Lord. We entered a middle-class residential neighborhood and parked in front of an ordinary looking, green shingled house. At the front door I noticed a brass plate screwed into the shingles that read, The Athanagorus Brotherhood Church

Inside the house, things looked normal until we walked through the living room and I saw the indoor swimming pool. It was lit in blue, surrounded by rock and hanging ferns, and had a waterfall at one end. The flat, slate rock edges merged into an office area in an alcove where yellowed newspaper clippings were thumbtacked all over one wall. Snapshots of boats, divers, and artifacts were thumbtacked all over another wall.

There was a display table in the alcove where giant, square nails, colored rocks, and small, rusted pieces of metal were arranged on it, with little typed descriptions taped below each item. Milo motioned me towards an empty chair beside the table and I sat down, still scanning the display.

"These artifacts are off the *Maravilla*," he said proudly. Then he leaned closer, as if to reveal a secret. "The wreck isn't in Rodney Baron's lease area. It's in mine. I have seventy-five square miles under concession directly south of Rodney's site." Milo watched me intently, waiting for my reaction to this startling information, knowing I didn't believe it. Then he said, "I want you to excavate the wreck for me."

He let that statement sink in before continuing. "I've studied thousands of pages of documents over the last five years, and I can prove to you that the wreck is in my lease area."

"But Robert Marx found the wreck, and he says it's in Rodney's area. He brought up real treasure to prove it. What have you got?" I said.

91

Somebody was lying. Which one was it? Was I getting suckered into something here or was I uncovering new information that would lead me to the real location of the *Maravilla*? Maybe this is what Anderson had known and refused to tell me. My sense of adventure was returning. I was feeling the anticipation of the hunt again. My fingers were twitching.

"I have more than sufficient data to prove it to you," Milo said. "But I must have your trust first. There is something much bigger at stake here than just uncovering a Spanish galleon - something that will change the world. Are you prepared to see this project through to the very end?"

"Sure," I chirped. "I'm not a quitter."

"You'll be severely tested before this ordeal is over."

"Look, Mr. Zorbas," I said, assuming my most convincing manner. "I have the resources to do the job. My proof is the *Coral Sea* sitting at the marina. I still have to see your proof."

"I'm prepared to show you my proof," Milo quickly replied. "Please understand the delicate nature of shipwreck information. You have nothing to lose by listening, and I have everything to lose by telling you."

Over the next two hours he unrolled charts, laid out dozens of books containing old drawings, and related to me in detail how one Sir William Phipps had recovered a large portion of the *Maravilla* forty years after it sank. Phipps left a log book showing the location of the *Maravilla* as well as that of four other shipwrecks along the Little Bahama Bank. Milo showed me government seismic charts of the area, aerial photographs, underwater pictures of large dark objects on the ocean floor, and Bahamian government documents stamped with several blue ink seals. The sheer weight of his evidence was very convincing. I started to think that even though this guy drove a weird car and had an unusual house, he might actually possess some valuable facts on the wreck I had come to recover.

"Do you know about the statue of the Madonna and Christ Child?" he asked me when we took a break from studying documents.

"No, nothing," I said, bracing myself mentally for more monumental information.

"I'm sure you've researched the wreck enough to know that King Philip IV of Spain was almost broke when the *Maravilla* was loaded with treasure. Her delivery of gold and silver from the New World was expected to save the Spanish throne from bankruptcy. Well, in addition to her manifested cargo, she was carrying a five-foot-tall, solid gold statue of the Madonna and Christ Child. The king had ordered it for the Holy Church. The statue was loaded onto the *Maravilla* in complete secrecy in Vera Cruz, Mexico. It has never been found.

"Very interesting," I said in a level voice, hoping I didn't sound like I hadn't done my research. Actually, I only knew what I had heard from Anderson and Glenn, and that hardly qualified as research. Then I started mentally calculating how much the statue would be worth.

"I'll tell you why I'm obsessed with recovering this wreck," Milo went on. "Three years ago I was caught in a terrible storm in my fishing boat, the *Republic*. The winds had blown me way off course and I was taking on too much water, almost sinking. Just when I had given up hope of making it back alive, the clouds parted slightly and an amazing shaft of bright light shone straight down onto the water. Instantly the storm cleared and I was able to save my boat and myself. I threw a buoy overboard on the spot then dove down in the shallow water. I found a cannon and a big treasure box sticking up out of the sand just like this one." Milo held out a book opened to a picture of a seventeenth-century trunk.

"All the things on this table are from that wrecksite. These stones here are unpolished rubies and jade." He rolled his finger through a small pile of red and green stones on the table. Then he picked up a thick square spike that looked like a bronze chisel. "Only a vessel built to carry valuables would have been made with spikes like this one. Normally the spikes were just iron. I've also studied the wind and weather systems and I can prove that the main section of the *Maravilla* would have drifted south from the point where it was struck by the other vessel and broken in two. Rodney Baron's wrecksite is only the bow section of the *Maravilla*. My wrecksite is the main cargo hold."

Milo had my complete and undivided attention now. The quantity of data he had showed me was enough to give him some real credibility. Even if his wreck wasn't the *Maravilla*, it was worth checking out. I wanted to see the cannon and treasure box.

"After that experience I was 'born again'," Milo continued. "I knew I had found the *Maravilla* and that it was my task to bring up its treasure in the name of God. But I'm not a rich man. I can't afford the vessel and equipment needed for the recovery. So God showed me your vessel motoring under the bridge. He brought you here to help me complete this task. If we are going to work together, you must be willing to give God the credit for recovering the wreck."

"God can have the credit," I joked. "How much do we get?"

"The Bahamians will take 25 percent and the balance will be divided equally between the Athanagorus Brotherhood Church and you."

Very intriguing, I thought. Here's another twist to the game. Is the church thing just a tax cover? What does he have to gain if all this stuff he's telling me is a lie? There's so much data here it can't all be a hoax, can it? Am I holding his born-again enthusiasm against him? It wouldn't be a bad thing having God on our side, but what would the crew think about all this?

I was really baffled. I certainly couldn't ignore what Milo was telling me. If his wreck really was the *Maravilla*, I'd look like a real idiot for passing up this chance to excavate it. At the very least, I ought to eliminate the possibility.

Milo sat down in the desk chair and swiveled it around to face me. Then he handed me an artist's rendition of a galleon being battered by a huge wave.

"That's the cover drawing for my book," he said. "It's all written. The world is coming to an end but all good Christians have nothing to worry about. They will all be taken up to heaven. That's the message of the book. The recovery of the treasure will simply bring world attention to it. Margaret, we are but tools for God's use. He is the real salvage master to recover the *Maravilla* treasure."

The crew is never going to believe this one, I thought. This is just too ridiculous. "Look, I have to be getting back to the boat," was all I said.

I called a crew meeting the next morning and gave a vague outline of Milo's wrecksite and his proposal that we dig up the treasure for him. I left out the part about God. The issue was pretty clear-cut; did we want to stay tied to the dock in Florida or check out Milo's wrecksite? In a show of hands, the whole crew, even Glenn, Zach and Katie, voted for investigating Milo's site.

"I've got a message here from the man who has the second lease on Baron's site," Glenn smiled as he passed me a piece of paper. It said:

I'LL BLOW YOU OUT OF THE WATER IF YOU TRY TO WORK MY SITE!

❦

During the following week, I spent hours and hours in the phone booth at the end of the dock. I was receiving advice from lawyers, investors, Anderson, and my mother. Meanwhile, Milo was proceeding with the details. He had a contract typed up and convinced Glenn that his seventy-five-square-mile Bahamian lease concession was completely legal and absolutely uncontested. Glenn then had his attorney put in writing that if the *Coral Sea* was going anywhere, it was going to Milo's site. So I signed the contract with Milo and the crew started preparing for another voyage.

"Why'd ya go and make a deal with that wino?" Rodney Baron roared the day I visited him to say we'd be working Milo's site until the double-lease situation was cleared up on his site. "The man's a raving lunatic! A Jesus freak! Don't tell me you believed his cock-and-bull story about the *Maravilla* being in his lease area? He's been telling that shit to the press for years. I told you to stay away from the kooks! Jesus! I knew I never should have made a deal with no woman! Wait'll I tell Marx about this. He'll laugh his fool head off."

Rodney exhaled a smoke cloud around himself as he paced his family room. I sat in his Lazyboy™ recliner and hung my head in shame.

Back on the boat, I brooded over my situation. I couldn't back out of the deal with Milo, it was already signed and the investors had been told we were leaving for the Bahamas. I had taken Glenn out to dinner at the Breakers, the fanciest, most expensive hotel in Palm Beach, and settled our charter dispute by finally agreeing to let his girlfriends come out on the boat with us, one at a time. I had to make a move. Sitting at the dock was costing me five hundred dollars a day. I figured it couldn't hurt to take a look at the cannon and treasure box Milo had found. We were all itching to get in the water. So, in the second week of April, we pulled out and headed for the Bahamas with Milo Zorbas as our new lease partner and God as our salvage master.

Chapter Seven

To reach Grand Bahama Island, the northernmost island in the Bahama Islands chain, you have to steer southeast when you come out of the Palm Beach Inlet, even though your destination lies northeast. That's because the Gulf Stream current will carry your boat so far north you would miss the island completely if you steered straight for it. We were heading for the northern tip of Grand Bahama Island, the last vestige of the New World that a Spaniard would have seen on his way across the Atlantic towards home.

When the vessels of three and four hundred years ago drifted up the Gulf Stream current, catching the wind whenever they could, their captains used sextants to calculate what latitude they were crossing. The only other navigational aids were a few crude, hand-drawn maps, a compass and the captains' memory. The vessels were big, clumsy, and so heavy with gold and silver that they were almost impossible to steer in bad weather. Besides all their valuable cargo, they were obligated to carry thirty to seventy cannons to protect themselves against attacks. All the artillery was mounted near the top decks, which made the ships so top heavy they were ready to keel over at the first opportunity.

It was scary business sailing across the ocean in a galleon. Everybody went to church before they got on board. They had no idea when a hurricane might brew up and no way to communicate with other ships except by running up flags or firing shots in the air. They were completely at the mercy of Mother Nature.

I had gone on a reading binge at the Palm Beach library to learn all I could about galleons. I figured it was about time I found out what I had gotten myself into instead of relying on someone else to teach me, which hadn't worked too well. I also checked out books on the theory and use of magnetometers and metal detectors and whatever there was on underwater excavations. To my surprise, Robert Marx had written a great number of the books available. At least one of the people I had met on the project knew what he was doing.

Now we were sailing across the Gulf Stream in our modern-day vessel. The wind whipped at our faces and the sun warmed our skin. A saltwater mist flew off the crests of the white-tipped waves as we plunged forward through dark blue water. We were finally on our way again to dig up treasure and the whole boat was alive with the feeling. Everyone was anxious, spiked with excitement. Even I was sparkling again, dreaming of the treasure that would soon be mine. This was a prime example of the glorious, but temporary, highs that characterize the up-and-down roller-coaster ride of a treasure hunting expedition.

Eight hours of open ocean brought us within sight of a thin white crust of land topped by a row of wispy green pine trees bent to the wind. The dark blue of the water gradually lightened to aquamarine as it approached a white, soft-sand beach. This was West End, an isolated village of Bahamian fishermen and conch divers. The main attraction was a large, bustling hotel that catered to the package vacation crowd from the midwestern United States and graduating high school girls from Canada.

The hotel, with its restaurants, shopping arcade, recreation facilities, theater, swimming pool, private beach, and concrete-walled commercial dock, was a city in itself, where weekly shipments of food and convenience items arrived from Florida. Its yacht harbor teemed with party-loving weekend sailors and sailboat live-aboards. We motored through the narrow harbor entrance and pulled up to the commercial dock. For the next four months, this would be our link to civilization.

Our arrival attracted no special attention. The Bahamian townspeople had seen plenty of treasure hunting boats over the years. And since the *Maravilla* had been discovered, several ships equipped with odd-looking tubes on their sterns had appeared during the calm-weather season. The hotel management gladly collected its reasonable dock fee, and the hotel employees gladly offered us anything we needed at a negotiable price.

After we were cleared by customs officials and given a Bahamian cruise permit, Milo rented a hotel room and went off in search of the manager to arrange for a display of shipwreck artifacts in the hotel lobby. The crew went off in search of female hotel guests. Glenn and Zach went off in search of other captains to talk to. And Kevin and I were left with Katie, who cornered me in the galley to complain that she had now cooked two hundred and eighty-two meals since we left Santa Barbara and deserved a week's vacation.

Pine trees surrounded the commercial dock, and the wind rustled through their tops, creating a pleasant whistle that soothed the nerves and dulled the senses. Time seemed to slow down. The Bahamians were in no rush to change their lifestyle, the hotel guests were in no rush to go back home, and the boat dwellers

101

were in no rush to end their parties. Harmonious procrastination abounded. The term island time took on real meaning. Among the crew, bicycles became the favored mode of transportation, and everywhere the breeze and salty sea smell combined with the bright sun and vivid blue sky to make the perfect image of a tropical heaven.

Across from the hotel was a liquor store manned by a skinny, inattentive Bahamian content to play backgammon nine hours a day in the shade of the store doorway. Mathuselum Rum, distilled and bottled in Freeport at the south end of the island, became the preferred beverage of the crew. It mixed with anything and was always available if you had time to play a game of backgammon. You might even get it for free if you managed to win the game - an event as rare as snowballs on the beach.

The Bahamians spoke a Jamaican-style English, accenting the vowels and calling everybody mon. Even Glenn was enjoying himself in West End, no longer considering me a threat to his authority. In fact, he was making plans to fly one of his girlfriends out from Santa Barbara to keep him company while we were digging up treasure. We spent a grand three days, but our bubble burst on the fourth morning when we woke up to find two smaller vessels tied to the dock just in front of us. The names *Scrounger II* and *Scrounger III* were painted across their sterns.

"Wonder what happened to *Scrounger I*?" was Steve's rhetorical question as we all gathered in the galley for a meeting with Milo.

"I'm going to introduce you to several people today," Milo began. There was a trace of excitement in his voice. "But first I'm going to show you the silver we've recovered from the wrecksite." Milo lifted a cloth to reveal a five-pound oblong disk of pure silver resting on the galley table. "The two boats tied up in front of the *Coral Sea* have been working the ballast pile of my wreck for the past three weeks. They've found two other pieces of silver besides this one. I've arranged for you to return with them to the site so they can show you how far they've progressed."

"Why didn't you tell us you had other people working for you?" I blurted out, suddenly angry that I hadn't been told the whole story. The rest of the crew were drooling over the silver.

"It's of no consequence. They'll be leaving for good the day after tomorrow," responded Milo, as if I were out of line questioning him at all. "God has chosen *this* crew to have the glory of recovering the *Maravilla* treasure."

"God, my ass," scoffed Glenn. He picked up the silver and tossed it in the air a couple of times. "Why are they leaving if they've just found this silver?"

"You are not to question my decisions," reprimanded Milo. He looked furious. "I am God's representative here and I know how He wants the excavation to proceed!"

During that one outburst I suddenly realized we were working with a complete madman who actually believed himself to be the right hand of God.

"Now, I've drawn up a diagram here of the chain of command," Milo continued in a calmer voice. He held up a chart he'd made on poster board. "As you see, I'm at the top with four stars. Glenn and Zachary are under me with three stars, I've appointed two of my most loyal church members to be on board as my representatives, and they each have two stars. Over here I've put Marc and Duane as leaders of the divers and I've assigned them one star. The rest of the crew is listed down here under Marc and Duane. Margee, you don't seem to fit in anywhere, so you're down here at the bottom." I was outraged but silent. My crew members were starting to snicker under their breath.

"I'll be standing by at our base station here at the hotel," Milo went on. "We'll stay in contact by radio so I can get you any supplies you need." He pulled a Mohawk CB radio microphone out of a box he'd brought with him and placed it on the table. It was at least thirty years old, from the era of Amos and Andy. The crew had to cover their mouths to hide their laughter.

"Aren't you coming with us?" asked Duane earnestly, oblivious to the humor in the situation.

"I wish I could," was Milo's sorrowful answer, to which the crew breathed a sigh of relief. "But I can't abandon our daily Christian radio show. That's why I'm sending Pete and Randy with you. They're good divers and they've been with me since the start of this project. I want you all to treat them with kindness and courtesy."

"This meeting is over, as far as I'm concerned," Glenn growled emphatically. He got up from his usual place under the air conditioner and headed for the rear galley door. "This is a bunch of hogwash, if you ask me." The crew was snickering again.

"You can laugh if you want to," yelled Milo, waving a warning finger in the air. "But each of you will be severely tested by God before you're finished. He will decide if you are deserving of this treasure, not I."

The crew looked longingly after Glenn, wishing they had the guts to leave too. But they were curious enough to hear what else Milo might say and greedy enough not to upset the fragile accord we had struck with this obsessed religious man with the five-pound silver bar in his hand.

"Now, there's one more thing you should know," Milo resumed after Glenn had gone. "There's an old Bahamian legend that says that when the solid gold statue of the Madonna and Christ Child is found, it will signal the beginning of the end of the world. But do not fear!" He took on a thunderous preacher's tone. "All good Christians will be saved and taken up to heaven!"

When the meeting was finally over and Milo had returned to his hotel room, Bubby, Steve, Marc, and Kevin called a meeting of their own on the helicopter pad with me as a captive audience.

"Margee, you can't be serious about this guy," was Bubby's desperate opening line.

"Yeah, no one said anything about causing the end of the world when I signed onto this misadventure," added Steve sarcastically.

"Did you see Duane lapping up every word Milo said?" asked Marc. "He's really believing this shit. That could be dangerous."

"I think the real question here is, are you gonna tell if you find the statue?" said Kevin. "Maybe we could melt it down before anybody saw it."

"Naw, biblical prophecy wouldn't disappear just because nobody else sees the statue. I think the world would still end," concluded Steve.

"This isn't biblical prophecy, it's Bahamian prophecy," Marc corrected him.

"Gentlemen," I said. "I had only one goal in mind when we started this whole thing and that was to find the treasure of the *Maravilla*. The goal is still the same. We've just changed the players. I know Milo is a kook, but we're going along with him - and God - until we see what's in that treasure box. Agreed?"

"I'll stick it out," smiled Steve. "I've got nothing to lose."

"Me, too," Kevin chimed in. "It's getting interesting now."

"I've come this far," sighed Marc. "I'm not going to back out now."

"Bubby?" I prodded.

"Oh, all right," agreed Bub, twisting the bottom edge of his torn tee shirt. "But if there's no treasure I get to kill Milo."

"Bub, that's not a Christian thing to do," I reminded him in a motherly tone.

"Then let me kill Katie," was Bub's quick alternative. "I swear I'm gonna do it if she tells me one more time to go on a diet."

"Hey, Bub," said Steve. "Just wait until dinner when she's looking right at you. Then pour ketchup all over the meal. That'll cause her more pain than death would."

"You're right!" cried Bub, his eyes lighting up at the thought. "Okay. Her life is temporarily spared."

In the morning Milo showed up all twinkle-eyed and merry with his "authorized representatives" and a case full of neon orange and electric yellow spray paint. He soon had the dive crew painting numbers on our cement blocks and marking off one-foot increments on a fifty-foot length of chain. Then he had the crew paint each foot of chain in alternating colors. After the painting, construction began on wood-framed screen boxes to be used to sift sand for coins and gems Glenn watched the whole process with amused detachment. He still thought Milo was an idiot but as long as his boat was safe, and he was getting his charter fee, he didn't object to checking out Milo's wrecksite.

Needless to say, we all gave Milo's two "representatives" the once-over when they came onboard. Pete, the older one, was constantly chewing on a wad of tobacco and always carried a tiny ceramic cup in his left hand to spit in. Randy was a spindly seventeen-year-old who stuck close to Pete and rarely spoke. We accepted the two of them for exactly what they were, spies for Milo.

By noon we had loaded the chains, blocks, and screens on the back deck and were waiting with varying degrees of patience while Milo blessed the boat. He prayed out loud for a safe voyage and bountiful recovery and then stood soberly on the pier as we pulled away.

The *Scrounger III* led the way, turning northward outside the harbor towards the submerged continental shelf known as the Little Bahama Bank. This shallow bank juts north from Grand Bahama Island for almost fifty miles before it drops away into deep ocean. Its western edge is littered with wrecks from the Spanish period and the Civil War, when blockade runners and rum and gun powder smugglers dashed back and forth across the Gulf Stream. The bank was so shallow in some places that if a ship hit it and sank, its mast would still be sticking up out of the water. In the case of the *Maravilla*, its captain actually headed for the bank after she was struck by another ship. He wanted her to sink in shallow water so she could be easily salvaged.

According to Bob Marx's account, it was 1656, and the *Maravilla* was traveling home to Spain with several other ships loaded with treasures from South America, Mexico, and Cuba. In the middle of the night, a lookout shouted that the ship was in shallow water, too close to the bank. The captain ordered the ship turned left, back out toward the deep Gulf Stream, and had a cannon shot fired to warn the other ships that there was danger ahead. But the vessel just behind the *Maravilla* misunderstood the warning shot and sailed headlong into the *Maravilla's* port side, snapping her in two. She started taking on water through the gaping hole just behind her bow section, and the captain frantically ordered the vessel to come about and head for the bank, knowing her sinking was inevitable. The Spaniards never recovered all her cargo, and Sir William Phipps renamed her the Plate Wreck when he found her, because of all the silver plates he recovered from her wreckage.

When Robert Marx rediscovered the *Maravilla* in the early 1970's, he reported finding only the bow section, speculating that the main cargo hold must have drifted farther east. Milo was claiming that the hull had drifted slightly southward into his lease area, and it was towards Milo's site we were now heading on this balmy afternoon voyage.

After four hours of traveling, the *Scrounger III* slowed to a stop and radioed us that we had arrived at the wrecksite. There was nothing around us but blue ocean and blue sky.

Underwater, the Little Bahama Bank formed a barrier reef that was too shallow for our vessels to pass over, but the *Scrounger III* had found a cut in the bank wide enough for us to pass to the inside of the reef and anchor in eighteen feet of water over the wrecksite. Glenn was noticeably nervous as we inched our way between the coral outcroppings on either side of the cut. He insisted that we attach one of the bright orange Norwegian buoys to a coral head to mark the entrance permanently.

As the sun flattened out on the horizon, lighting the bottoms of the distant clouds with a fiery bronze light, we set out three anchors to hold us stationary for the night. The sea was as calm as a lake on a windless summer evening and a billion stars made their appearance on a black velvet sky.

The captain of the *Scrounger III* invited Glenn and me over to his vessel for a drink. We motored over in the rubber Zodiac and climbed aboard the back deck, where folding chairs were scattered haphazardly around a massive air compressor. Four men in dirty tee shirts were already seated, holding coffee mugs full of liquor and smiling at us as if our legs were caught in a beaver trap.

"So you're Milo's next victims," one of the men exclaimed as he shook our hands. "Welcome aboard." The rest of the men just nodded their heads slightly in greeting. Two more coffee mugs were handed to Glenn and I as the ship's captain stepped through a hatchway, carrying a liquor bottle.

"Welcome to the rock wreck," said the captain, raising his coffee mug. "We've uncovered almost the whole ballast pile for you. What you do next is up to you."

"What about the silver?" asked Glenn anxiously. "That's what we're here for, ya know what I mean?"

"Shit, we found that silver three weeks ago and nothin' since," said the captain.

"Do you guys think this is the *Maravilla*?" I cut in, already wincing at what the answer might be.

"If it is, it was stripped and burned to the water line before it settled here practically in one piece. That ballast pile is perfectly intact, and there ain't nothin' but cannon balls and pottery shard scattered all around. I'm just glad we're getting off this damn project tomorrow."

"Why did you sign up with Milo in the first place?" I asked, gripping my cup and hoping for a sane response. The captain got up from his chair and started pacing like a caged lion.

"It wasn't my damned idea," he growled. "The guy who owns this boat had his tit in a ringer and we got stuck with this job. He'd raised a lot of money from investors but didn't have a site to work. The investors were screaming because he'd already taken his 25 percent of the money, so he made a deal with that lunatic Milo, and here we are."

"You mean the boat owner got 25 percent of the investor's money before any work was started?" Glenn asked. I could see the wheels spinning inside his head as he tried to calculate what his amount would have been.

"Shit, yes," one of the other men piped up. "That fucker lives on the money he raises. He don't give a damn about finding treasure, long as he has a boat and a site to work. He just keeps raking in the bucks."

"Where're you headed next?" Glenn asked.

"Back to beautiful Florida," said the captain, his attitude suddenly changing to mirth. "This boat's goin' into drydock. That's the other thing the guy does with the money - he keeps his boats fixed up."

"How does he get away with it?" Glenn asked, as if he were taking notes on the guy's scam.

"Hell, Florida's crawling with fools looking to invest in a treasure hunt. And this guy's got a real talent for finding 'em," answered another man.

"What percentage of the recovery do you guys get?" I asked.

"Recovery, my ass. You think we're stupid enough to fall for that shit?" laughed the captain. "We get a nice fat salary, guaranteed, even when we're in drydock. Anybody who'd do this work for a percentage oughta have his head examined."

Glenn and I looked at each other silently and the captain changed the subject.

"Now, Glenn, I'd advise you to anchor south no matter what the wind is doing," said the captain. "This current is stronger than you think and any bad weather will come at you from that direction. 'Course the squalls will come at you from any direction. Best thing to do then is just hold your ground. And whatever you do, don't go east. It just gets shallower. I'd keep a weather radio on all the time if I was you. First notice of any hurricane, you get your ass back to West End, pronto. As far as the excavation is concerned, if you're gonna use those blasters you got on your boat, you'll blow whatever's down there to smithereens. Not that it matters any. There's nothing down there to find."

"Don't forget to tell 'em about the electronics," added one of the men, taking another gulp from his coffee cup.

"Oh, yeah," the captain continued. "You know you're sitting in the Bermuda Triangle, don't you?" Glenn and I flashed another quick glance at each other. "Some days all the electronics just go crazy. Nothin' works. Beats me what causes it. In a day or two everything goes back to normal. It's the damnedest thing."

The conversation stretched on for another hour. The men got to talking about vessel equipment and Glenn invited them over to the *Coral Sea* to take a look at his engine room. I never asked about the treasure box Milo had discussed with me. I thought I ought to keep something secret. Or maybe I just didn't want to hear any more bad news.

In the Zodiac, on the way back to our boat, Glenn only said one thing, "Remember, it was *your* idea to work on Milo's site."

Chapter Eight

Glenn wasted no time informing the rest of the crew about the pessimistic observations made by the men of the *Scrounger III*. Lots of whites showed around everybody's eyeballs when they heard we were inside the Bermuda Triangle, where many ships and planes have mysteriously disappeared over the years. Not only were we inside the triangle, we were at the apex of it. This realization started discussions about the lost city of Atlantis and other eerie, unexplained phenomena. Someone even asked whether there might be ghosts from the shipwreck guarding the treasure. I had nothing reassuring to add to the conversation except to remind everybody that we would be on Milo's site only until the duplicate-lease situation was cleared up on Rodney Baron's site. Of course, if we found treasure at Milo's site, we'd reconsider.

There was no lack of enthusiasm the next morning as we all dragged out our dive gear and Zach fired up the air compressor to begin filling tanks. Kevin was really in his element now, checking gauges, adjusting straps, and repairing regulators. He preferred the operational side of treasure hunting, leaving the never-ending battle of management to me.

Katie made a special breakfast partly to commemorate our first day in the water and partly to remind everybody that, unlike the rest of the crew, she had been working at her job since we had left Santa Barbara. She had already decided that we would never find any treasure and that I didn't know what the hell I was doing. She had visions of a little yarn shop she would open when she got back home, resolving that she would cook her gourmet meals only for people who would appreciate them, not for ketchup-loving bums like us.

In record time the whole crew was jumping off the back deck into the crystal-clear, eighty-five-degree water. No wetsuits were needed here. It felt like bathtub water; in fact, you had to get out of the water to cool off.

The ocean floor was a snow-white, sand desert dotted with random outcroppings of elkhorn coral. In some places only five feet of water covered the coral's rigid branches, which felt no remorse at slicing the skin of a careless diver. A hundred times more painful, was the fire coral, with its smooth-looking vertical branches. The surface of fire coral is covered with millions of microscopic hair-like thorns that attach to the skin like nettles, causing a burning sting that lasts for hours. Only one encounter with fire coral was needed to teach a diver respect for that small, easily hidden growth. Moray eels and the sharp-toothed barracuda could be scared away, but not fire coral. It respected nothing, and burned every fool who came in contact with it.

The highest branches of the elkhorn coral marked the top of the reef, which swooped down into a giant pit of sand that stretched off into the distance. The color of the water was iceburg blue.

Swimming underwater in the direction of the sand, one suddenly came upon a huge depression neatly filled with a pyramid-shaped pile of rocks ten feet high and thirty feet long. It looked like a monument, a tombstone of round, smooth, toaster-size river rocks all stacked up in a neat pile. This was a ballast pile, the hundreds of tons of heavy rock that filled the bottoms of wooden vessels to keep them balanced upright. This was the wrecksite.

But there was no ship, no piece of a ship, not anything resembling a ship. Just that pile of rocks. Sand had been cleared away in all directions from the rock pile right down to the hard, limestone ocean floor. Pieces of worm-eaten wood glazed over by a thin crust of white coral-growth lay scattered around the rocks. Lots of broken pieces of clay pottery the size of soda crackers could be found around the outer edges of the depression and in the cracks and crevices of the coral reef. That was it.

On later dives, using the underwater metal detectors, we found square, green nails eight inches long and some wafer-thin pieces of rusted metal. That was all that existed within 200 hundred feet of that pile of rocks.

After three hours underwater combing over the bottom, using my dive knife to flip things over or poke into crevices, I returned to the boat disenchanted. I had expected something a little more glamorous than this. I had known we would not find a whole vessel waiting for us, but I had thought some pieces would be lying around.

I got a full tank of air and went down again just to sit on the bottom opposite the rock pile and study it. The first thing that bothered me was how small the rock pile was in comparison to the size of the galleons I'd seen in pictures. The second thing was that if a ship had sunk here, in eighteen feet of water, the Spaniards would have had no trouble at all recovering the treasure. My third thought was, this couldn't possibly be the *Maravilla*.

After diving all morning and finding nothing new, we pulled up the anchors and prepared to head back to West End. Already bored with our treasure hunting activities, Zach turned on the stereo and tuned in the radio station Milo had told us to listen to at noon. Milo's familiar voice came booming through the speakers, preaching something about projects in the name of God and how the Athanagorus Brotherhood had been blessed with the arrival of a salvage vessel from California.

"... Let us praise the Lord for providing us with our newfound Christian friends and the magnificent vessel that the Lord will use to recover what He buried so long ago. At this very moment our friends are busy working at the site for us, facing dangerous underwater perils to accomplish God's will. I hope they're listening. Hi, Margee, hi, Glenn, and Zach and Katie and the whole crew of the *Coral Sea*. Our prayers are with you. Praise the Lord. This is Milo Zorbas signing off until tomorrow at our lunch time Christian broadcast. Tsssss ..."

"You sure know how to pick 'em, Margee," was Glenn's snide remark as we motored back out through the cut in the coral and Zach picked up our buoy with a fish gaff.

"Yeah, I picked you," was my sarcastic reply.

"It wasn't my idea to work Milo's wreck," Glenn added, making sure none of the blame would land on him.

"That's a lie!" I snapped back, "You had it typed right into our amended charter agreement that Milo's site was the *only* site you'd allow the *Coral Sea* to work."

"You're damn right! It was the only one where no one was threatening to blow us out of the water!" barked Glenn, firing up for another yelling match.

The ugly side of treasure hunting had again reared its nasty head. When the chips were down and no treasure was being found, the first instinct was to find somebody to blame. Katie started rolling her eyes up to the ceiling every time I walked by, and the rest of the crew avoided talking to me. I felt like a leper. The flip side to fortune and glory was disgrace and ridicule. Treasure hunting was a black-and-white world, you either found treasure or you didn't. We didn't. Since God was the salvage master on this job, I decided to blame Him.

Back at West End, after everyone had scurried off the boat, Milo showed up, anxious to tell me his good news.

"The hotel is going to put up a display right in the main lobby," he beamed with pride. "We will announce to the world from here that the *Maravilla* has been found. I've arranged for international press coverage."

"I wouldn't get so excited if I were you, Milo," I told him. "Everything we found says your wreck is not the *Maravilla*."

"Of course it is," Milo insisted. He sat down beside me on the bunk and patted my hand consolingly. "You don't think I'd be silly enough to show you its treasure on your first trip out, do you? I had to make sure you were going to keep your end of the bargain before I revealed God's secrets. Did you hear my broadcast today? Our whole congregation supports you. Pete and Randy gave me a wonderful report of your work and the way you treated them."

"Milo, this is a business deal, not a religious field trip," I spat back in a harsh tone. "When are you going to tell me the location of the treasure box?"

"Very well," he said sharply, "Here is a map showing where the box is located. But I want you to agree to return to port every Saturday evening so the crew can attend church on Sunday."

"You gotta be joking," I smirked as I took the map. My crew would be chasing girls on their day off, not kneeling in prayer.

"God must be given the praise that is due Him if you are to succeed in your excavations," Milo concluded, sounding like a minister.

I ended up agreeing to Sunday in port, and just as I had predicted, the crew spent the day carousing. Duane was the only one who actually went to church, and after that he went carousing too. When we motored out of the harbor again heading north, we had two extra passengers on board. One was Glenn's vivacious, dark-tanned girlfriend Vicki, and the other was a psychic who had flown out from California at the request of one of my investors, to help locate the treasure.

Vicki was one of the first blond cooks Glenn had ever hired. He had always told her that someday he would take the *Coral Sea* treasure hunting, and he had flown her out to the Bahamas to prove it to her. He had figured she would be impressed enough to want to sleep with him, but the plan backfired when she brought out her sleeping bag after the first night in his cabin. She spent two weeks on the boat before Glenn exchanged her for a plumper girl from Fort Lauderdale who was more easily impressed.

The psychic turned out to be a gangly man with pale white skin and dark brown eyes that seemed to have no pupils. "I get a gritty sensation between my teeth when I'm near gold or silver," he told us. "It's never failed me."

The crew thought I was going off the deep end when I allowed the psychic on board. They started chanting "ooooWEEEEoooo" whenever they saw me and, when he wasn't around, took to calling the psychic Oowee for short. His real name was Jack Smith, or so he told us. He had a clinic in northern California, where he used his hands to generate healing powers over patients' bodies. He liked helping people, but there too many

118

disbelievers in the world, and he wasn't making any money. If he found treasure for us, I had to agree to verify his story when he made the announcement public. He wanted the glory before the fortune.

"Milo isn't going to like this one bit," Pete told me nervously, after we had motored back out to the wrecksite. "I don't think he would ever have allowed it."

"Aw, c'mon," I jested. "Aren't you fascinated by psychic phenomena? Don't you want to see if Jack can really do it? What can it hurt?"

Pete wet his lips with his tongue, turned his head to look out to sea, and slowly, believingly, said, "Psychics are agents of the Devil."

Oh boy, I thought, another weirdo. What is it about treasure hunting that brings them all out? Or was I just the lucky one who kept finding them? I shrugged off Pete's remark as that of a fanatic and turned my attention to the activity on the back deck.

When it came time for Jack to do his thing, it was Marc who maneuvered the Zodiac rubber boat in the direction the psychic pointed to with his finger.

As the Zodiac drifted away from the *Coral Sea,* we all rushed to the railing to watch the historic event. Even Glenn came out of his wheelhouse to puff on his pipe nonchalantly and glance at the spectacle. Katie, wiping a bowl with a long white dishtowel, came out of the galley to stand beside Zach and witness what she knew would be another fiasco. Only Pete and Randy stayed inside, afraid to watch the Devil at work.

Jack, with his eyes closed tightly, was stretched out on his belly across the front end of the Zodiac holding his hands, palms down, out over the water. Thirty minutes ticked agonizingly by while the Zodiac traveled back and forth over an area the size of a football field. Our attention was starting to wander when Jack suddenly jerked up and shouted, "Right here! Throw a buoy right here!"

Excitement electrified us all at the railing. Suddenly everyone was believing Jack could find treasure. He closed his eyes to concentrate and stretched out prone again across the front of the Zodiac. We could see him wiggling his jaw from side to side and we imagined the grittiness he must be feeling between his teeth.

"Over here, over here!" Jack shouted impatiently, pointing to a spot close to the first buoy. "I feel silver over here!" Marc zoomed the Zodiac to the place and hastily threw over another cement block. It kerplunked into the water, leaving a Styrofoam donut to float on the surface.

"Back up a little, a little more, a little more. Okay, here! Put a buoy here! It's gold here!" shouted Jack.

By the end of the day there were at least twenty Styrofoam donuts bobbing up and down on the ocean's surface. Marc brought the Zodiac alongside the *Coral Sea* and the psychic climbed triumphantly up the boarding ladder sporting a crimson red sunburnt nose and a mile-wide smile. "The place is littered with gold and silver!" he told us.

By seven o'clock the next morning, we had all eaten breakfast and were standing on the back deck in our swim suits, charged with treasure-fever. "This is it!" I squeeled to myself. "The treasure is almost in my hands." I couldn't stand still. I was prancing in place like I was going to wet my pants. I wanted to be the first one in the water. As I looked at the anxious faces around me, the only one missing was Glenn. He was still sleeping.

"We'll have to wait until ten o'clock, when the sun is higher, before we take the *Coral Sea* back inside the reef," Zach announced timidly. "My dad says the sun shines in his eyes too much this early."

"You gotta be kidding," scoffed Kevin. "Tell him to put on some sunglasses."

"No, really," Zach said defensively. "He says the sun reflects off the water and shines right in his eyes. He can't see where he's going."

"Let me at him!" roared Bubby thundering forward, making fists. "I'll show him some sunshine!"

"This could get messy," Steve whispered in my ear. "Glad I'm not in command here. You'd better do something quick, Margee."

"You tell him to come up here," Bubby roared again. Kevin and Marc were holding him back by the arms.

"Oh, boy! Maybe we'll see some blood," said Duane, clapping his hands and partially hiding behind one of the air vent tubes.

"This is ridiculous, Margee," shouted Katie, who had come running out of the galley when the argument started. "Bubby is a raving monster. You have to control him!"

"He's only expressing what we all feel, Katie," Marc snapped back at her. "And you know it."

In the space of thirty seconds, our treasure hunting high had disintegrated into all-out war. It was the boat crew against the dive crew once more, and Glenn slept through the whole thing. When he finally appeared, at nine-thirty, he slowly ate his breakfast then went up to the wheelhouse to wind his brass clock. At ten he started up the engines and slowly motored inside the reef, positioning the boat over a cluster of Styrofoam buoys.

Whether or not the sun was in his eyes was beside the point. Glenn had chosen that particular moment to remind everybody that he was the captain and he had the final word. Throughout the rest of the week, we motored inside the reef at ten and back out to deeper water by three in the afternoon. The sun reflected into Glenn's eyes when it set, too.

After Glenn returned to his cabin the crew went about lowering the starboard blaster into the water. When everything was set and locked into place, the starboard engine was started and revved up to 1000 RPMs. Billows of white sand clouds churned up in the water behind the boat as it strained at the stern anchor lines. The ocean current carried the suspended sand northward in a long flowing tail that stretched away from us for half a mile. After fifteen minutes of blasting, the engine was shut off and we dove down to see what we had uncovered.

Other than the areas of eel grass, the entire ocean floor under the boat was devoid of sand. It was stark, bare, limestone bottom with no sign of treasure. We figured there could only be one explanation, the treasure was still hidden under the eel grass.

Like a wire-mesh barrier impervious to our mechanical ingenuity, the eel grass remained undisturbed. Eel grass is a sea plant that grows in thick patches of singular, slimy green shafts that stick up out of the sand like flowerless daffodils. We cut out huge sections of the grass with our dive knives so the water blast could get up under the roots and undermine its strength. Then the engine was turned on again for another fifteen minutes. This time five-foot-deep craters were scoured out in the places where the eel grass had been cut away.

We repeated the tedious process for two days and found nothing, not one piece of gold or silver, not one piece of anything. The underwater metal detectors remained stubbornly silent. Oowee had failed. In disgrace, the psychic stayed in his bunk till we returned to port.

We quickly shook off our psychic disappointment by maneuvering the boat to excavate Milo's treasure box. We found a corner of it peeking out of the sand roughly in the place marked on Milo's map. The water was too shallow there to use the *Coral Sea*, so the crew mounted a miniature propeller blaster on the Velveeta boat and blew the sand away from the edges of the box. I was waiting eagerly on the back deck when Kevin surfaced to tell me the results.

"It's steel, it's got threaded holes and welded corners," Kevin said breathlessly. "And it's empty."

My heart sank. I felt betrayed. I was smart enough to know there had been no welding in the days of the *Maravilla*. The box was obviously something modern, it had nothing to do with seventeenth century treasure. So we returned to port empty handed with a pissed-off dive crew, an arrogant boat crew, a washed-up psychic, an unimpressed girlfriend, and two very nervous spies for Milo.

As usual, when we pulled into the harbor, the hotel golf carts were lined up at the dock to whisk half the crew off to a backgammon game with Luther, in the doorway of the liquor store. It was late afternoon when I finally changed into street clothes and went into town. As I walked by the hotel pool on my way to the lobby, I noticed Zach and Duane lying comfortably on lounge chairs, watching females in wet bathing suits climb out of the pool. I would have kept right on walking without saying a word, but Duane saw me coming and sat up with a mischievous grin on his face.

"I called Milo and told him you had the Devil on the boat," said Duane with a mixture of sassiness and defiance. "He's calling the Bahamian Coast Guard to stop you from returning to the site. What do you think about that?"

I was speechless. What do you say to a disloyal asshole? What words are appropriate for a back-stabbing weasel who happens to be a crew member and an investing partner. What do you counter with when a sniveling, spineless snake-in-the-grass tells you he snitched on you?

123

"Fuck off, Duane," I blurted out and stomped off to the hotel lobby.

It was completely out of character for me to say something like that, out loud, in public. What was happening to me? I felt like I was drowning. I was being smothered by idiots, and my only crime was that I wanted to find some treasure. Why did I deserve an egomaniacal captain and a three-hundred-pound fisherman who wanted to kill him? Why was I blessed with a witch disguised as a cook who had prepared three hundred and sixty-one meals since we started this comedy of errors? Why was I having such terrible luck with salvage masters? What colossal mistake had I made that was keeping the treasure out of my reach?

"God will never show you the treasure while you've got the Devil on board!" was Milo's thunderous statement when I called him from the hotel lobby to find out where I stood. He had returned to Florida the day we left for the wrecksite. I got a mini-sermon over the phone, ending with his demand that I come to Florida to settle things before we proceeded any further.

That was fine with me. It was time for some reorganization anyway. I marched back to the boat and found Duane in the wheelhouse, necking with some girl from the pool. That was all I could take.

"Pack your bags right now, Duane! You're off this boat!" I commanded. "And you'd better get your ass back to the hotel, honey," I said to the girl.

I'd just passed another milestone as a treasure hunting trainee. Not only did I have to *think* like a man, I had to *fight* like one too. The only thing assholes respect is strength, so stand back. I started wearing a tee shirt with big block letters across the chest that said, "HERE COMES TROUBLE."

I shipped Duane back to Florida that very afternoon on a small chartered plane and made arrangements for the pilot to pick me up the next day. I let the psychic bid an apologetic farewell to the crew and took him back to Florida with me. Bubby also left claiming he really would kill Glenn if he stayed on the boat any longer.

When I phoned Rodney Baron, I learned that the Bahamian government had finally canceled the second lease, and after renegotiating a few percentages, Rodney agreed to work with me again, even if I was a woman.

With a clear path ahead of me, I met Milo Zorbas on a park bench facing the Intercoastal Waterway, not so far from the marina where he had first stepped aboard the *Coral Sea*.

"Margee, my child, what evil has possessed you?" began Milo in his soppy, sermon voice. "I have consulted at length with the Lord on what to do with you," he went on. "I've prepared a list of things you must do before God will permit you to return to His wrecksite."

"Milo, your wreck is not the *Maravilla* and your treasure box is a steel gasoline tank," I interrupted, trying to shock him into listening.

"I want you to erect an altar in the galley and fly the Athanagorus Brotherhood flag on the main mast. I also want you to sprinkle holy water off the back deck before anybody goes in the water each morning. And no fornicating aboard the boat. If you agree to these things, God will reinstate you in our project," said Milo, smiling.

I had to laugh. I couldn't hold it in any longer. I handed Milo back his list of demands and said, "No thanks. I don't want to be reinstated. Good-bye, Milo. And God bless you." I left him sitting on the bench, starring at his piece of paper.

Never lose faith in divine providence, I remembered Captain Red saying in a pirate movie once. After all I'd been through, I still had a shot at the real wrecksite of the *Maravilla* and I was feeling great.

I raced back to the *Coral Sea* to tell everybody the good news and got onboard just in time to hear the weather radio announce the approach of Hurricane David.

Chapter Nine

My idea of a hurricane was tumultuous winds, uprooted trees, horrendous rains and television reports of death and destruction. In West End, Hurricane David was a three-day party. Within hours of the radio announcement, the harbor had filled up with every kind of sailboat, yacht, fishing sloop, and dope-smuggling vessel you could think of. The bigger boats lined the sea walls on the commercial dock and the smaller vessels were crammed into the yacht harbor. There were so many boats tied up alongside each other and wedged into every available space, you could barely see the water. Ropes and lines were strung back and forth like spider webs connecting all the vessels, and the boats actually berthed in a harbor slip or next to a wall were secured with four and five lines more than usual. Canvas tarps used as sunroofs or siding were all put away and masts were reinforced with extra staywires. When all the work was done, out came the rum.

The impending catastrophe made everybody instant buddies. Glasses clinked, bottles passed from vessel to vessel and a different Jimmy Buffett song was playing on every stereo. The wind that had started whipping the branches of the pine trees surrounding the harbor didn't affect the party. Warm rain began to swirl with the wind, signaling the outer edge of the storm, and still the intoxicated shouts echoed off the cement sea walls. "Hell, we'll either live through it or die from it!" yelled one beer-bellied sailor just before he yanked his baseball cap over his eyes and fell sideways into the water from the bow of his dinghy.

At the hotel, storm shutters covered all the windows and anything that wasn't bolted down was brought inside. Worried-looking guests milled around the lobby or sat for hours in the hotel theater watching the movie Animal House, which was to run continuously for ninety-six hours. It was the only movie they had. Luther, at the liquor store, was doing big business. "Day bot ahl dee rum dis moning, mon," he told Steve, "Where you bean, mon? Ahl dats left is tequila."

On the *Coral Sea* Glenn was barking orders at everybody to tie everything down and run mooring lines clear across to the other side of the harbor. Extra tires, rubber bumpers, and the Norwegian buoys were hung from the railing along the entire length of the ship to keep it from smashing into the dock when the swells started rolling into the harbor. The swells were so powerful they ricocheted off the sea walls four times before being consumed by the following swell. All night long the boat rolled from side to side like a cradle being rocked too forcefully, and the wet rubber of the tires screeched and moaned as the boat squeezed them against the dock. Sleep was sporadic if we got any at all.

The winds were stronger in the morning. Someone had strung a rope around the marina as a safety line for pedestrians to hold onto. It became a common sight to see people's feet slip out from under them so that they landed with a thud on their butts like fallen ice skaters. The pearl-gray sky overhead was dense with rainclouds. Waves of raindrops sifted over the landscape, sometimes in light sprinkles and sometimes in torrential downpours. Through it all, the music kept playing and the rum kept flowing.

By the end of the third day the weather radio reported that the hurricane was headed out to sea. It had passed just south of Grand Bahama Island, leaving hundreds of bamboo shacks lying in rubble. The only damages at West End were fallen power lines and flooding in some of the buildings. The fact that we weren't all blown to pieces gave us reason to continue celebrating and the party went on for another day.

Everyone in the harbor suffered from too much liquor and too little sleep. We all looked the same with our wet hair, wet clothes, wet shoes and wet smiling faces. A certain camaraderie permeated the harbor atmosphere, the result of surviving a catastrophe alongside someone you never knew and would probably never see again.

On the fourth day, the sun finally peeked through isolated breaks in the clouds. The rain ceased its relentless barrage and was carried away by the dwindling winds to the east. The ground was left pockmarked with puddles of all sizes reflecting the darting sunlight in blinding flashes. Vessels, the bravest ones first, were slowly making their way out of the harbor. It looked like a parking lot emptying after a rock concert.

Most of our crew was out on deck untying ropes or hanging something out to dry when Rodney Baron and his partner, Mike, strolled up to the boat carrying rolls of charts and a few bags. I was a little surprised to see them so soon after the storm had receded, but then I remembered that Rodney was the type that liked to get right down to business.

Mike was a short, feisty fellow with a blond porcupine beard that outlined a deceiving smile. He was small-boned and muscular like a middle-aged surfer who looked too old to be hanging around the beach but who could still ride the gnarliest wave out there. Windblown blond hair covered his narrow face and dangled in front of his eyes like pine needles. He seemed a likable sort, easy to get along with, but also the type that never showed you all of his cards. You always got the feeling from him that there was something he didn't want you to know, some secret that was none of your business. He threw his battered suitcase and dive bag on the deck as if he'd done it a thousand times and soon made friends with everybody on board, even Katie.

"You were with Bob Marx when the *Maravilla* was first rediscovered, weren't you?" asked Zach, unable to contain his curiosity any longer.

"Yeah, I was," answered Mike proudly. "I've been on every vessel that ever worked that site. I know the wreck like the back of my hand."

"Do you know where the main hull is?" asked Steve eagerly.

"Nah. We've found bits and pieces scattered everywhere. All you can do is keep excavating. There's a lot of area out there that's never been looked at."

"Is there really a solid gold statue of the Madonna and Christ Child down there?" Kevin asked, still worried about the end of the world.

"That depends on who you talk to," said Mike, rubbing his beard. "Marx says it's a bunch of crap, but more than one person says it's there. Then there are other people who say it was on a completely different ship. I wouldn't lose any sleep over it."

We motored out of West End harbor with the sunrise and headed north again, this time right passed Milo's wrecksite. It was another hour before the engines slowed and we started circling until Rodney's coordinates lined up with the satellite navigation readout. Mike already had his mask, tank, and flippers on, and was waiting on the back deck for Rodney's hand signal to jump overboard and check out the bottom. After several tension-filled minutes, Mike surfaced with a thumb's up sign and Zach released the bow anchor securing us to the ocean floor right over the only discovered remains of the *Nuestra Señora de Las Maravillas.*

It had now been six months since we left Santa Barbara with the idea of anchoring on this very spot, but there was no time to wonder if it had all been worth it. We were all too busy getting on our diving gear. Once the stern anchors were set, even Glenn donned his tank and mask.

It's a magical feeling to be on the deck of a vessel getting ready to look for treasure. Your mind flies away with visions. You see your hands holding chains of gold; you see yourself kneeling on the sandy bottom bringing up silver coins. Adrenaline is surging through you. Your heartbeat is pounding in your throat. You rush to get ready, check your air, make sure your mask fits tightly, pull on your fins, and duck-walk over to the opening in the railing. You stare down into the inviting warm water, actually seeing two divers swimming downward, way below you. Then you grab the regulator, push the purge button a couple times to listen for the familiar gusts of air, then insert the mouthpiece and clasp it hard between your teeth. "Shit! I'm really looking for sunken treasure," is the last thing you think of as you lean out over the edge of the boat and fall into the crystal-clear water.

I pinched my nose and blew through my ears as I sank downward. It was fifty feet to the bottom, almost three times deeper than Milo's site, and much more rewarding.

As soon as my feet hit the smooth sand I saw an enormous, ancient, crescent-shaped anchor with one of its flukes buried in a flat, pink reef. Its long, square shank rose upward to a thick wooden crossbar. Above the crossbar was a giant iron ring that measured at least ten inches in diameter. This was the *Maravilla's* bow anchor, which marked the wrecksite. Beyond the anchor the pinkish reef disappeared under a huge sand pocket that stretched for a thousand feet to the east.

The place looked completely serene and untouched. There were no disturbances or bulges in the sand, no odd shapes, nothing that made this patch of white ocean bottom look different from any other in that part of the world. But when we turned on the blasters and blew the sand away, the place looked like a junkyard. A jumbled heap of rocks, planks of wood, and hunks of white coral lay crisscrossed at the bottom of the blast hole, waiting to be investigated.

In this first hole we blasted, on the first day we had arrived on the site, we found our first silver bar! Lordy, Lordy! We were no longer treasure hunters, we were treasure finders! We jumped up and down, hugged each other profusely and smiled till our cheeks hurt.

Everybody on the boat shared the exhilarating rush of discovery. The bar was passed around a thousand times to be fondled and inspected. It was the shape of a Twinkie™, about two inches high and six inches long, with a flat bottom and rounded ends.

This was contraband silver, what the Spaniards used to call "finger bars." The bars were illegal because they had no markings and the King's tax was never paid on them. Such bars were formed at the silver mines in Bolivia by pouring molten silver into a tiny ditch dug out by two fingers in the dirt. The bars were left to cool in secret and then hidden in the pockets of the thieving ingot maker. Later they would be sold to a seaman boarding a galleon who would smuggle them onboard and then hide them somewhere in the ship's interior until he reached Spain, or, in this case, until the ship sank and the silver was found 325 years later by an inquisitive diver.

132

During the next week, we blasted ten holes that looked like inverted volcanoes fifteen feet deep in the sand. The crew needed no prodding. They cheerfully worked from sunup to sundown without complaint. The back workbench started filling up with pieces of silver serving dishes, broken clay pottery, round steel musket balls, and curious coral-encrusted shapes that we kept immersed in water until they could be inspected further.

Round, black, grainy disks resembling Oreo cookies were brought up and, when cleaned off with a mild solution of muriatic acid, turned out to be silver pieces-of-eight. Steve and Kevin found green emeralds, and Marc brought up a unique ball-shaped lock with a tiny key. Everyday somebody climbed back up the boarding ladder with something interesting in his hand or bulging in his goodie bag.

We started using plastic, thirty-gallon garbage cans full of seawater to hold the objects. The stern crane was now being used to haul up coral-covered spikes, stanchions, and rifle barrels. In our greedy haste, we were using hammers to break open coral globs, looking for more coins and destroying whatever else the globs contained. For every ounce of precious metal we were finding, we were rummaging through fifty pounds of coral crust. A layer of coral rubble was settling on the sand underneath the boat as we cast overboard what we didn't want.

Sometimes we uncovered a mound of coral with a short piece of yellow polypropylene line tied to it, reminding us that other treasure hunters had been there before us. Only the fact that we were finding valuable artifacts told us that a particular spot had not been uncovered before.

In one hole we found two coral-covered swords completely intact. One was a rapier sword with a four-sided blade and a protective hilt that we could barely fit our twentieth-century-sized hands into. We played swashbuckling pirates with it on the back deck. We found pewter plates, bent cups, twisted spoons, and white, clay smoking pipes with initials stamped in the bowl or designs etched around the broken-off stems.

At one point we uncovered part of the *Maravilla's* keel, a three-foot-thick rectangular hunk of dense wood sitting upright on the limestone bottom, surrounded by ballast rock on all sides. This piece was at least twelve feet long and an end had snapped off, probably when the ship crashed into the bottom the night it sank. Not too far from the keel we uncovered an iron cannon that we subsequently covered up again when we blasted the next hole.

For one brief week we were all a happy family, helping each other and congratulating ourselves on our bountiful recovery. Katie stopped griping and started baking bread, and the galley dinner table was a pleasant gathering of noisy, chattering divers recalling the day's activities and planning the next. Glenn was back to telling his funny stories, since Rodney and Mike had never heard them. And for the first time since Santa Barbara, Glenn and I weren't fighting. However, like all states of perfection, this one had a limited life span. Our blissful private world was unexpectedly invaded the day the *Tropic Bird* motored into view and dropped its anchor scarcely a mile away from us.

"Who the hell is that?" asked Steve, pointing off the stern of the boat at a 125-foot, passenger-carrying vessel floating in the distance.

"Poachers," hissed Rodney, who had come out of the galley for a better look at our visitors.

"Nah, they wouldn't be so obvious," Mike remarked. Marc hurried up to the wheelhouse to get the binoculars and inform Glenn.

"Why else would they pick this spot to anchor?" Rodney asked, lighting a cigarette and never taking his eye off the vessel.

"It's got a work deck in the middle and people walking all over it," Marc called down from the top deck after he'd taken a look through the binoculars.

"Should we keep diving?" Kevin asked, waiting at the ladder with all his gear on. "I'm next in the water."

"Okay, but don't bring anything up," Mike replied cautiously. "They might be watching us with binoculars too."

"Have they got the right to anchor here?" I asked Rodney, expecting him to have all the answers.

"They can anchor, but they can't be treasure hunting," said Rodney. "I'll bet they're just marking down the coordinates for future reference. The only way to know anything for sure, is to go over there and check them out. What do you say, Glenn? You up for a ride?"

"Well, hell, Rodney," Glenn hesitated. "Maybe we oughta just watch 'em for a while, ya know what I mean?"

"I say they're pirates and we oughta go over there and see what they're up to," Rodney insisted.

"Let's see if they make a move first," was Mike's sound advice.

We all nodded in agreement and cautiously resumed doing what we were doing before the vessel had been noticed. It was late afternoon anyway, and the process of pulling everything up for the night kept everybody busy for the next hour or so. Still, not a minute passed without someone twisting his head to check on the unidentified vessel.

The wind was picking up and clouds were bunching together as the orange sun began its westerly descent into the ocean. There seemed to be no way around a reconnaissance mission. Five of us decided to join Rodney in the rubber Zodiac to go check out the other vessel. Glenn mumbled something about having to stay behind to protect his own boat.

It was a long, bouncy, wet ride across the mile of open ocean with six of us weighing down the Zodiac. By the time we reached the *Tropic Bird*, whitecaps were forming on the water and the sky was darkening with the sunset. We were met at the boarding ladder by a young captain who gladly showed us around his vessel and brought out some rum to welcome us properly. Then he explained he had amateur scientists aboard who were recording dolphin noises and told us he'd be cruising the whole Bahama Bank for the next month. After actually seeing graphs, recording equipment, and photographs of dolphins all over the boat, Rodney relaxed and we all swallowed our rum a little more easily - so easily, in fact, that it was midnight when we realized we'd drunk half the night away and had to get back to the *Coral Sea*.

"Wow, get a load of that lightning," Steve said, when we were standing at the railing about to climb down into the Zodiac. On every side of us, flat-bottomed clouds were lining the horizon, shooting bolts of lightning down towards the ocean.

"You sure this is a good idea?" I said in a chicken voice.

"Quit your whining, honey," Rodney bellowed, leaning slightly and obviously drunk. "We'll get your cowardly ass home safely."

"Yeah, Margee, where's your sense of adventure?" slurred Marc, equally drunk.

Once we were all in the Zodiac and had waved good-bye to our gracious host, Marc started up the outboard motor and we inched away from the *Tropic Bird* into the darkness. The tiny lights of the *Coral Sea* seemed a long way away as we bobbed up and down in the water, getting splashed from all sides. A hundred yards into our voyage Rodney suddenly stood full upright and shouted at the night.

"You damn spirits of the *Maravilla*, you can't hide the treasure any longer!" he screamed, waving his arms wildly and making the Zodiac tip and rock.

"Sit down, stupid!" Marc shouted at Rodney. "You'll drown us all."

"You gotta know how to deal with spirits," Rodney yelled back at him, still standing but half falling over.

Lightning flashed again and we heard the distant thunder crack. The ocean was tossing and rolling the Zodiac with tremendous force as I braved a glance at my backside to see that I was riding on a rubber cushion only inches above the water's surface.

"You can't show a spirit any fear," Rodney raved on, waving a threatening fist at the night. "You gotta show 'em who's boss!"

"Oh, darn, we forgot the life jackets," Steve said, tapping his cheek like a forgetful assistant.

The ocean bounced us around like a bucking bronco. Water was splashing on my back like bursting water balloons. Primitive fear gnawed at my insides as I hung onto the ropes, knowing we'd be swallowed up by the raging ocean if anything went wrong. Rodney was yelling his fool head off like a drunken witch doctor, and the lights of the *Coral Sea* were still a long way off. I was scared to death.

"You've guarded that treasure long enough," Rodney shouted at the spirits. "Now its time to let us have it!"

"You really think they're researching dolphins?" I asked Mike.

"It's a cover," Rodney broke in, still refusing to sit down.

"There is a school of dolphins out here," Mike said. "About thirty of them." He wiped water off his face as his side of the Zodiac rose up over a wave and we all gasped and grabbed on tighter.

"They're watching over the treasure," Rodney warned. "They're probably possessed by spirits too."

"You gonna calm the weather?" Mike yelled out to Rodney.

"You got that right!" Rodney assured him.

The ocean pitched and heaved until Rodney finally fell backwards onto the floor of the Zodiac. Marc had to catch him and steer the outboard at the same time. The stern of the Zodiac sunk downward from Rodney's weight and the bow rose up, lifted by the wind, and we all screamed in horror at the thought of being dumped into the merciless black water. It was still too far to swim to the *Coral Sea*, the Gulf Stream current would carry us out of sight. I was shivering with fright.

"Just hold on and close your eyes," Kevin yelled above the thunder. "We'll either live through it or die from it!"

"There's nothing to worry about, woman," Rodney howled at me. "I've got my mojo beads."

By some miracle, we made it back to the *Coral Sea*. Nobody was up to greet us. If we had tipped over, no one would have known. Marc of course denied that we were ever in danger. Kevin and Steve just rolled their eyes.

As we pulled the Zodiac out of the water with the boom winch, swinging it over to the helicopter pad where we kept it at night, we saw Rodney heading towards the bow. A few minutes later we heard him chanting and caught a glimpse of him dancing on one foot and shaking something in his cupped hands. I went to bed thinking no one would ever believe this. I'm seeing it with my own eyes and I don't believe it. In the morning the water was perfectly flat and calm, and Rodney took all the credit.

Throughout the following month, the *Tropic Bird* appeared several times, and each time dolphins appeared shortly afterward. As if performing a ritual, they played with us for a while before swimming toward the visiting vessel, which was always anchored a safe distance away.

We returned to West End after ten days at the site and the first one off the boat was Glenn. He was leaving for three weeks to attend his daughter's wedding and check on things in California. He left Zach in charge of the boat. Rodney got off too, claiming that his business needed him and that he had to report to the Bahamian government.

"They'll be expecting us to turn in that treasure in a couple of weeks," Rodney told me. "Have them sign an inventory when they take it," he advised. "They'll hold it in Nassau until we're ready to divide."

When the *Coral Sea* headed north to the wrecksite again after taking on fresh food and rum raisin ice cream from the hotel, there were only seven of us on board; Steve, Marc, Kevin, Zach, Katie, Mike and myself. We were the hard-core survivors. Treasure hunting had a way of skimming off the lightweights.

Chapter Ten

Bubby had once told me that women don't belong on boats. He said that the ocean is a jealous mistress that demands the full attention of any man who would dare to cross it. Some even go so far as to say that a female on board is bad luck. After six months of incessant nagging from Katie, I thought I understood why they said such things. However, with the arrival of Judy and Lisa, I learned the real reason why women don't belong on boats - it's because men are too easily distracted.

Judy was a twenty-five-year-old blond with a great figure and a playful personality. She had wide cheekbones and a perpetually sunburnt nose that wrinkled when she laughed and made her eyes squint into two tiny crescents. Marc liked her because, not only was she tantalizing in her skimpy bikini, but she also had a brain. They claimed they were studying whenever I found them snuggling in some obscure corner of the boat.

Lisa was much younger than Judy, with long curly blond hair and a baby face full of freckles. She was somewhere in her first year of college with an undecided major. Steve liked her easy-going manner and the fact that she was still young enough to be moldable. He wasn't into intellectual challenges, which made Lisa perfect for him, since she was into unicorns, rainbows, and poetry.

At nineteen she was still wide-eyed and trusting, traits that Steve took full advantage of during her visit.

The whole atmosphere on board changed, now that Marc and Steve had their girlfriends on board. For an incredible two weeks every aspect of our excavation work proceeded with gaiety, laughter, cooperation, and genuine satisfaction. The girls did whatever chores were assigned to them, thanking their lucky stars, and me, for the golden opportunity to be part of the crew. The only down side was the distraction factor.

I found a gas transfer hose leaking all over the deck once while one of my crew members was being distracted by feminine attention. Then there was the plastic guard on the crow's nest that smashed to the deck while two lovers were trying a daring new position. It took extra dives to inspect a blast hole when the girls were involved. And at the end of the day, when the moon was casting romantic light over the outside shower on the back deck, one could usually find two naked bodies giggling and splashing under the curtainless showerhead.

With the girls on board, the crew deftly displayed the talents they had acquired during the previous weeks of treasure diving. The tasks of anchoring and lowering the blasters were performed with ease. Everybody found something of value on the bottom each day, and the finds were cleaned and inspected with care each evening. I stored emeralds and coins in a big steel safe we had mounted in a corner of the galley. The rest of the objects we kept in wooden boxes on the top sun deck. I typed inventory sheets of everything we found, describing in detail the size, type of material, and quantity. For the first time since we had left the ranch, I felt proud of myself. I had actually found treasure.

To document our finds, we spread plush, purple bath towels on the deck and artistically arranged rows of coins for picture taking. None of the "pieces of eight" were round. The edges had been crudely shaped with a knife and the Spanish markings - a raised cross with lions and castles on one side and single letters, numbers, and parallel pillars on the other - had mostly worn away. When a date was visible, it was an old-script-style 55. What impressed you when you held these coins was their weight. A piece of eight was a solid ounce of silver. It made the coins of today feel light and cheap. Back in 1655, a coin was worth something.

We spent so much time underwater that we got to be friends with some of the marine life. There was an ugly brown grouper fish we named Spot who would eat anything you brought down for him, including the plastic bag you brought it in. If you were hanging around the edges of the blast hole, you could sometimes get run over by a blind stingray.

The fish that weren't our friends were the barracuda. They had long, slender bodies that reflected the sunlight and menacing angular mouths they held open to reveal their sharp, pointed teeth. A barracuda will swim in circles around you, always keeping his eye on you, and wait for the moment when you look away. Then he moves in closer. He swims around and around keeping that eye on you, making you really nervous. These fish aren't attackers, they're prowlers. You have to frighten them off with your fins or have enough guts to swim right toward them. It's the only way to get rid of them.

The worst dive I ever had was the day I spent a whole tank of air running away from sea creatures. I had jumped into the water with Marc and Judy but lost track of them when a small remora fish decided he wanted to cling to my leg. These fish are only about ten inches long, but their backs are covered with rough ridges that allow them to attach to bigger fish for a free ride. I had no intention of giving this remora a lift. I tried swimming away but he followed me everywhere I went. I swam behind coral, then up to the surface, then back into the blast hole, but whatever I did that little sucker kept heading for my leg. I shooed him away and poked at him with my knife, and still he swam toward my leg. I ended up turning around in one spot like a twirling ice skater, keeping my leg just inches from his determined suction cups.

The remora chased me for half an hour before he finally dropped out of sight. I hung onto the *Coral Sea's* anchor chain to catch my breath and started pulling myself towards the surface hand over hand when I caught a glimpse of a large gray fish hovering in the distance and I froze stiff. A shark, I thought. Oh, God, what do I do? Should I dive for the bottom or hang onto the chain? He seemed to be moving very slowly. Maybe he doesn't see me, I thought. Then I remembered that sharks sense things rather than see them. I started backing down the chain. I felt myself breathing rapidly, almost hyperventilating. Don't panic, I thought, and don't move too quickly. The shark just hovered. I felt my heart pounding. I checked my pressure gauge, I was almost out of air. I would have to go to the surface and then he would attack me. Now I was starting to panic. I was looking all around me to see if other sharks were around. My hands were going numb because I was holding the chain so tightly.

Then it struck me that the shark had not swum past me once since I spotted him. And then I remembered sharks don't hover. They have to keep moving to breath. I cautiously moved up the chain, straining my eyes to see better. I got all the way to the surface before I realized that the "shark" was just a winged hunk of metal that was hanging by cable from the *Coral Sea's* outriggers. These metal weights help keep the boat stable in the rolling swells. What a fool I thought as I climbed back onto the boat exhausted and out of breath. Of course Marc, Kevin, and Steve had seen the whole thing, and I had to confess that I'd run away from a ten-inch fish and had been scared out of my wits by a hunk of steel.

The other hazards of being underwater so often are not as obvious. Your skin gets waterlogged and forms wrinkles. Microscopic organisms grow in your ears if you don't clean them out with medicine every night. Your ears can get infected and hurt deep inside your head all the time, preventing you from going back in the water for three or four days. If you don't adjust your mask correctly you get "mask squeeze," which pops the blood vessels in your eyeballs. Also, several sicknesses develop underwater, like nitrogen narcosis and the well-known "bends" from staying down too long.

In the face of all these possibilities, it was comforting to know that Marc was a paramedic. He stitched up Steve's toe and Kevin's knee after minor accidents and administered what medicines we had on board. In three months we went through twenty-six boxes of Band-aids™.

Shells were the big item when we weren't finding treasure or playing with the marine life. Once we blasted all the sand off a piece of ocean floor, the heavier items like seashells and broken bits of coral usually fell back into the hole. Since we were carefully picking over everything, we always came across countless colored, perfectly shaped shells, and every crew member had a bucket or can full. The biggest were conch shells, with spiral horns and smooth rose-pink insides. You had to be careful not to pick up shells with the conches still inside or they would stink up the whole boat after a day or two on board. Seasoned divers know that keeping stinky seashells in a dive bag is the best way to get through customs quickly in an airport.

From the number of artifacts we had recovered, it was clear that we had not yet found the main hull of the *Maravilla*. We spent days in the Velveeta boat with the magnetometer traversing back and forth over quarter-mile sections marked off with buoys, but nothing we passed over gave a strong signal. Judy drove while I kept my eyes glued to the jumping needle on the slowly advancing chart paper. It came to me after days of fruitless effort what a tedious, time-consuming task it must have been to find this wreck in the first place.

Anderson had told me that Bob Marx had searched for eight months with a magnetometer over fifty square miles of ocean, but he found this part of the *Maravilla* solely by accident. His crew was ready to give up, and when they pulled up their anchor they found two ballast rocks stuck in the anchor flukes. That's how they actually found the wreck, good research and luck.

Our finds though, were diminishing. On one dive Marc came bounding out of the water with a goodie bag stuffed with silver coins, but for several days we sat idle waiting out strange periods of time when the compass would start spinning around all by itself and none of our electrical equipment would function correctly.

Sometimes we would have to stop work completely when a rogue mini-storm, called a squall, would suddenly descend on us with blinding showers of rain. For twenty minutes we wouldn't be able to see each other or the buoys or anything more than ten feet away. Then, as quickly as it had come, the storm cloud would drift away and everything would return to sunny normality. Whenever such strange things happened, the crew would form triangles with their thumbs and forefingers to symbolize the Bermuda Triangle. Nothing would have to be said.

One morning we woke up to five U.S. Coast Guard boats motoring in circles around us and a uniformed man with a bullhorn telling us to stand by to be boarded. A large Coast Guard cutter was waiting in the distance in the deeper water of the Gulf Stream. The smaller boat that came alongside us had six green marijuana leaves painted in a row on its bow, evidently recording the number of busts this particular vessel had made. We told the officers that we were treasure hunting but they searched our boat thoroughly anyway.

"Your artifacts might have been decoys," they said, apparently satisfied that we weren't drug smugglers. They told us to report by radio if we saw any "square groupers" floating by. That was their term for bales of marijuana.

That night, long after supper, when everything was dark and still and the only noise was the ever-constant hum of the generator, we heard a voice whisper on the VHF radio.

"Is that you?" the voice asked as if questioning someone in a dark alley.

"Yeah. Where you at?" another voice whispered back.

"Fifteen minutes away."

"Usual place then," was the last thing we heard.

Ten minutes later a huge plane with no lights flew low over our boat and Mike knew exactly what was happening.

"They're making a drop," Mike informed us. "Probably at Walkers Cay. Ha, ha, the Coast Guard was too early."

"How do they know where to drop it?" Steve asked with a gleam in his eye.

"They signal with lights," Mike said, watching the sky intently.

Steve and Kevin ran up to the wheelhouse and started flicking the lights on our mast. The plane made another low pass over our vessel but continued on towards the east.

"Nice try," said Mike when the two returned to the galley. "There are probably twenty Bahamian fishing sloops out there formed in a circle. They'll drop the stuff right in the middle. And tomorrow you'll see cigarette boats zipping over here from

Florida. They can make the trip in forty-five minutes. Some of them go seventy miles an hour."

Sure enough, all day long the following day, bullet-shaped speedboats trailed streaks of white water as they skimmed over the water's surface traveling east. Not long afterwards they streaked by again, heading west back to Florida. We never saw any "square groupers" floating by.

Day after day, we blasted the sand on the ocean floor and dove down to inspect what was left. If we stayed in the water while the blaster was blowing, we had to hold onto the bottom with three-foot fish gaffs hooked into a crevice or coral head, our bodies flapped like flags in the wind. If your hand slipped you were blown clear out of the hole and fifty feet beyond the perimeter. Then you had to swim, struggling against the blast, to get back to your position. Your arm felt like it was coming out of its socket most of the time. Your fingers lost all sensation and froze in a permanent grip shape for hours. But it was all worth it when you watched a piece of treasure magically appear in front of your eyes as the sand particles were whisked away from its edges.

Finding emeralds was a little trickier. As soon as you saw one, the blast was carrying it away. You had to instantly capture an emerald in your hands and hold it down in the sand until the blasting stopped. If you were too curious or wanted to make sure you had captured it, you raised one side of your cupped hands and ran the risk of the emerald flying away from you. It was better to sit there with your hand over it until the blaster was shut down. Then you could lift your hand to find a brilliant, green six-sided emerald stone resting in the sand. The biggest one we ever found was as thick as a thumb and more than an inch long. Some of the stones started out white at one end and then progressed from transparent to light green and, depending on the quality of the stone, finally dark, rich emerald green.

At the end of September the Bahamian government informed us that they were giving our area to the person who had held the duplicate lease. "He must have paid them a shitload of money," was Mike's learned opinion. We later learned that the sum was fifty thousand dollars. Since the good weather season was over anyway, we decided it was wiser, and cheaper, to head home.

We had been working the *Maravilla* site for a total of eight weeks. We had forty emeralds, a few hundred coins, two swords, and an assortment of coral-encrusted artifacts and broken bits of pottery to show for our time. We had blasted more than sixty holes in the twenty-foot-deep sand and still had no idea where the mother lode was hiding. As far as I know, no one else after us has ever found the main cargo hold either.

"This treasure-hunting stuff is harder than I thought," I admitted one night when we were all sitting around the bow listening to Mike play the guitar.

"Patience and persistence," Mike said, like a college professor summing up the two main points of his lecture. "That's what it's all about."

The mood on the *Coral Sea* was sorrowful yet dignified as we returned to West End for the last time. At least we had a few trinkets to show for our efforts. Steve pointed out that we may have actually saved the world by not finding the gold statue of the Madonna and Christ Child.

The police car met us at the commercial dock, just as it had every time we returned to West End. Both the officers in it signed my inventory sheet, and we sent the last few things we had found off to Nassau on the weekly mail boat. We sold our extra food, the extra refrigerator, and the Velveeta boat to local Bahamians and crossed the Gulf Stream to Florida, docking in West Palm Beach at the same marina we had left four months before. The world didn't notice.

Most of the crew flew home, but Steve and Kevin volunteered to drive a U-Haul truck home with all the gear that had to be returned to California. Glenn had returned and decided that the *Coral Sea* would remain in Florida. He had big plans for chartering to more successful treasure hunters.

I put an advertisement for a going-out-of-business sale in the local paper to sell off the remaining equipment. The only people who showed up were a used marine supply dealer and the county sheriff, who had a court summons for me. Milo Zorbas was suing me to have an injunction forbidding me to return to his lease site for one hundred years. I laughed so hard I was in tears. Eventually his suit was thrown out of court. The remainder of the equipment was sold at flea markets.

Two weeks later I flew to Nassau with Rodney Baron to divvy up the treasure we had recovered with the Bahamian government. We entered a stark, olive-green office that looked like a police interrogation room. There we met the Permanent Secretary to the Minister of Transport, a slight, composed man, plus several other men carrying all the plastic crates and plastic bags we had delivered to the West End Police. The hundreds of pounds of coral-covered metal objects, we were told, were to be donated to the National Museum.

"I have something here that may affect our division process," the Permanent Secretary said. He opened an envelope and handed a letter to Rodney. "A Mr. Milo Zorbas has herein stated that one hundred coins were stolen and smuggled to Florida by this young lady." The secretary turned to glare at me. "The letter is countersigned by someone named Duane."

I suddenly felt sick, my shoulders cramped. So this is what disgruntled treasure hunters do, I said to myself. I made a mental note never again to trust anyone who says he's treasure hunting for God.

"Now, that just isn't so," Rodney asserted, tossing the letter on the table. "You know Milo is a kook just as well as I do. He's just sore at her because she wouldn't work his site. It's a damn lie, I guarantee it."

"Rodney, we've never had any problems with you," said the secretary, returning the letter to its envelope. "Are you willing to vouch for the actions of this lady and her innocence?"

"I most certainly am."

"Then we shall proceed."

The treasure was set out on the table in four piles. One or two items were added or subtracted from each pile until no one cared which pile went to whom. The Secretary picked the first pile and Rodney and I took the other three. We repeated the process until all the emeralds, coins, unusual artifacts, porcelain pottery pieces, plates, cups, and silverware were divided. Clay items were simply counted and the Secretary picked out one quarter of them. The whole business took less than two hours. We placed the items we could carry in four large suitcases and walked out into the bright Bahamian sunshine.

Rodney left immediately for Florida with the suitcases and I stayed behind to arrange for the larger items to be shipped by cargo carrier. It was all very civil, very quick, and very unspectacular. I wondered how different it might have been if we were dividing tons of gold.

As I was wandering around the shipping docks looking for cargo companies, I was riveted to a halt in front of several piles of what appeared to be broken pallets. There, underneath the splintered wood and rusty carriage bolts, were the hundreds of coral-covered iron objects we had recovered from the *Maravilla* wrecksite. At least half the pieces were cracked and crushed, an orange-colored liquid oozing from the broken parts, spilling onto the pieces below, staining the white coral.

It felt like someone had punched me in the chest. A sadness came over me, a devastating sadness that twisted my stomach into knots. Then I was furious. I thought of all the hours and money and back-breaking labor we had spent to recover these things, and this is where they ended up. I asked a passing dock-worker if he knew what these items were and he said he thought they were garbage. I asked inside several open doors in the surrounding warehouses and nobody knew anything about the piles of pallets and "iron junk." National Museum, my ass, I thought. These things will probably rot right here. Nobody really cared.

The sum total of all the things that were finally divided between Rodney and our Caribbean Gold Company, was about $350,000, the same amount we had ultimately spent on the expedition. Financially we had managed to break even. I packaged everything in padded boxes and sent each investor his share of the booty, consoling myself that it wasn't bad for my first time out.

On the day I finally returned to the *Coral Sea* to settle up the fuel escrow account with Glenn, I was dressed as a landlubber again in comfortable pants and a pretty silk blouse. I walked to the end of the marina and found Glenn washing off some rubber mats with a garden hose. He pretended not to see me, and as I came closer, he bent over and aimed the hose right at me, drenching me with water from head to toe.

"Shit, Margee, I didn't see you coming," he lied. "I was too busy cleaning, ya know what I mean?"

"Of course you were," I lied back. "Feel better now?"

"Made all the difference in the world," he smiled, turning off the water and heading for the galley.

Now, don't get into a fight with him, I told myself. Remember with Glenn Miller, your first deal is your best. The more time he has to think, the worse off you'll be. I took a deep breath and followed him into the galley. We sat opposite each other at the galley table with a pile of notepad papers and repair bills between us.

"I figure you owe me all the money in the escrow account," Glenn said, scrutinizing me with a wary eye as he puffed on his pipe.

"Well, since you didn't take the crew and equipment back to California, I should at least be able to deduct their airfares and freight costs," I countered.

"What about my nylon line that was cut in four pieces when we went through the Panama Canal?" he barked. "And how about my broken ten-ton winch?"

"It's a five-ton winch and it was broken when we came on board," I barked back.

"It's gonna cost you twelve hundred dollars to fix my gyro stabilizers, you know." He started shuffling through the bills.

"Why? We never used them."

"And what in the hell did you do with the clamps for the blasters? I want those clamps," he was yelling now.

"Those are my clamps, Glenn. I'm keeping them as souvenirs."

"They were specially made to fit those blasters, you imbecile. They belong to me," he snarled.

"Right, specially made by *my* crew. Make your own clamps if you want some." I snarled back.

It was too late now for a peaceful settlement. We were both going for the throat.

"You have to pay me fuel money to get back to California," Glenn shouted, poking his finger repeatedly on the tabletop.

"Why? You're not going back there."

"I will someday."

"Fine. Someday I'll pay you."

"All right. We'll call it a draw!" Glenn shouted, thrusting out his arms like a baseball umpire signaling "safe."

"I'll give you the clamps and half the escrow money," I said calmly.

"Three-quarters of the escrow money."

"Done."

I was still dripping wet when I walked out of the galley, but I knew I had gotten off easy. Chuckling to myself, I walked down the dock leaving the *Coral Sea* and its crazy captain for the last time. I was all the way to the parking lot when Zach came running up behind me.

"I wanted to say good-bye," he said softly. "Will I ever see you after today?"

"I'm sure our paths will cross again," I answered, wondering if they ever really would.

"What will you do now?" he asked.

"Well," I said, looking up at him with a sly little grin, "I know where there's a wreck in Ecuador."

PART TWO

". . . you survived because you decided against
quitting when the battle wasn't much fun."

Richard Bach
A Gift of Wings

Chapter Eleven

The casually dressed man behind the podium tapped on the microphone to quiet the room before he spoke. After checking his notes one last time, he leaned closer to the microphone and said, "As conference chairman, I'd like to welcome you all to the annual Conference of the International Underwater Archaeology Society. As most of you know, this is a week-long conference dedicated to the cooperation and further understanding of those involved in the preservation of our historical underwater resources. Besides the various workshops throughout the week, on Tuesday there will be a general meeting to bring you up to date on the Abandoned Shipwreck Act and Senate Bill S-858."

It was January 1982. The biggest snowstorm in a century had just dumped six feet of new snow on Denver the day before the conference opened. As usual, I had no idea what I was getting into, but Bob Marx had insisted that I learn about some of the archaeological aspects of treasure hunting. He was scheduled to give a paper on sunken Phoenician ships on Wednesday.

Six months earlier, I had gone to see Bob just before I left Florida, more out of curiosity than necessity. Our *Maravilla* treasure had been divided, the equipment had all been sold, and I was going back to California to decide on my future. Before I could ask him any questions Bob grabbed my arm and hurried me into his spacious living room filled with shipwreck artifacts.

"Let me show you something," he said as I sat in the chair next to some Roman amphora lying on the floor.

He reached into a binder and pulled out an eight-by-ten glossy color photograph of a tabletop covered in gold - gold chains, gold bars, gold crosses, coins, and jewelry, all lying on a crimson-red cloth.

"I brought all that up in one day," he said as he quickly grabbed another chair. "I found two wrecks side by side off the coast of Guam. Seventeenth century. Now, tell me what happened with your expedition. Sounds like you never got off the bow section of the *Maravilla*."

"Well, Anderson quit, and Mike took us right to the area you already worked, and I spent most of my time dealing with Glenn. The man's a lunatic!" I laughed.

"Yeah, I've heard about most of it. Listen, if you can sit here and laugh after what you went through, you're a real treasure hunter."

"Treasure finder," I corrected him.

"Absolutely. Now, what are you going to do about the Ecuador wreck?"

"Is it really there or did you make up the information?"

"I can't believe you'd ask me that, Margee!" He suddenly got mad. "I don't need to make up information! If you'd do some damn research yourself you'd know it's there!"

"I'm sorry if I offended you, but I'm through assuming things. I got into a lot of trouble assuming things."

"Listen, babe, that's one of my top ten wrecks. It's loaded. Remember, our agreement says if you don't go after it within five years, all rights revert to me."

"I've got four years left."

"Well, do me a favor. Get acquainted with some of the historical aspects of what you're doing. When you find that wreck, the archaeological community is going to descend on you like flies on shit. Do some research, for Christ sakes!"

"I paid *you* to do the research. Why do I have to do it too?"

"Because I think you're gonna hit it big. And it'll help if you know what you're talking about when those vultures come to pick you apart. Study Spanish, nautical history and proper excavation techniques. See if you can find more info on the wreck in Ecuadorian or Peruvian archives. Research never ends. Now, the next Underwater Archaeology Conference is in January, in Denver. I'll be looking for you there."

So here I sat listening to lectures, watching slides, studying graphs, slowly coming to realize that the difference between what I had done and what these archaeologists were doing was record keeping - they went slower and made maps and drawings of everything before they brought it up. Here it was 1982 and they were presenting work they had done in the sixties and early seventies. Lack of money was the reason they all gave. Institutions couldn't afford to fund too many projects. They also made it clear that their recoveries went directly to museums and university laboratories. However, not one project presented had recovered gold and silver. It was all ceramic pots and silverware, shoe buckles and everyday utensils.

The information was interesting at first, but after a while I got bored. Once a particular wreck from a particular time period was reconstructed, what was the sense in doing the same thing over again ten times? These archeologists spent a lot of time discussing minuscule points, like the difference between the angles at which two spoons were sitting when they were uncovered, or the significance of a square-cornered shoe buckle versus a round-cornered one. Granted, this might be interesting data to archaeologists, but in the scope of world events, does it really matter? The fact that marine archaeologists were having trouble finding jobs and that public funding was scarce told me that the rest of the world wasn't all that interested in the angles of two sunken spoons.

The full brunt of the raging controversy between marine archaeologists and treasure hunters hit me at the general meeting on Tuesday. The archaeologists were lobbying in Washington to pass the Abandoned Shipwreck Act, which, they believed, would stop treasure hunting in the United States once and for all.

"These grave robbers are selling off our historical heritage!" the archaeologists shouted. (Apparently, you aren't a grave robber if you measure and draw something before you take it.)

"Looting a shipwreck is the same as looting the Pyramids," they cried. (I guess it was irrelevant that there are only a handful of Pyramids but there are hundreds of thousands of shipwrecks.)

"We need to preserve shipwrecks for the public good." they insisted. (Well, if the entire public really agreed with that attitude there wouldn't be a controversy.)

The Shipwreck Act would declare every sunken vessel in U.S. waters to be property of the federal government. Anybody taking anything off a wreck (anybody except marine archaeologists, of course) would be fined and thrown in jail. (Well, that was one sure way of establishing job security for marine archaeologists).

It was obvious that the archaeologists wanted the wrecks all to themselves. Their attitude was made crystal clear to me when I lingered after the general meeting to talk with the chairman, a marine archaeologist from Florida.

160

"Excuse me, Mr. Chairman," I said when the crowd around him began to disburse. "I have a question to ask."

"What is it?" he asked, scrutinizing my name tag.

"If I was going to excavate a wreck, are there any manuals or textbooks available that would tell me precisely how to do it?"

"Are you an accredited marine archaeologist?" he asked without hesitation.

"No."

"Then keep your fucking hands off the wreck!" he said angrily and walked away.

Bob Marx never showed up on Wednesday. His report was read by somebody else. I saw no point in staying amongst the enemy any longer, so I caught the next flight back to California.

A few things Bob had told me earlier kept swimming around in my head. First, fully 90 percent of all the shipwrecks ever found were found by people who weren't marine archaeologists. Second, every year government agencies and local port authorities destroy hundreds of wrecks and artifacts when they dredge waterways and enlarge port facilities. And modern ships dragging anchors across the ocean floor destroy more sunken wrecks than treasure hunters do. Finally, for every marine archaeology project, there are at least a hundred privately financed treasure hunts.

Couldn't some compromise be reached? If treasure hunters would let archaeologists retrieve their data while excavating a wrecksite, couldn't archaeologists let treasure hunters sell some of the recovered items? After all, compromise is the essence of progress.

When I arrived back home, I went straight to my safe and pulled out the map and summary information on the Ecuador

161

wreck. Bob Marx had sold me the information as a backup site for the *Maravilla* expedition. I had put it away thinking I would never need it, now it captivated me. The summary information read as follows:

The galleon was built in 1587. The name of the galleon was *Santa Maria de los Remedios*. In 1588 it served as the Almiranta in the Armada de Mar de Sur, which carried the treasures from Callao to Panama and then returned with merchandises from the fair of Nombre de Dios. In February 1590 the ship was careened at Callao. A visita (inspection and survey) was performed on the ship on April 3rd and the ship was listed as being 740 tons, carrying 8 anchors of between 12 and 29 quintals (100 pounds), and possessing 42 cannons (20 iron and 22 bronze), plus six pedreros (small stone-throwing cannon). By order of the Viceroy of Peru, the vessel was selected as the Capitana for that year's armada going up to Panama.

On April 15th, this Armada set sail from Callao consisting of four ships: The Capitana (Santa Maria de los Remedios), the Almiranta (Nuestra Señora de Guia), the San Juan Bautista and the Santa Maria de Gracia. Aboard all four ships they were carrying a total of 12,480,000 ducats in treasure.

Aboard the Capitana they had 5,250,000 ducats in gold and silver. Of the total in gold and silver the breakdown was as follows:

3,782,000 ducats in silver bullion
1,130,250 ducats in specie of silver (coins)
337,750 ducats in gold bullion (tejos)

In addition there were 176 chests of plata labrada, which means objects such as silverware, plates, candlesticks, etc., all made of silver. No value was placed on these pieces. Also seven chests of gold church plate were carried on the Capitana. No value placed on this gold. The register also lists 313 cajones de regalos (boxes of gifts), but no mention of what they contained nor their value.

Remember that usually ships of this period carried about 50 percent more in contraband of the total amount registered on each ship and that most of the contraband was in the form of gold, since it was less bulky to carry and hide, and there was a 16:1 ratio in the value between gold and silver.

The above figures for the registered gold and silver do not take into account all of the personal treasures carried by the crew, passengers and merchants. Since the merchants from Peru were going to attend the Fair in Nombre de Dios, they had to be carrying at least another million ducats in treasure to make their purchases at the Fair. The registered treasure mentioned in the total was only the amount already consigned to be sent back to Spain on the Armada and Flota of Tierra Firme.

The Captain General was Don Juan de la Coroña, the Captain was Don Domingo de Uribe, chief pilot was Luis de Endeva. There were 89 sailors, 64 marines, 18 religious, 124 passengers returning to Spain, 46 merchants from Peru and Chile, and 29 slaves.

They had a slow but uneventful voyage until reaching the Bay of Manta, Ecuador on May 2nd, where they stopped for several days because of calms.

Around midnight on the third night, a furious tempest sprung up, placing all four ships in danger. The Almiranta and the other two smaller ships managed to cut their cables and head out to sea. By sunrise the following morning they were over five leagues from Manta Bay and continued on their voyage up to Panama, expecting to meet up with the Capitana along the way - not realizing that she had been totally lost.

When the storm struck (which the assistant pilot later claimed was "the worst I have ever witnessed in 33 years of sailing") the Capitana was closer to shore than the other three ships and was unable to veer away from the shore. On each tack the huge seas caused the ship to be forced closer and closer to the coast. Finally the ship struck bottom and great panic ensued. The captain ordered all of the masts cut, but even before this could be done the ship began "going to pieces." Two chalupas and a lancha were lowered to try and get the crew and passengers ashore. Such a large number of persons jumped into the lancha that it was swamped and sank. Both chalupas also overturned in the surf. Of the total number of persons aboard the ship, only 23 persons survived.

By dawn no part of the ship remained above the water and the shore was strewn with bodies, timbers and other things from the ship.

During an investigation conducted several months later, it was also discovered that treasures had been found in chests of clothes which had been washed ashore.

The ship was lost "midway between the anchorage off Manta and Cape San Lorenzo on a placel (shoal or reef)" in one document; another states that it "pounded out its bottom on some rocks a league, more or less, to the west of the village." Both of these locations correspond to what is shown on the chart of Manta Bay, which says "amongst which rocks was cast away a ship in which was a prodigious treasure."

Word reached the President of the Audencia of Panama of the disaster on May 19th, and he quickly ordered a salvage effort to be initiated without delay. Three pataches with 44 divers from the pearl fisheries in the Pearl Islands, and 85 soldiers were sent down to Manta Bay. Contrary winds forced them back to the Perico Islands three weeks later. It wasn't until September 9th that they finally reached the site of the wreck. Rough seas prevented them from starting their search until September 22. They reported that very few traces of the ship were to be seen on the bottom (one letter said in six fathoms and another eight fathoms) except for some cannon and two "piles of silver bars." During the next eight months they were only able to work about a third of the time because of rough seas, but they did recover 16 of the bronze cannons, 295 bars of silver, and 64,387 pesos in loose coins. They reported that all of the rest of the treasure was hidden under the sands.

Three years later, another expedition was sent to this wrecksite by order of the King of Spain. Expert divers from the pearl fisheries of Isla Margarita off the coast of Venezuela were sent. Six weeks of intensive search only produced seven large silver bars, two more bronze cannon, and a gold chain "four codos in length." Again they reported that everything was hidden under the shifting sands.

Nothing more on this wreck until 1618, when a Spaniard petitioned the King of Spain for a "patent" to try and salvage this shipwreck and several others in the "South Seas." No mention if he was ever granted the concession or if he ever found anything.

The only other mention of this shipwreck occurs in 1764, when a group of Spaniards enlist the help of "a Dutch engineer with a new machine for recovering lost sea treasures" and petition the King of Spain for permission to "find and salvage the treasure nao [galleon] lost off Manta Bay in 1590" as well as others lost along the Pacific Coast of South America. They were given a contract, granting them one-third of what they could find. No further mention if they ever went on the expedition or of any success. However, if they would have had great success some documents would still exist proclaiming the event.

I worked out ducats to ounces to pounds to tons and came out with 174 tons of silver and 11.9 tons of gold, not counting the stuff that might have been smuggled aboard. Bob had told me that in thirty years of shipwreck research he'd seen fewer than a dozen charts that pinpointed a wreck's location as precisely as the chart I was holding in my hands.

What should I do? Send all the material back to Bob and forget it? Be content with a normal life, making a comfortable living at some monotonous job? Should I give up adventure? Where is Ecuador anyway? I didn't speak Spanish. I didn't even have enough money for a plane ticket. Was I really crazy enough to fly off to South America with a treasure map? Hadn't I learned anything from my last treasure hunting experience?

I hemmed and hawed and baked cookies and waited for Kevin to come home from work. He had found a job back in the sport scuba diving industry and hated it. We had taken our furniture out of storage and rented a small two-bedroom house in the hills east of San Francisco not far from the ranch we had sold. We were broke. Since we had had to pay back the investors first from the *Maravilla* treasure, and the amount of treasure only covered the costs of the expedition, Kevin and I got nothing. Out of boredom one day, I drove up to the local State University to visit with an old friend, a professor of anthropology and archaeology.

"I just don't know what to do, Alan," I told him as I fumbled with the papers on his desk. "I'm sitting here with a map showing me where tons of gold and silver are, but I've already lost my shirt going after one shipwreck."

"Hey, in blackjack, when you lose one hand, the only way to get your money back is to bet double on the next hand," Alan advised me. He always had interesting advice.

167

"Geeze, you're in the archaeology department and you're talking about shipwreck excavation like it was a gambling game. I thought you'd be telling me to keep my hands off the treasure."

"Listen, eighty percent of the people who get into archaeology want to do exactly what you're doing. They just learn to make detailed drawings while they're doing it."

"OK, I agree that the historical data should be recorded, but I also think the excavators should get to keep some of the recovered items. A lot of good archaeology could get accomplished if it could be combined with business somehow. Of course, some of the stuff should go into museums, but why all of it? There must be a way to excavate shipwrecks correctly and get paid for it, don't you think?"

"Are you talking to me or yourself?" Alan asked.

"Very funny."

"I'd go for it if I were you, Margee."

"Do you know any Ecuadorians?"

"No."

"You got any money for an expedition?"

"No, but I might know somebody who does."

"Are you serious?" I suddenly sat up. "Don't kid me, now. I'm in a real quandary here."

"Really. The guy is a multimillionaire. He's got a foundation in San Francisco and he'd probably love to fund a shipwreck excavation. Especially if there was something in it for him. He's Latin too."

"What kind of foundation is it?"

"It's to promote arts, sciences and humanities. It's called XSABA."

"What's the guy's name?"

"Laisder Benito Roberto de Medoza. Want me to call him?"

"Not yet, I gotta think about this for awhile."

As I drove home from the university I tried to analyze my feelings. Alan's offer was another entrance to the treasure hunting world and it was forcing me to decide what to do with the shipwreck information. If I went to see this Medoza guy, it would mean I had decided to go search for the shipwreck. It was as simple as that. I had no other reason to meet the guy. And if I decided to go after the shipwreck, I would have to see it through to the end, whatever happened.

Kevin wanted to go for it, we'd already discussed it. I couldn't think of anything else I'd rather be doing. If we didn't go after the Ecuador wreck, Marx would just sell the information to somebody who would. This was an opportunity to prove that archaeology and business could work together to the benefit of both. I suddenly realized that this was another one of those solitary, pivotal moments in life that irretrievably change your destiny.

"Okay," I said to myself as I pulled into my driveway. "I'm going to lead an expedition to recover the shipwreck in Ecuador."

❦

Alan made the appointment with Mr. Medoza and I dressed in my conservative business suit for the occasion. I wanted to appear as level-headed and business-minded as possible, not like an adventurer infected with gold fever. I'd learned a long time ago that 'It's all in the presentation.'

Thank goodness Medoza wouldn't be seeing my mode of transportation. I was driving *La Bamba*, the sky-blue 1956

Chevy pickup truck we had bought from Jake. I crossed the San Francisco Bay Bridge, and followed Alan's directions to the very top of Nob Hill, to one of the ritziest, most expensive apartment buildings in San Francisco. The place was right across the street from the Pacific Union Club, commonly known as the millionaires club. This is looking good, I thought to myself.

Black wrought iron gates with shiny brass embellishments marked the entrance to the brick-paved courtyard in front of the building. Two statue-like doormen stood on either side of the main doors. Plush carpets and etched glass windows adorned the interior of the building, radiating the heavy, elegant atmosphere of old money.

"Is someone expecting you, madam?" one of the doormen asked in a butlerish tone.

"Yes, a Mr. Medoza," I replied, trying to sound rich myself.

"I shall announce your arrival," he said, bowing slightly before he walked to a marble desk to use the telephone. "Mr. Medoza will receive you on the fifteenth floor, madam," the doorman told me.

I thanked him and walked to the elevator with my chin slightly raised and my hands starting to sweat. On the fifteenth floor I found the right apartment and was about to knock when the door swung open and I was greeted by a four foot tall man in a white suit and bright red tie. He had an oversized forehead, wide noticeable ears, and full protruding lips, all contributing to a boyish impression.

"Please come in," he said, extending a delicate hand to guide me through the doorway. "I am Roberto."

I entered a large room furnished in antiques and oil masterpieces in gilded frames. One entire wall was a window with

170

a breathtaking view of the Fairmont Hotel, Grace Cathedral, San Francisco's financial district, and the bay.

"Welcome to XSABA," smiled Roberto, taking a seat opposite me. "May I offer you some champagne?"

"No, thank you," I said sweetly. I wanted to keep my wits about me.

"Alan tells me you need funding for an expedition to Ecuador," he said, crossing his legs and leaning back on his chair. "You wish to excavate a sunken Spanish galleon, I believe?"

"Yes, that's correct," I answered. "I have the historical information from the Spanish archives that pinpoints the wreck location to a five-mile area. The vessel was carrying over ten tons of gold and 170 tons of silver."

"How much money do you need to excavate it?"

"Half a million dollars."

"What is the name of the ship?"

"I'll tell you that when you put up the money."

"I see. Have you ever worked with a foundation before?"

"No, only private investors."

"I have a proposition for you," said Roberto, clasping his hands together. "I'll put up six hundred thousand dollars for your shipwreck recovery if you will lead a scientific expedition to Ecuador first, on behalf of our foundation. Are you interested?"

"What kind of scientific expedition?" I asked suspiciously.

"I'll leave that up to you," said Roberto. "I will put XSABA's facilities at your disposal. You may use this office if you like. My only requirements are that you donate your time for free and that the expedition be something that will be beneficial both to the country of Ecuador and to the field of science."

"Of course I'd be interested," I said, fighting the urge to ask hundreds of questions. I settled on just one. "What does XSABA stand for?"

"The X is the Greek symbol for strangers. XSABA stands for Strangers, Science, Arts and Business Allied. Your project fits in nicely with our theme. I'm assuming XSABA would receive a percentage of any recovery from your shipwreck."

"Forty percent of whatever Ecuador gives us, if you fund the entire project," I said flatly.

"My offer still stands," said Roberto, as he rose from his chair. "Why don't you come back tomorrow, after you've had some time to think it over, and give me your answer? Shall we say noon? I would enjoy your company at lunch."

I was on cloud nine driving back over the bridge towards home. Good ol' Alan. Working with a foundation would be the perfect way to combine archaeology and business. What a lucky break!

Before the week was over I had a set of keys to the XSABA apartment and a private office with a seventeenth-century, gold inlaid, French provincial desk. I had a window with that magnificent view of San Francisco and a Rembrandt painting hanging on the wall. A telephone, copy machine, and green BMW automobile were at my disposal, and, I had a signed agreement that I would be reimbursed for any expenses I might incur, provided I fill out a form and attach the receipts. It must have been the smell of money that made me accept Roberto's offer so readily. Kevin wasn't so easily impressed. He didn't trust Roberto at all. "The guy's got shifty eyes," Kevin warned me.

The following week I was introduced to local priests from the Franciscan, Jesuit, and Salesian Orders. Each of them headed a separate project funded by XSABA and they all accepted me without question as the chairwoman of the science committee. In a foundation, I learned, everything was done by committee, and committee meant party, most of the time.

Twice a week, in the evenings, the cut crystal glasses were filled with Cordon Negro champagne and the XSABA apartment was filled with richly dressed, exotic guests.

There were Lords and Ladies from France, a consul general from Central America, a famous surrealist artist from Czechoslovakia, art critics, a priest or two, the wife of a prominent Philippine doctor, and several minor people without titles. Alan was usually there for the free booze, and of course Kevin and I attended every bash. It was at one of these parties that Roberto introduced me to Angela Julieta Vega Nazur de Kampa, an Ecuadorian lady who spent six months out of the year living in Ecuador.

"This is how we get things done at XSABA," Roberto told me. "The right connection is much more valuable than money."

Angela was a real party animal. She bubbled like the champagne, flashing her jewelry and mingling with all the guests whether she spoke their language or not. She was a middle-aged "Charo" with an ample bosom that filled her deep, V-neck dresses to overflowing and never failed to catch men's attention. She wore a Carmen Miranda-style hat, with colored straw fruit bunched high on one side like a delicatessen fruit bowl. She had a round face, friendly eyes, cinnamon skin, and a heavy Spanish accent that flowed with her carefree personality and happy disposition. Underneath all the flamboyance though, Angela was a businesswoman who missed nothing. If the conversation was money, Angela was in on it, and once she heard the word *treasure*, it didn't take her long to get involved in our expedition.

Roberto advised me to assemble a group of my friends, and my science committee soon consisted of Angela, Alan, Kevin, two investors from the Bahamian expedition, my mother, and a priest. At

173

our first meeting, in March 1982 we sipped champagne, nibbled on finger sandwiches with the crusts cut off, and decided that oceanography would be the theme of our scientific expedition to Ecuador. I made it very clear to everyone that my goal was the shipwreck, that I was organizing the scientific stuff to fulfill a bargain and nothing more. There were no objections. They were all in it for the shipwreck as well. Then Angela stood up, announced she was leaving for Ecuador in June, and asked who wanted to go with her? I cautiously raised my hand.

In three months time I assembled a group of scientists whose research had something to do with Ecuador. I did it with the trusty telephone by calling oceanographic and marine-oriented institutions, and telling them we had a research vessel scheduled to cruise Ecuadorian waters. I was overwhelmed with projects. They ranged from tagging seabirds, to studying zooplankton. One scientist wanted to record the oxygen content of ocean-bottom sediments. The director of a local aquarium wanted to capture specimens for a display of South American fish. A Harvard University professor wanted to get blood samples from Galápagos Island sea lions. Scripps Institute of Oceanography wanted to study the food chain in the ocean and collect dinoflagelates, the microorganisms that sustain all life in the sea. A specialist in nudibranchs (brightly colored slug-like sea creatures) had collected specimens from everywhere in the world except Ecuador and begged me to let him go on the cruise. And no cruise would be complete without studying the El Niño phenomena, a severe change in the weather pattern that occurred every six to seven years.

It seemed the world was starving for Ecuadorian oceanographic research. I was suddenly a very popular person, receiving phone calls and letters from all over the country. I was really having fun. I was also getting a crash course in oceanography, studying books every evening so I could understand what the hell these scientists were talking about.

Every weekday I rode the electric train into San Francisco then hopped on a cable car that climbed to the top of Nob Hill. I was a regular. The cable car brakeman always saved the end seat on the outside for me and he let me ring the brass bell if he was busy with the hand brakes. The cold, crisp, San Francisco air made my nose red by the time I strode past the doormen at the XSABA apartment building and took the elevator to the fifteenth floor. By mid-day I was usually finished with my phone calls, so I chatted with the new secretary, Lina. She had arrived scarcely a week after I had joined XSABA.

Lina was a tiny woman with frail hands and an upper-class background. She was one of the "blue ladies," I was later told, a woman of wealthy blood lines. She had owned a finishing school in the Philippines and before that had distinguished herself in literature, receiving an award from the French president, Charles de Gaulle. Our friendship grew out of our mutual love of gossip and our gossip was fueled by our endless curiosity about Roberto and his strange foundation.

"Oh, Maggie," Lina would call me affectionately. "Come sit beside me, dear. I've heard something new about Roberto. The poor thing is three months behind on the rent for this apartment."

"Really?" I mused. "As a matter of fact, yesterday I got a phone call from some guy who said the lease payment on these fancy memory typewriters is overdue. You don't think Roberto is broke, do you?"

"I hope not," Lina said coldly. "I heard he was inheriting thirty million dollars, but he borrowed money from me to buy lunch today."

"Well, he always reimburses me when I turn in my receipts. Of course, the total has never been more than a hundred dollars."

"He promised to have a limousine take me to and from the office everyday, but I haven't seen it yet. Roberto has a kind heart, but I think he might have overextended himself."

"Have you ever met any other XSABA staff people?" I asked as if we were looking for clues in a mystery novel. "Isn't it strange that we're the only two people here?"

"I did meet the old secretary once," Lina said. "But I think you are XSABA's only current project."

"I suppose I should be grateful."

"I suppose so. But take my advice dear. Don't loan Roberto any money."

Perhaps it's human nature to want answers to all your questions. On the other hand, you should never look a gift horse in the mouth, they say. I busied myself with putting the final touches on a presentation binder that contained descriptions of each science project going to Ecuador. Yet the closer it got to June, the more uncertain I felt about traveling to a country where I didn't speak the language. Since Kevin had to keep working to pay our bills and didn't know a word of Spanish either, we convinced our friend Mac to make the trip with me.

Mac was a famous doctor who'd studied in Mexico for years and spoke Spanish like he was born to it. He was energetic and kind, with a quick mind and a mischievous personality. Medicine was serious business to him, but outside the office he was a jokester. The first time Kevin and I met him was at a dinner party, where he convinced seven well-dressed guests to get on their hands and knees and form a human pyramid, three people high, before dinner was served. I could trust Mac. If nothing else, he could tell jokes in Spanish.

Everything was now set. XSABA was going to Ecuador, represented by Angela, Lina, Mac, and me. Roberto gave us all letters of introduction with the XSABA seal on them. With wide-eyed anticipation and a twinge of suspense, I boarded the plane for my first flight to South America.

Chapter Twelve

"Attención, damas y caballeros. Estamos llegando al aeropuerto Simón Bolivar en la ciudad de Guayaquil. Por favor abroche su cinturón y no fumar. Attenchon, ladies an gentleman. We are arriving at dee Simon Bolivar airport een de city off Guayaquil. Plees fasen you seat belt an e no esmoking," said the airline sterwardess.

It was 6:30 a.m. as we descended into Guayaquil airport through a hazy yellowish-gray sky. Yawning and stretching after the all-night flight, I peered out the window at a river delta landscape, flat and green with thick veins of milk-chocolate-colored water stretching everywhere. Rickety split-bamboo shacks dotted the countryside perched precariously on the relatively dry areas. It was hard to tell if the water was encroaching on the land or vice versa.

The stifling heat was the first thing I noticed as we walked across the tarmac toward the terminal. A general sense of urgency permeated the crowd as people pressed against each other, elbowing for space, claiming overstuffed luggage and waving at relatives waiting outside the double glass doors. Angela was everywhere at once, gabbing with other passengers, directing the luggage carriers, watching out for Lina, Mac, and me, and explaining to the customs inspectors in ninety-mile-an-hour Spanish that the jumbled mess inside her four gigantic suitcases was all personal belongings.

Finally we passed onto the street and into the throng of yelling people frantically waving their hands. Three carloads of Angela's friends had come to the airport to receive her, and they descended on us all at once, hugging us and kissing our cheeks. Young boys trying to earn a tip kept clutching at our bags. A newspaper reporter hastily took our picture before we were crammed into cars and driven into downtown Guayaquil. My clothes were already soaked with sweat.

The car bounced through chuckholes, swerved around people and debris, and jockeyed for position at every stoplight. There were no lines on the road to designate lanes, and most of the cars around us were dented, scratched, and rusted, a clear result of the traffic free-for-all. The city was dirty and crumbling. People were everywhere, like ants, filling the sidewalks, crossing between the cars, sitting in doorways, staring out of barred windows, flagging down buses, and loitering on street corners. None of them looked happy.

We parked in front of a four-story building and rode an elevator not much larger than a telephone booth to the top floor. There to greet us was Angela's mother, a small, plump, affectionate woman with a smiling face and outstretched arms. The hugging and cheek kissing started all over again as the room filled with noise and laughter. When the guests finally left and the four of us had a chance to talk, Angela asked me, "Well, how do you like my country?"

"It's overwhelming," I said with enthusiasm. "And hot. I wish I knew what everybody was saying."

"It doesn't matter," Angela told me. "Tomorrow we go to Salinas. There you will find more people who speak English."

"Angela, I noticed everybody calls you Julieta here," Mac said.

"Well, that is also my name," Angela said as if it were obvious. "In United States I'm Angela, here, I'm Julieta. Doesn't matter. Now you better get some sleep. On Thursday we go to Quito. I will make an appointment with my good friend Admiral Lario. He will help us. In this country you have to have your connections or you can't do anything."

"Thank you, Angela," I said sincerely.

"Call me Julieta," she replied.

In the afternoon, when it was even hotter, Mac and I went for a walk into the commercial center of the city. Like any big metropolis, it was full of traffic and signs and tall buildings, but above all Guayaquil was dirty. Men spat on the sidewalk, people threw their garbage down, and everything dried into black splotches of gooey filth. The rancid smells of rotten fruit and urine combined with diesel exhaust from the buses to attack our noses. I found myself taking short shallow breaths to minimize the amount of air I took into my lungs. Carefully avoiding random holes in the sidewalk that would break your leg if you fell into them, we picked our way among the street vendors selling coconut juice, or cooking bananas on blackened metal grates. Sometimes there was no sidewalk at all, just rocky dirt or broken-up pavement. I clasped Mac's hand for reassurance, ignoring the men who stared at me or beckoned me with a hissing "tsss, tsss, tsss."

The next day we left the city for the coast, a two-hour trip through green countryside, thick with vines and tropical plants. There are no freeways in Ecuador, only wide paved roads with no center line, and everybody, regardless of direction, drove down the middle to avoid the chuckholes on the edges. The whole trip was a never-ending game of chicken at fifty miles an hour.

As we approached the coast, the greenery gave way to dry, desolate hills covered by thorny scrub brush being grazed by an occasional wild donkey. On the Salinas peninsula, Ecuador's main resort area, a large, calm bay and a shoreline full of white high-rise condominiums stood before us. Julieta owned a fourth-floor condo right on the beach.

It was Julieta's plan to relax in Salinas for a few days, but I was too anxious to investigate Manta Bay, the site of our shipwreck. So Mac and I thumbed a ride back to Guayaquil, where we rented a car and drove northwest on another singular paved road with no center line.

We passed herds of cattle guided down the road by men on skinny horses, and sometimes miles of pavement would be sectioned off with rocks to protect rice or cacao beans drying in the sun. I felt we'd regressed at least a hundred years to an era when everything was done by hand. Five hours later we knew we were approaching the coast again when the landscape turned brown and barren. I pinched Mac's arm when we passed a sign saying Bienvenidos a Manta (Welcome to Manta).

For some reason I had been expecting a quaint, isolated little fishing village, but Manta was a bustling city of seventy thousand people with a mile-long breakwater protecting a sizable harbor full of fishing vessels and cargo ships.

We cruised the main street along the water's edge, looking for a salvage vessel to charter but couldn't find one. Then we got out our treasure map and set out to check the coastline, attempting to estimate where the underwater rocks would be. We had two landmarks - the city itself, which used to be the old 'village', and a point with a rock off it, five miles to the west. According to the historical data, somewhere in between was the wreck, and its *prodigious treasure.*

The map showed five points, jutting out from the coastline, but we only found three. We climbed to the top of hills and followed every soft dirt road we could find out of the city, but they all dead-ended before we could see a point with a rock beside it. We did learn, at least, that the water was calm and a boat could work in the area.

On the way back to Guayaquil, scarcely ten miles out of Manta, we passed through a town called Monticristi that sat at the foot of a steeply rising, cone-shaped mountain. Suddenly I felt the sting of excitement. My insides started buzzing as if my whole body was filled with bees.

"That's it! That's the mountain!" I shouted, as I fumbled for a piece of paper and scribbled down the words that were written on the old chart Marx had given me.

Mount $x f$ to

The big X meant cross, or cris, the oversize 'f' was the archaic form of 's' and the 'to' meant 'to' - Mount of Cristo - Monticristi! This was the mountain on the chart, that stood behind the village of Manta.

All around me, scattered over the hillsides, were tall, thick-trunked trees that looked like the menacing forest just outside the Emerald City in the Wizard of Oz. The branches looked like crooked fingers and the tree trunks formed ridges that looked like swollen blood veins on the back of a hand. A local hat weaver told us that they were ceibo (say-bo) trees. On the old chart they were called zeyba trees. The mountain, the ceibo trees and the bay - everything fit! We were in the right place. I was beaming smiles the whole ride back to Guayaquil, eager to finish the scientific stuff and start looking for the shipwreck.

A few days later, Mac and I took the thirty-minute flight to Quito, where we rendezvoused with Lina and Julieta. We were admitted inside the Ministry of National Defense and taken to the office of the navy commander, Admiral Lario. Handsome and stately in his dark blue uniform, the Admiral motioned us to be seated on a leather sofa while we talked about XSABA and our proposed scientific project. A wall size map of Ecuador hung opposite the Admiral's desk, and Mac used it to explain in Spanish the locations our scientists wanted to study. I showed him my presentation binder, noting the prestige of the institutions involved with the project. It was all very formal and important sounding, however the Admiral took Julieta aside to ask what the hell we were *really* here for.

I guess Julieta convinced him we were legitimate, because he called the Oceanographic Institute in Guayaquil and told them to receive us and start planning the joint project.

After we dropped Mac off at the airport for his trip back to California, Julieta turned to me in the back seat of the taxicab and softly said, "The Admiral has invited you to dinner. You should go if you want this project to proceed."

The Admiral picked me up at eight from our hotel. I wasn't nervous at first, I figured admirals were gentlemen and that dinner meant dinner. We drove a few circles around Quito, finally stopping in front of a restaurant that looked like a house except for the discreet sign in French, hanging from a wrought iron hook. "Muy exclusivo," the Admiral told me, he didn't speak any English.

A waiter in a white tuxedo conducted us to a small corner table. In the dimly lit restaurant I was trying my best to appear calm and sophisticated as I was seated opposite the Admiral.

I have no idea how he moved so fast, but as soon as the waiter left, the Admiral's hand zoomed up my floor-length skirt, down inside my pantihose, and forcefully grabbed a fistful of my pubic hair. *Holy shit!* I froze stiff as a board. I was frightened, then I was raging mad. Who does this bastard think he is? I had to clench my teeth so I wouldn't scream out. How... savage, I thought, how... presumptuous, how... painful. The Admiral was holding on tight to those pubic hairs and grinning at me like a poker player who'd just laid down four aces. What would the protocol books have to say about this I wondered? I tried to wiggle backwards, losing a few hairs in the attempt. I was furious because I didn't know how to say *'Get your filthy hand out of my pants'* in Spanish. I felt trapped, like an insect in a bottle. I had to do something, quick, but I didn't want to cause a scene in the restaurant.

Finally, in desperation, I picked up my menu and held it in front of my face so I didn't have to look at the Admiral, or say anything. Begrudgingly he released my hairs, drawing his hand out as quickly as it had slithered in. I was in such shock that I actually ordered my meal and ate it before I pulled myself together and insisted he take me straight back to my hotel.

I was thinking how glad I was that this "dinner" was over when, a block short of the hotel entrance, the Admiral parked the car, threw his arms around me, and started kissing me anywhere his lips could touch. I struggled, resisted, and squirmed out of his grasp, and when my hand found the door handle, I backed out of the car and escaped. I never looked back, and I never saw the Admiral again.

The following week the Oceanographic Institute accepted our project with open arms. Apparently I had somehow stumbled through my initiation into Latin business practices.

185

On the flight back to California I was already planning my strategy to locate the shipwreck. I figured I'd be through with the scientists in two or three months. Roberto, on the other hand, had a completely different idea.

"Margarita, you don't understand the Latin mentality," Roberto told me when we met at the XSABA apartment to discuss the trip. "They will need time to study our proposal."

"What's to study?" I said. "The Oceanographic Institute loves the project."

"The decision will be made at the higher levels," Roberto said calmly. "We have entered through the front door. Now we will have to manipulate things through the back door. Trust me. I know how these people think. It will be our task to make XSABA indispensable to them. Then, when we ask permission to recover the shipwreck, it will be granted without question."

"Just how long do you anticipate all this will take?" I asked, gripping the arms of the chair to maintain my composure.

"Perhaps six months, if we're lucky. We have much work to do. I would like you to go to Houston to meet some business acquaintances of mine. They own an international shipping company. I'll expect them to ship all the equipment to Ecuador for free."

"Why would they do it for free?" I questioned.

"Because of the enormous tax benefits they would receive by helping a nonprofit foundation. In time, Margarita, you will understand how foundations work." Roberto patted my arm as if to say, don't fret.

Okay, I thought, I'll admit I don't know anything about foundations. Maybe I should just go along with this whole thing for awhile. After all, I did meet Julieta and get a free trip to Ecuador. That was something.

So I went to Houston, stayed at a lavishly expensive hotel, and delivered Roberto's proposal to the president of the shipping company. I also traveled to New Orleans and Los Angeles, all at XSABA's expense. I attended more parties and wrote more letters and kept up a running Telex communication with the Oceanographic Institute in Ecuador.

Meanwhile, Roberto changed all XSABA's phone numbers when several people called regarding bounced checks. Then we received a repossession notice for the BMW. I was just about to demand some explanations when Roberto informed me that XSABA should have an oceanographic department.

In Sausalito, a small community just north of San Francisco, Roberto leased a houseboat and hired workers to turn its interior into an office. One room was filled with computers, microfiche, telex, mobile phone units, and copy machines. Another room, with a velvet couch and lots of filing cabinets, became my office. The upstairs became a library.

"Roberto, this whole thing is a farce," I said one day when nothing was making any sense to me. "I haven't seen XSABA complete any projects or help anyone. In fact, I haven't seen XSABA do anything in the year I've been here."

"That's no way for an Xsabian to talk," Roberto scolded me. "Why, we've spent thousands of dollars on your project alone."

"Then why are there so many bounced checks? I'd like to see the money for the scientific expedition before we go any further. All you've ever given me is that approval paper from some anonymous finance committee."

"Margarita, this is a poor foundation. We don't have money just lying around. We'll have to raise it."

"*Raise it?*" I shouted, recalling all the months and miles it had taken to raise the money for the Bahamas. "You told me you had it."

"Don't worry," said Roberto in a placating tone. "We can raise all the money in a single night. I'll buy a yacht, we'll have a fancy party, invite all of XSABA's rich benefactors, and we'll have all the money we need for both the science project and your shipwreck salvage work. Two million dollars should cover everything. Don't worry."

Maybe this is the way rich people do it, I told myself. Kevin wasn't as easily convinced. He hadn't trusted Roberto from the start. We agreed between us to give this XSABA thing one last chance by playing the yacht party game. At least it sounded logical to invite rich people to a fancy party and hit them up for a contribution. It just might work.

Two weeks later, Roberto told us he was purchasing a 110' yacht he had found in Los Angeles and would like Kevin and I to check it out and motor it back up to San Francisco. A captain and engineer would be sent to join us when the vessel was ready to sail.

❦

"This is a joke, right?" was all Kevin could say when we stood on the dock in Los Angeles facing a World War II Navy subchaser that somebody had painted white.

"Somehow I don't think so," I answered turning to smile at the ship's owner, who had left his army-navy surplus store to meet us at the marina.

"Isn't she a beaut?" the man said with pride glistening in his eyes. "They sure knew how to build 'em back in '41. I bought her at auction two years ago but I just don't have the money to finish fixing her up. That Roberto is getting a real deal here. Well, if you've got the check, she's all yours."

The captain and engineer Roberto had sent, arrived at the marina just as the boat owner was leaving with his check. The captain was a spindly, elderly man with a long, white, handlebar mustache that curled up in a circle at each end, reminding me of Salvadore Dali. He said we could call him Captain Eddy. When we asked him about his experience with older vessels, he was quite taken aback, assuring us that he'd been captaining vessels in San Francisco Bay for the last twenty years. His friend, the engineer, was a younger, fatter, less sociable man who immediately disappeared into the engine room.

Four hours later, while we were cleaning and preparing for the voyage, the engineer came up from the engine room, handed me several pages of written recommendations about the ship, and said he would *never* go to sea in this vessel. He flew back to San Francisco that afternoon.

"Don't let that bother you," Captain Eddy counseled me. "He's just a fussbudget. Everything's gotta be perfect with him. We can get this damn boat to San Francisco ourselves. We could use another person to man the wheel though. There's no auto pilot on this boat. I say we pull out tomorrow."

Kevin talked our friend Larry into making the trip with us. It was easy, Larry didn't know anything about boats. Being six foot tall, he would spend most of the boat trip bumping his head on ceiling beams and doorway hatches.

At 6 a.m. we started up the engines and crashed into another boat as we backed out of the berth.

"Well, we're off to an ignominious start!" Captain Eddy remarked, twisting the ends of his handlebar mustache.

"What kind of a boat do you captain in San Francisco?" Larry asked off-handedly.

"A dredge," Captain Eddy replied. "It's really great to be going out to sea again after twenty years in the bay."

Larry, Kevin and I looked at each other with fear and trepidation, but we figured, what the hell, we'll either live through it or die from it.

The compass read south, as we passed the last buoy, heading out of the L.A. harbor. After we turned 180° to the right, heading north, the compass still read south. "Aw, we don't need a compass," the captain told us.

We decided to motor straight through to San Francisco, taking turns at sleeping and manning the wheel. The fire we put out in the engine room the following day just added some spice to the trip.

After awhile it occurred to us that the captain seldom looked at the navigational charts. Bad eyesight, he told us. He knew where we were at night by counting the light flashes per minute from the lighthouses we passed. In the daytime he was guessing.

After fifty-five hours of rolling like a log and praying we wouldn't sink, we passed under the Golden Gate Bridge into San Francisco Bay, thankful to be alive.

Roberto had told me to take the boat up to a marina at the north end of the San Francisco Bay where a new dock had been built just for the Regina XSABA, the name Roberto had given to our new "party yacht." When we got there, there was nothing but a big open lagoon.

Captain Eddy dropped the anchor in the center of the lagoon, shut down the engines, and saluted us goodbye. Just after he left, the wind came up, blowing the Regina XSABA across the lagoon and straight toward the beach. I panicked. We had no other anchors. I zoomed over to the marina office in the dinghy, and soon had the boat tied off, like a hammock, to a dump truck at one end of the lagoon and a water truck at the other end,. It was then that Roberto showed up with champagne and crystal glasses to celebrate our arrival.

"Well done, well done," Roberto toasted us.

"Roberto, this boat is old and ugly," Kevin wasted no time in telling him.

"Ah, but we got it at a good price," Roberto countered. "New carpets, some chandeliers, a few paintings, my furniture, in a month you won't recognize it. We'll moor it at the guest dock at the St. Francis Yacht Club for the party. I'm having the invitations printed on gold leaf paper. Even the press will be there. We'll have all the money we need for your expeditions."

Since we'd come this far, Kevin and I thought, we might as well see it through. Kevin moved on board the Regina XSABA and spent two months fixing things up and installing the carpets. He even stapled white Christmas lights to all the railings and up the mast in a big triangle. The result was really impressive.

From the Sausalito houseboat I made the reservation at the St. Francis Yacht Club and finally learned the truth about Roberto.

"Okay, Roberto, the yacht's ready and the guest dock's reserved. Let's have the party," I urged him.

"Margarita, haven't you learned anything about foundations yet?" Roberto asked, sounding exasperated. "We're not actually going through with the party, we're just generating expenses for our files, a cover for the IRS. A nonprofit foundation can spend ninety-six percent of its income on expenses as long as a minimum of four percent is spent on charitable activities. My rich friends donate to XSABA so they can take the write off on their taxes, then spend ninety-six percent of their money as they please, through the foundation."

"So this whole thing is a fraud?" I concluded.

"Not at all. XSABA has paid all your expenses. You are our charitable activity. We'll eventually fund your expedition in another year or so. Don't you want to be an Xsabian?"

"No! I don't want to be an Xsabian. I quit!"

I stomped out of the houseboat, taking my books and personal things with me. I drove straight to the Nob Hill apartment to pick up a few more things and found the door padlocked with an eviction notice taped to it. I had wasted a year and a half with that bozo, I was thinking as I drove to the marina to pick up Kevin.

For a week I moped around in despair and self-pity. What a fool. I'd been used. Roberto called twice begging me to come back to XSABA. On his third call he told me what an idiot I was for throwing away the best opportunity I would ever have. He said he had taken a peon from the lower classes and introduced me to the world of wealth and that I had proved to be nothing but an ungrateful wretch. I hung up on him. I sent a copy of my resignation letter to all the scientists, and finally called Julieta and invited her to lunch.

"Julieta, I want to thank you for taking me to Ecuador, but Roberto is full of shit. I don't think he ever intended to put up the money," I said truthfully.

"So you're through with Roberto?" she asked, eyeing me sideways. "You have no written agreements with him?"

"No, nothing!"

"Good!" exclaimed Julieta, "Now you and I will go to Ecuador and get all the treasure!"

Chapter Thirteen

The muddy, brown river meandering through the green rice fields was now a familiar sight as we landed again in Guayaquil. Julieta's friends greeted me like family. Her mother, Amelia, kissed me vigorously on both cheeks.

As if performing a ritual, after we'd unpacked our things, Julieta made arrangements to travel to her beachfront condominium in Salinas for a weekend rest. Two men accompanied us this time; Julieta's lifelong friend, Francisco Baquerizo, and his business partner, Daniel.

Francisco, whom we called Pancho, had been General Manager of the Central Bank of Ecuador and had traveled the world on government missions. Now in his sixties, he was a distinguished man who spoke fluent English and knew the workings of Ecuadorian politics inside and out. His face was narrow, strong looking, with aristocratic features. He walked erect and always wore suits, even in hundred degree heat. He was the very definition of an Ecuadorian gentleman.

Daniel, on the other hand, was more gregarious and funny, with a few spare tires around his waist and a thick gray mustache that looked like a whisk broom when he smiled. He was a hardy fellow who'd spent fifteen years as a commander in the Colombian navy and was now in Ecuador to make some fast money. Daniel was always wearing his captain's hat and cracking jokes in broken English. He made me laugh and he loved to dance. But the day he invited me to the coastal town of Palmar to look at boats, was the day I almost drowned.

Daniel was looking for fishing boats and I was looking for salvage boats. We had headed north out of Salinas, along the road that paralleled the Pacific Ocean, driving in a small pickup truck that Daniel had borrowed for the day. The tiny truck bumped and bounced us through ditches and ruts left over from the El Niño rainstorms. In most places the roads and bridges were completely washed out, so we drove down into the now dry riverbeds. Sometimes the road was so bad, all the traffic drove on the hard-packed beach for miles. Occasionally we came upon shallow streams flowing across the beach on their way to the ocean. I would grip the armrest, thinking we'd get stuck in the wet sand, but Daniel, like Moses entering the Red Sea, just picked up speed and splashed right through the streams, sending up rooster tails of water on either side of us.

In Palmar, a village of dirt streets and bamboo houses, we were directed to a stretch of beach where huge, wooden fishing boats were literally dragged up onto the sand by hand. The boats were all keeled over to one side and men worked on them, replacing sections of rotten wood and pounding coconut-shell hair into the cracks between the hull planks, where it would swell into a seal when immersed in water. Farther up the beach, men were chiseling canoes out of tree trunks.

The village was stinky and dirty. Grayish-black pigs and skinny chickens chased by barefoot children ran everywhere, and the beach itself was covered in decaying fish parts. I kept my hand over my nose trying to filter out the stench, but it didn't help. At the end of the day, when Daniel finally determined that none of the boats was big enough for him, I ran to the truck and rolled up the window, holding my jacket over my nose. Just two more hours and we'll be back in Salinas, I told myself. You can make it.

The little truck rattled and shook down the dirt road until we reached the spot where we could get to the beach again. We sped across the damp sand at fifty miles an hour, but I was used to it now, not grabbing the armrest as much, that is, until I saw the river ahead of us.

"Daniel, that doesn't look like the same rivlet we passed through this morning," I gasped.

"Don't worry. No problem." he said, downshifting to gain more speed.

"I think the tide has come in," I warned him.

"We'll pass. Don't worry," Daniel smiled, both hands firmly on the wheel.

"It's too deep. We'll never make it!" I shouted, bracing against the dashboard. My pounding heart sounded like a woodpecker attacking a tree trunk. I sucked in a deep breath and held it.

In the last second before we splashed into the water, I saw uncertainty flash across Daniel's face, but it was too late. The truck plunged downward and water swooshed up the sides like a fountain and covered the hood. In an instant my feet were underwater and we were sinking. I pressed frantically against the door, but the force of the water was too strong, I couldn't open it. I was panicking. Now the water was over my knees. Desperately I rolled down the window, put the straps of my camera and purse between my teeth, and wiggled out into the cold, salty ocean water that was backfilling the mouth of the river. I swam for dear life.

Only the cab of the little truck was still above sea level when I waded out of the river, soaked and exhausted. Daniel had escaped out his window and was standing at the waters edge, hands on his hips, knowing the salt water would completely ruin the engine. "Mala suerte," he muttered under his breath. (Bad luck.)

The beach had been deserted but it quickly filled up with people, who stood around giggling and pointing at the submerged truck. An hour passed before someone found another truck and some rope. It took twenty men in the water lifting and pushing, with the second truck's tires spinning in the sand, to drag our little truck out of the water. They towed it up to the roadway and left it beside an old building to dry off. Daniel handed out all the money he had to the people who had helped, then the beach was deserted again.

"I thought you were a commander in the Navy. How could you sink a truck?" I asked as we stood beside the dirt road with our thumbs out, trying to hitch a ride.

"That's nothing," Daniel smiled. "I sink two boats in the merchant marines. Big ones."

"Oh, wonderful," I said, stifling a smile. "At least you're a survivor."

"Survivor, yes," Daniel assured me, his head bobbing vigorously up and down. "I passed seven days in a lifeboat until rescue. Tengo fe," he said. (I have faith.)

For an hour we stood beside the road, taking turns sticking out our thumbs at the one overloaded bus and three cars that rumbled by. Finally a dinged-up, little red pickup truck with a fat green parrot and a family of five crammed in the front seat, stopped to pick us up. We climbed in the back and sat on the wheel wells as the little pickup truck headed towards Salinas at a pace that gave the dust plenty of time to settle all over us.

Not far down the road, our driver stopped again to help a pathetic group of people staring at a broken axle on their lop-sided vehicle. We picked them up too. Now we had two goats, four chickens, and a family of six, including Grandma, sharing the three-by-four-foot truck bed with us. I was handed a stinky chicken with a bloody eye to hold. Soon it grew dark and it crossed my mind that this was probably as bad as it gets. Then it started to rain.

At 10 p.m. Daniel and I finally burst through the door of Julieta's condominium and stood in the doorway, dripping a puddle at our feet like a couple of drunks who'd fallen overboard.

"You'll never guess what happened to us," I blurted across the room to Julieta. She was seated with a half dozen well-dressed people nervously waiting for some word from us. "We sank the truck in the mouth of a river!" a raved on. "What an adventure!"

Everyone immediately turned to look at an angry-faced man in the corner who got up and led Daniel out of the room. He was the owner of the truck. Neither of the men came back.

The next time I saw Daniel, he was in the hospital with a broken shoulder. He had rented another truck and run into a dead donkey in the middle of the road at midnight, sending the truck careening over an embankment into a deep gully. He had lain bleeding, upside down, for six hours before he was rescued. The man was definitely a survivor.

On this second trip to Ecuador with Julieta, my goal was to learn everything I could about the country, its people, its politics and its rules for salvaging shipwrecks. I also had to learn the twisted path, through the spider web of relationships, that underlies Ecuadorian society.

Ecuador is as much a melting pot as the United States, with one important difference. In North America, the Indians were killed off and their influence snuffed out, but in South America, the Indian population still flourishes, stubbornly clinging to a centuries-old way of life. The indigenous Indians still outnumber the descendants of the outsiders who came to Ecuador to conquer and exploit. The Incas came first, then the Spaniards, then the Dutch, English, Germans, Swiss, Lebanese, Asians, and North Americans, all looking for wealth in the jungles and mountains and shores of Ecuador.

Of course, the Spanish influence had the most impact. Ecuador's language, government, church, and social hierarchies were all established by Spaniards. The importance of blood lines and the first born son, were also Spanish legacies.

The primary question in Ecuador is: Who are your relatives? Money and relatives determine whether or not you will succeed in Ecuador. The poor, uneducated Indians living off the land, don't have a chance. It was my good fortune to have stumbled into the hands of Julieta, who traversed the spider web of social connections as easily as she turned the pages of her little black telephone book.

During the month I stayed with Julieta, dancing and partying, traveling here and there, and meeting all her friends, I was forming essential bonds of Ecuadorian trust, though I didn't know it then. I was too busy worrying about what I was eating and recovering from what I was drinking. My cheeks were sore from smiling so much as I tried to camouflage the fact that I didn't know what these people were saying to me in Spanish. I stuck close to Julieta, doing everything she told me to do and never repeating any gossip. It was too easy to say the wrong thing to the wrong person, so I said nothing. For a whole month, I just smiled.

In the wee hours of the morning before we returned to California, during the last of many goodbye parties for Julieta, we attended to business. Julieta had decided that Pancho was to help us with all the government paperwork for our shipwreck recovery. Through bloodshot eyes, Pancho penned out an agreement among the three of us. I had to wake him up a couple of times during the procedure. At four a.m., just two and a half hours before our flight, the three of us put our drunken scrawls to the bottom of the paper, forming our partnership in true Ecuadorian style.

❦

I passed the last months of 1983 living in California but contemplating Ecuador. As a fisherman busies himself with daydreaming until the fish bites, I immersed myself in Christmas and New Year's merriment, waiting to hear what progress Pancho had made with the government paperwork. Kevin was still wrapped up in the diving industry, building displays for trade shows to pay our bills, while I put the expedition together. He preferred to stay in the background, avoiding third-world politics as much as possible.

In the bustle of the holiday season I found myself having lunch one afternoon with my friend John, a college professor who had taught me everything I knew about computers. He and I never talked about current events or family problems or latest loves, we discussed mind control, thought projection, and the astral plane. John was obsessed with understanding man's reason for existence and how to get what we want in life. He believed there had to be some mathematical equation or discoverable process that would bring us fulfillment and happiness.

"I've been reading some fascinating books lately on the process of thinking," John said. "They all end up saying that the mind is the path to getting what you want."

"So, have you learned what to do with your mind" I asked, munching my hamburger.

"No, but I've boiled it down to two concepts," John said. "First, there's no getting around the fact that you must be able to control your thoughts."

"And the second concept?"

"That every human being has the same power of the mind."

"Well let me know when you've figured it all out." I teased him. "Then you can teach it to me."

I dropped John off at the college after we finished our hamburgers. Normally I would have spent more time talking with him about his new concepts, but I had to get home to change clothes. I had to be at a meeting in an hour.

After parking *La Bamba* in the driveway, I noticed that John had left his jacket in the truck bed. I grabbed it quickly, and a small, white, soft-cover book fell out of the jacket pocket and landed face up at my feet. Curious, I read a couple of lines as I walked up the porch steps, and the next thing I knew I was sitting on the top step reading random paragraphs throughout the whole book. When I finally stopped reading, I was two hours late for the meeting and I didn't care. The last words I read were these:

"Be STILL - and KNOW - I AM - GOD"

I AM in You as the oak is in the acorn. You are I as the sunbeam is the Sun. You are a phase of Me in expression.

I first give you the Key that will unlock every mystery that now hides from you the secret of my Being.

The Key is

"To THINK is to CREATE", or

"AS you THINK in your HEART, so is it with you."

A Thinker is a Creator.

A Thinker lives in a world of his own conscious creation.

... your body, your personality, your character, your environment, your world, ARE what they APPEAR to be TO YOU, because you have thought them into their present status.
Therefore YOU CAN CHANGE THEM BY THE SAME PROCESS, if they do not please you; you can make them whatever you will, by THINKING them so.

For it was by your unconscious thinking or thinking unconscious of the control your desires exercised over your creative power, that your world and your life are now what you sometime in the past desired them to be.[1]

In a kind of trance, I closed the book and flashed back to Florida, to Milo Zorbas telling me God was my salvage master. Now this book was telling me that God dwells within us - that we form our physical world by what we think and believe - that the truth of the universe is simply this: "Thinking is creating."

At the time, I didn't think this had anything to do with sunken treasure.

Chapter Fourteen

"Hi, John, it's Margee calling." I said into the phone the next day. "I just wanted to let you know that I have your jacket. You left it in the back of my truck yesterday."

"What a relief. I thought I'd dropped it somewhere."

"I also want to confess that I read the book that was in your pocket. I thumbed through it and ended up reading the whole thing. Who's the author?"

"God."

"Right."

"Really. Look in the front."

"Uh-huh, and is this the only book that says stuff like this?"

"Of course not. This book just explains the process of the mind in spiritual terms. I have another one that explains it in more or less scientific terms. I'll drop it off when I come to get my jacket."

❦

In January of 1984, Pancho called to tell us he had finished investigating the procedure for finding shipwrecks. All Julieta and I had to do was return to Ecuador and get started, no problem. Of course, at this stage I still thought "no problem" really meant "no problem". I later learned that "no problem" meant absolutely nothing, that an Ecuadorian day is measured in weeks, and that if Ecuadorians say three or four weeks they mean four to five months, if they rush it.

In February, Julieta and I and her five gigantic suitcases got on the flight to Ecuador. "Some Christmas presents," said Julieta, indicating her suitcases. "You say these two are yours, okay?" I had only one medium-size suitcase and a carry-on. I had packed for a two-week trip, which, after you apply the Ecuadorian time equation, adjust for Julieta's parties, and extrapolate to the closest available return flight, works out to be three months.

We landed in Guayaquil in the middle of the hot, summer, rainy season. The humidity was 95%, the temperature was 95°. Breathing was like inhaling thick vapors. While Californians are wearing overcoats and going snow skiing, Ecuadorians go to the beach and drink beer. It was also Carnival time, when the kids throw water balloons at everybody in sight and the grown-ups throw parties in their beach condos.

Naturally, after dumping the suitcases at Amelia's apartment, we headed for Salinas, where the rich and famous of Ecuador flaunt their imported possessions. It was also a chance for Julieta, Pancho, and me to finally discuss our strategy for finding my Ecuadorian shipwreck. Pancho started off the discussion.

"The Civil Code Law of Ecuador says that any Ecuadorian who finds treasures in the ocean is entitled to fifty percent of the findings. The other fifty percent must be given to the government."

"Has anyone ever brought up treasure in Ecuador before?" I asked.

"Sure, but they didn't give any to the government," Julieta cut in. "They keep it quiet and take all the treasure. That's the way you do things here in Ecuador."

"I can't do it that way," I said looking down at the table. "I'm not here as a thief. I'm here to prove that business and archaeology can work together, and make a lot of money in the process. If you two want me to steal, we better stop right now."

"Okay, okay," said Julieta, "you do it your way."

"We're talking a large recovery here," I said. "We're talking big vessels sitting in the same spot for months. People from the beach will be able to watch us. I wouldn't be able to hide what we were doing even if I wanted to. And if we got caught stealing anything, we'd wind up with nothing."

"We understand," said Pancho in a calm voice, patting Julieta's hand. "You have control over the expedition, Margarita. Julieta and I will get the permission papers. Now, this law only applies to Ecuadorians, not foreigners."

"I thought so," I said. "Actually, it would be better for you and Julieta to deal with the government and make it look like I work for you. When can we get the permission papers?"

"We should wait until León is President, in August," Julieta asserted strongly. "This administration is going out, and they won't give us permission."

"That's true," Pancho agreed. "Julieta and I have many connections with the next government. We should wait. Have another beer."

"Pancho, I'm not playing games here," I said as I pushed the beer aside and scooted my chair closer to his. "There is a lot of gold and silver on this wreck and it will take time and probably millions of dollars to excavate it. The three of us will have to stick together till the very end. Are you sure you want to make that kind of commitment?"

"Margarita, I have been waiting for a commitment like this ALL MY LIFE."

❦

Back at Amelia's apartment, a young man sat down at the breakfast table very carefully and sipped a glass of orange juice. His right eye was bruised and swollen, a deep cut closed with dry blood ran across his forehead. His hands were wrapped in white bandages, leaving only his scratched and swollen fingers exposed. This looks like a guy I should stay away from, I was thinking to myself, until Amelia told me he was part of the family.

"My name is Hugo," he said in perfect English, raising a bandaged hand, but not extending it for a handshake. "Please excuse the way I look. I just spent the last three days in jail."

"What did you do?" I asked timidly.

"I threw a policeman through a plate glass window. He deserved it. He stole my gold bracelet."

"Are you really part of the family?"

"Sure. I've been at school in Boston for the last six years though. I just came back to take a look around. I think I'm going back to Boston. This country is full of pendejos (assholes). It never changes."

Hugo had coal black eyes that seemed to trap you, while his innocent grin calmed you like a tranquilizer. I felt he was equally harmless and dangerous, protective yet destructive. In our afternoon discussions while his hands were healing, he helped me understand the Ecuadorian point of view on life, and politics.

206

"There are at least sixteen different political parties in Ecuador." I said. "What's the difference between them?"

"Nothing. Same shit, different flies. They all want to gain the power so they can steal money."

"What's most important to the people of Ecuador?"

"The family. Relatives are the only ones you can trust. The family is more important than business, or money, or politics, or anything."

"Tell me about the conquistadors," I said eagerly. "What did they teach you in school about the history of Ecuador?"

He told me that the country's known history started with the Incas. Before that there were only stories of tribes in the jungle and on the coast. The last Inca ruler, Huayna Capac, had two sons - Huascar, who stayed in Peru to rule the southern Inca Empire from Cuzco, and Atahualpa, who ruled the northern part of the Inca Empire from Quito. In 1533, when the Spaniard, Francisco Pizzaro, came to conquer the Incas, he captured Atahualpa and held him for ransom in Quito. The ransom price was all the gold from the Inca temples in Cuzco. This treasure was sent up to Quito, but at the last minute, one of the Inca generals, Rumiñahui, decided not to trust the Spaniards, and he ordered the treasure to be hidden in a cave in the Llanganati (yahn-ga-nah-tee) mountains outside Quito. So Pizzaro killed Atahualpa and the Spaniards took over for almost three hundred years. Spain ruled the entire west coast of South America. All the land of Venezuela, Columbia, Ecuador, Peru, and Bolivia, was called Gran Columbia. In 1821, Ecuador broke with Spanish rule when the Great Liberator, Simón Bolivar, united all the people of Gran Columbia and fought the war with the Spanish. Ecuador has been independent ever since.

"So what happened to the treasure?" I asked, inching forward attentively.

"It's still up in the mountains somewhere. Lots of people have tried to find it, but you have to pass through dense forests, high up, where the fog is really thick. The Llanganatis, are on the eastern corridor of the Andes Mountains. The place is covered with lakes and deep ravines. Only the Inca knew how to get to the cave where the stuff is hidden. Hey, you're not here to look for that treasure are you?"

"Me?" I pointed at myself with raised eyebrows. "Nah."

"Then why *are* you here? And don't tell me you're just traveling. Nobody comes to Ecuador as a tourist more than once. You must be in some business."

The two things an Ecuadorian will always ask you are, one, 'How many children do you have?' and, two, 'What are you doing here?' It's inescapable. They keep asking aggravatingly direct questions until they're satisfied with some answer, which they usually assume is a lie. I had been realizing for some time that I needed a cover, so I didn't have to tell everybody about my treasure hunt.

"What kind of business would you suggest?" I asked Hugo.

"Caramba! We've got shrimp, oil, bananas, flowers, coffee, fish," Hugo counted on his fingers.

"That's all big-time stuff, too established. You need a lot of money to jump in, which I don't have. We'd need to start smaller. You know, everybody likes the hand-crafted things I bring back. I bet I could sell things like that."

"Artesanias?"

"Yeah, hand-made tapestries and baskets, that kind of stuff. We'd have to find the people who actually make it, though. I don't want to pay store prices."

So Hugo and I started an import business, the perfect cover. We spent a few days hitting all the folklore shops and tourist hangouts, picking out what was cheapest but still looked pretty. I only picked things I liked, figuring I'd be stuck with it, if it didn't sell. Hugo was busy calculating his profits.

Our walking trips turned into bus trips as we had to go farther and farther away from Guayaquil to find sources. We made deals with basket makers, pottery makers, Panama hat makers, and people who brought things in from the jungle like macaw headdresses, shimmering green beetle necklaces, wooden spears, and things made out of crocodile or iguana skin.

Outside the big city, the busses followed narrow roads that stretched like single, isolated threads across a countryside of rice fields, banana trees, and unspoiled land. We rumbled through small towns, catching glimpses of thin, saddled horses tied to trees. Sleeping men swayed gently in straw hammocks while scruffy children ran around a yard unseparated from its jungle surroundings. There were no neckties or high-heeled shoes, just slow moving, black-haired, dark-skinned people existing in their own version of the world. A version that perpetuated itself generation after generation. Change was not welcome here. The people found security in doing things just as their elders had done.

The buses were dusty and crowded. Cumbia music, whose predominant percussion instrument is the cow bell, blared at high volume through scratchy speakers. Baby pigs squealed inside tied gunny sacks under the seats. Whenever we stopped to let off passengers, five or six kids jumped on board with cokes, empanadas, corn, or candies to sell. They yelled out what they had as they squeezed and squirmed passed the people standing in the aisles. The bus jerked and jostled on its way until the kids had sold all they could and then jumped off in the middle of nowhere to catch a bus headed in the other direction. When the bus broke down, everybody got off to see what was wrong and chatter amongst themselves about how to fix it. A hammer was usually involved. If a bus was three or four hours late in arriving at its destination, nobody worried. This was Ecuador.

It was during these trips that I started reading the second book my answer-seeking friend, John, had given me. The book had this to say about thought and reality:

Experience is the product of the mind, the spirit, conscious thoughts and feelings, and unconscious thoughts and feelings. These together form the reality that you know. You are hardly at the mercy of a reality, therefore, that exists apart from yourself, or is thrust upon you. You are so intimately connected with the physical events composing your life experience that often you cannot distinguish between the seemingly material occurrences and the thoughts, expectations and desires that gave them birth.

What exists physically exists first in thought and feeling. There is no other rule.

You are in physical existence to learn and understand that your energy, translated into feelings, thoughts and emotions, causes all experience. There are no exceptions.

YOU MAKE YOUR OWN REALITY.

If you dwell upon limitations, then you will meet them. You must create a new picture in your mind.

This is done by combining belief, emotion and imagination, and forming them into a mental picture of the desired physical result. Of course, the wanted result is not yet physical or you would not need to create it, so it does no good to say that your physical experience seems to contradict what you are trying to do.

As it took awhile for the unsatisfactory beliefs to become materialized, so it may be a time before you see physical results; but the new ideas will take growth and change your experience as certainly as the old ones did.

You must understand, again, that your ideas and thoughts do not exist as phantoms or shadow images without substance. They are electromagnetic realities. They affect your physical being and they are automatically translated by your nervous system into the stuff of your flesh and of your experience.[2]

In a trance again, I closed this second book as I mentally compared it to the first one. Both were saying that the events in our lives are not random; that they are produced by the way we think; that you can get what you want by creating it with your thoughts. "Oh sure." I mumbled, staring out the bus window at a third world reality. "Maybe I'll just *think* the treasure out of the ocean. Wouldn't that be a kick?"

Chapter Fifteen

All the time I was viewing Ecuador from bus windows, Pancho and Julieta had been searching for the best way to obtain a contract from the government. Asking for such a contract had to be done slowly, delicately, until we could see who was on our side and who wasn't.

Ecuadorians are leery of things that happen too fast. To them, if someone is rushing a project, it's only because there is something to hide, something that time will reveal. But if a project survives the test of time as it passes from hand to hand, Ecuadorians feel that it must be clean and that nobody will lose his job because of some yet-to-be-exposed, underhanded dealings. So we moved slowly. I had to repress my natural tendency to get on with things as quickly as possible. I had to learn Ecuadorian patience, the most nerve-wracking, teeth-gritting, time-consuming patience of all. We decided to ask for an exploration contract through the Department of Geology and Mines, explaining that we wanted to survey the ocean floor for minerals.

Hugo's family invited me to live in their house in the capital city of Quito, while I was waiting for an answer from the Department of Geology and Mines. So I left the withering heat and humidity of Guayaquil for the bone-numbing cold and drenching rain of the Andean city of Quito. Actually I was glad to leave Guayaquil for awhile. I was starting to suffer from an invasion of microscopic bugs that work their way into your flesh from old mattresses. They were crawling inside my skin and leaving a dotted trail of round bruises on my legs that itched worse than poison oak. I had even felt cockroaches scurrying over my lips in the middle of the night. At those times, I had to remember not to scream or they'd fall into my mouth. All sorts of crawling things came out at night in Guayaquil. Usually they would be lying dead next to your face when you woke up in the morning.

In Quito things were much different. Hugo's house was a three-story corner building in the heart of the old colonial section. Cobblestone streets, white concrete buildings, red tile roofs, and carved wooden doors, all crammed close together, echoed the ringing church bells and shouts of the street vendors. The whole city oozed history and the house itself had once been part of a huge colonial hospital. In this section of Quito, it was illegal to change the architecture or use colors other than blue, white, and brown to paint. This was Ecuador's cultural heritage, to be preserved not only for Ecuador, but for all of humanity.

The street level of the corner building was the family business, a stationery store. The second level was partly rented and partly storage. The family lived on the third level, beneath wooden arches and twenty-foot ceilings hand painted with images of birds and flowers. All the plumbing pipes and electrical wires were exposed in the building and there was no fireplace or heating furnace.

The bathroom, done in original antique tiles, had a claw-foot bathtub in the middle of the room with a tiny, five-gallon, water heater set on a shelf behind it. Hugo's father always used all the hot water early in the morning, letting the rest of us freeze our tootsies off in the ice cold water that remained.

The large, main salon in the very center of the house had an angled, glass ceiling and a block glass floor, allowing sunlight to enter and pass through to the levels below. It was all very regal and historic and uncomfortable. To live in a century-old house, meant you had to adapt to a century-old lifestyle.

At 4 a.m. the nearby church bells began ringing to wake the Indians, house maids, and delivery people. By 6 a.m. the street below my bedroom window was alive with coal salesmen, newspaper boys yelling *"Comercio,"* babies crying, vendors arguing, dogs barking, and horns honking. The noise shook the thin window panes and ricocheted off the cement walls, finding its way to my ears even though I was hiding under four wool blankets to keep out the cold. I stayed under the blankets until 9 a.m., when the sun started warming the cement walls and Hugo's parents had gone downstairs to open the stationery store. I felt like an exchange student, thrust upon a foreign family, trying to learn the ways of another culture. I was forced to speak Spanish or starve to death. Hugo wasn't always there to translate for me. I bought a serious-looking book titled, *Spanish in Twenty Easy Lessons*, and for two months I spent my evenings wrapped in wool blankets, hunched under a circular fluorescent light.

I spent most of each day pacing around the house, waiting for Pancho's daily phone call. He'd tell me what office he was at, why there was another delay in the paperwork, apologize for Ecuador's slow pace, and promise to call me the next day.

So it went, day after day, week after week. On Mondays not much happened because people were just getting to their offices. On Tuesdays there was usually a little action, like papers being moved from one place to another. On Wednesdays we often talked to somebody who was involved with reviewing our project, answering whatever questions came up. On Thursdays we usually heard a firm statement from a higher official saying what would have to be done the following week, before our project could be approved. And on Fridays nobody was in the office at all.

On the weekends, Hugo and I would borrow the family car, drive out of the city, and search for handicrafts to sell. One night, in a bare-walled cafe in Latacunga, I got drunk on wine and spilled the beans about the treasure hunt.

"No kidding... I'm after a sunken Spanish galleon," I told Hugo over a flickering candle, as I took another sip.

"Bullshit," said Hugo.

"It's full of gold and silver," I slurred on. "And I have a chart that shows right where it sank!"

"How did you get the chart?" Hugo asked, squinting his eyes, expecting me to make up a story.

"I paid a lotta money for it," I answered truthfully.

"What about Julieta?"

"She's in on it with me. Pancho too. We've already started the paperwork for a contract with the government."

"Let me help you too." Hugo was getting interested now, calculating his profits again.

"Hell, I've already told you too much," I said, trying unsuccessfully to shake off the wine.

"I can keep a secret, Margarita. I knew you were here for something more than artesanias."

"Oh, geeze, now I've broken my own rule about drinking. I tell everybody else that 'loose lips sink ships,' then I go and do it myself."

"No, don't worry. You can trust me."

"Why should I trust you?" I looked him in the eye.

"Because I think you're the girl Señorita Luz told me about. A long time ago she said a blond North American girl would come here and that I would work with her."

"Who's Señorita Luz?"

"Well . . . she's like the seer for our family. She sees the future and knows how to stop the power of the black magic."

"Gimme a break." I sobered up for a moment. "Don't start with the black magic stuff. I thought everybody here belonged to the Catholic church."

"They do. The people here accepted the Catholic religion because it was brought by the Spaniards. But they accept the black magic because it has been here much longer. Believe me, it's real. I had a Colombian girlfriend who used it on me once." Hugo paused, to stare at the candle. "She was beautiful, but when I wouldn't go to Colombia to live with her, she got angry and violent. She said she would use black magic to punish me. About three days later, I got very sick, vomiting all the time. After that, things I touched would break, sometimes right in my hand. Everything in my life was going wrong. I was going crazy until Señorita Luz broke the spell and washed away the evil."

"Is this true?" I demanded, suspecting he was taking advantage of my intoxicated state.

"Swear to God! It's all true," insisted Hugo, "If you want, I'll bring Señorita Luz to our house. You can see for yourself."

It wouldn't be the first time, I thought to myself. I'd always been curious about card readers and psychics. They always saw me finding treasure.

"What can she do for me?" I asked, lowering my voice to a whisper.

"She can give you a cleansing. It's a bath that will protect you from negative influences."

I leaned back in my chair mulling over the cleansing idea in my wine-drenched mind. In the three months I'd been in Ecuador our project had passed from secretary to engineer to lawyer to secretary to sub-secretary to director to lawyer and then back to the first secretary, all because this or that detail wasn't right. My patience was wearing thin. I needed some action, so I agreed to the cleansing. I'd try anything if it would help. After all, I was living in a different culture here. Maybe I was being affected by things I didn't even know about. When we got back to Quito, Hugo called Señorita Luz.

She arrived at the house carrying a big, black, doctor's bag and after we hugged each other Ecuadorian style, she led me into my bedroom and locked the door behind us.

"I saw in the cards yesterday, many people who are jealous of what you are doing," began Señorita Luz intensely. "There are others who do not wish you to succeed unless they are part of your project. These negative energies are blocking your path. I will use the power of God to stop these energies from affecting you."

"Will it hurt?" was the only thing I wanted to know.

"No, my dear. Now, take off all your clothes and we'll get started."

Señorita Luz pulled two drinking glasses out of her bag along with a lemon, an egg, and a giant pickle jar. The jar was filled with slimy leaves, curly vines, round black things and twisted twigs all swimming in a greenish-yellow liquid. She filled the drinking glasses with tap water from the bathroom and set them on the desk. Then, whispering Spanish words I didn't understand, she rubbed the lemon over my whole body. She dropped the lemon into one of the glasses of water and watched intently as little air bubbles formed on its outer skin. Next she traced my whole body again, this time using the egg. Then she cracked the shell and let the egg plop into the other glass of water. Again she watched as the air bubbles formed on the round yellow yolk. Appearing satisfied with the diagnosis, she unscrewed the lid of the pickle jar, turned me around so my back was to her, took a mouthful of the greenish-yellow liquid, and spit it across my back in the sign of a cross. Boy, did that stuff stink! It smelled like spoiled milk.

"Now, take some of this and rub it all over your body, my dear. Cover all of your skin, don't miss a spot."

Reluctantly, I dipped my hand ever so slightly into the wide-mouthed jar and scooped up a portion of the rancid-smelling fluid. It was warm and runny, like liquid Jello™, and I rubbed it all over me while I held my breath. Then she told me I couldn't wash the stuff off for three days.

"I'm going to give you some of this to keep with you," she said as she started to clean up. "Put a small amount behind your ears before you go to any important meetings. It will bring you good luck."

The only container I could find was an empty plastic pill bottle in my suitcase. Carefully Señorita Luz filled the little bottle half full with the stinky liquid and replaced the cap. "Keep it in a safe place," she instructed, as she slipped out the door. I put the bottle in the corner of my suitcase and locked it. I got dressed, trying not to breath too deeply and wondering whether I was truly open-minded or just a gullible fool.

Although I sat alone at the far end of the dining table that evening, Hugo's family could still smell me. They acted as if it were just another normal part of life. Negative influences had to be cleansed away sometimes. Maybe they were used to the smell. I, however, couldn't stand to be in the same room with myself. I passed most of the three days sitting on the roof, hoping the wind would blow the stink off of me.

I held out the whole three days before I took a bath and returned to society. I figured I'd give the remedy every chance to succeed. When I opened my suitcase, I found that the liquid had eaten through the pill bottle and turned half of the inside of my suitcase black. I never put any behind my ears.

Our request for a contract was approved a week later and Hugo figured he'd earned a percentage of the treasure for making it happen. I didn't argue. I needed allies. Stranger things than Señorita Luz were bound to happen in the future.

Chapter Sixteen

After working like a dog all summer in California, I saved enough money to return to Ecuador with Julieta to attend the presidential inauguration in August of 1984. Only 133 people had been invited to enter the congressional palace balcony to witness the "Transicion de Mando," the passing of the presidential sash from the outgoing to the incoming president, which formally begins a new four-year administration. Our very presence at such an elite function exemplified Julieta's formidable political influence.

We waited outside the congressional palace in our fancy dresses and high heels as a caravan of black Mercedes pulled up to the wide, red carpet covering the sidewalk. A mounted honor guard stood at attention, the feathered plumes on the horses' heads, waving in the breeze. As the sun fell behind the volcano Pichincha, dignitaries from other countries passed before us on the red carpet. "Viva Leon!" shouted the jubilant crowd around us. "Todos con Leon!" We climbed the marble stairs to the balcony, taking our place among Leon's inner circle of friends. Hugo and his family were seated beside us.

The ceremony started with speeches, speeches, and more speeches, followed by the transmission of the sash. Leon put his arm through the wrong end, so this part took a little longer than planned. Fifteen minutes of clapping and shouting followed, until the President of Congress had to stand up and wave his arms to silence the balcony group.

Leon's inaugural address was forty-five minutes of a zealous forefinger wagging at the ceiling, like a furious father scolding his children. The balcony group loved it, but the dignitaries in the audience remained rigid and silent. When the ceremony ended and the dignitaries had all left, we picked our way through the horse shit that had accumulated on the sidewalk.

"Now you will see some things happen in this country," said Hugo as he guided us around the manure.

"Now we will get the contract signed," said Julieta, her spiked heels clicking on the sidewalk.

"Now we can go to the casino and gamble," said Hugo's mother, steering our group towards a fancy downtown hotel.

I've never gambled much. People laugh at me when I say that, considering my occupation. Treasure hunting has got to be the biggest gamble of all, they say, with its one-in-a-million odds. But I think of it as a calculated risk, not a roll of the dice. In treasure hunting you choose your target, use continually improving technology to find the wreck, and then divide the stuff in accordance with your initial agreements. All the scoundrels, pirates, greedy business partners, corrupt officials, treacherous sea conditions, lunatic captains and life-threatening situations, just add a little flavor to the endeavor. What's gambling got to do with it?

At noon the following day we attended a private picnic for the new president. Cinzano umbrellas dotted the picnic area as five hundred people milled about, chatting, slapping each other's backs, and toasting the new administration. A sense of victory and celebration glowed on everyone's faces as if they'd

222

all reached the summit of Mr. Everest together. The new vice president and the first lady strolled the grounds followed by clusters of people, but the president stayed in one place, ringed twice by blue-and-red uniformed soldiers.

An armed soldier approached our table. "Señora Julieta Vega? El Presidente desea hablar contigo." (The president wishes to speak with you.)

"Vamos, Margarita. Bring your camera," Julieta said rapidly as she fumbled in her purse for her lipstick.

The soldier led us through the crowd, parted the two circles of guards, and left us standing face to face with the president. In rapid Spanish that I didn't understand, Julieta and Leon greeted each other. I snapped two pictures.

"This is my north american friend," Julieta said, motioning me forward.

"Encantado," the President smiled as he held my hand and kissed my cheek tenderly. "Julieta has told me about your project. I think it's wonderful."

"See, I told you," said Julieta, as we were ushered back to our table. "Now you can dig up the treasure."

That evening we were all dressed up again, sipping champagne, having another celebration party at Hugo's house. Cumbia music started playing and Hugo's father, happily drunk, decided to teach me how to dance, Latin style.

"Feel the music, don't watch the steps," he kept saying, "Loosen those hips."

When I got the sway just right and the upbeat on the back foot, Hugo's father dropped down on one knee and whipped out his handkerchief. He whirled it around his head, over and over. The woman is supposed to dance around the man as long as he keeps whirling the handkerchief.

I was wearing my infamous long black skirt, the one I wore the night the admiral had taken me to dinner, and I swished it from side to side, dancing round and round Hugo's father. The guests started clapping to the beat so I showed off a few tricky steps, and finally some half-Latin, half-gringo improvisations. The music kept playing and Hugo's father kept twirling that damn handkerchief.

Abruptly, the music stopped, catching me off balance and I accidentally stepped on my skirt. My arms flew up in the air and I fell over backwards like a toppled bowling pin. Just before I would have crashed to the floor, Hugo's uncle, Ernesto, dashed across the room and caught me in his arms. The salon exploded in laughter, drinks were raised high to salute the rescue and I think at that moment, I became half-Ecuadorian. I understood the people in the room, saw the world through their eyes. I understood their manners, their feelings, and most of all, their belief that life comes first, and business second.

From then on, I was treated like part of the "family" and the permission papers for our ocean floor survey work were signed a few weeks later.

❦

The night I got home from Ecuador I had the most shockingly-real dream of my whole life. I dreamed I was diving down through a small hole on the ocean floor, and at the bottom of the hole was a giant room full of gold stacked from the floor to the ceiling. There were piles of gold chains, gold

224

coins, gold jewelry, gold plates, gold candlesticks and lots of gold bars.

In the morning I still remembered every detail of the dream. I couldn't get it out of my head. I started to believe that the dream meant I would find the gold on the bottom of the ocean.

Kevin and I were both working now, trying to save up money for my next trip to Ecuador. Finding the treasure was a goal we had chosen together, but I was the aggressor. I was the one who refused to give up. I had an iron grip on this quest, like a hungry old alley dog with its teeth sunk into a T-bone steak.

Kevin wanted the treasure too, but he was content to stay in the shadows, letting me blaze the trail. Our marriage was solid and comfortable and our hopes of finding treasure bound us together, even when we were apart.

In the evenings I would spread a giant map of Ecuador out on the kitchen floor, putting salt and pepper shakers on the corners to hold them down. In my negotiations with the government, I had requested a search area so large that it didn't matter who knew the coordinates written on our contract. We had been granted more than a thousand square miles of ocean to explore.

Since I knew a potential investor would want to see my treasure map, I made another photograph of it and cut out the compass rose and landmark names. In the narrative below the map, I cut out all the sailing directions, water depths, and compass headings, but I left in the part about the prodigious treasure.

"What makes you so sure you'll be able to find the treasure?" Kevin asked, putting the burden of discovery on my shoulders.

"That's easy," I grinned. "I believe someone will show me exactly where it is."

"With what?" He mused, curious about my strategy.

"I don't know." I shrugged. Then I thought of John's books and said philosophically, "It doesn't matter what they use to show me where the treasure is, just that they show me. I don't have to use precious thought time dwelling on the means. I just concentrate on the outcome."

"Yeah, right," snickered Kevin. "Hope it works."

❦

New Year's Day 1985 brought rain and wind, and a phone call from Hugo telling me to come to Ecuador quick, he was getting married. Julieta and I and seven more bulging suitcases were on the southbound plane in a week.

In one of the colonial churches in the old part of Quito, Hugo married a petite young girl from Romania, named Adina. At the reception I met Hugo's new mother-in-law, Marieana. Since Hugo's house was full of relatives, Marieana invited me to stay with her.

In Marieana's tiny, one-bedroom apartment, I slept on the living room couch and kept my belongings stuffed under the pillows. The third room of the apartment was the kitchen, whose barred windows looked down on a concrete washing trough in the middle of the patio.

Marieana was a struggling architect, determined to make it on her own after divorcing her Ecuadorian husband, and I was a struggling treasure hunter determined to find a shipwreck. She didn't speak any English and I didn't speak Romanian. We were quite a pair; two foreign women living above a liquor store, surviving on thirty-three dollars a week in combined money.

The nights were the worst part. The picture window behind the couch muted none of the street noise, and at midnight, when the taxi cab drivers got off their shifts, they congregated around the liquor store, brawling and laughing and pissing in the street. Dogs barked all night, roosters crowed at three a.m., and sunrise came at six. We only had running water from 6:30 a.m. to 8:30 a.m., so we had to fill up buckets to flush the toilet and wash the dishes. Only bottled mineral water was fit to drink, so every morning I filled a straw basket with the empties and took them to the corner store to exchange them for full ones. We cooked on a two-burner hot plate, usually dining on soup and a salad with hunks of cheese in it. We had no television.

Now that Pancho and Julieta had obtained Ecuador's permission to search in the ocean, I had to find investors again. I spent three months looking for them in Ecuador. I tried banana growers, bank owners and ex-generals but my most interesting encounter was with the owner of the mineral water company.

"Andrés is my name," he said in perfect English the night Pancho and I met him at his home. "I beg you to excuse the mess, but I am living as a bachelor right now."

"How's it going with the divorce?" Pancho asked. He and Andrés were long-time friends.

"I'm through with women," Andrés said, winking at me. "Now, tell me about this treasure."

I had all my documents with me, and I laid them out on the table one by one as I explained our entire project.

"I see here that Isla de La Plata is inside your contract area," he said pointing to the chart. "Do you intend to recover the silver that Sir Francis Drake left there?"

"What do you know about it?"I asked curiosly.

"That's why they named the place Island of the Silver. In 1578, Drake had to throw forty-five tons of silver overboard to lighten his vessel so he could make it across the Pacific Ocean and complete his circumnavigation of the world. It's all written in Nora Sterling's book. Let me call my friend Presley, he's got the book. He does a lot of archaeological work here in Ecuador and knows all about Isla de La Plata. He even knows a guy who was there a couple of years ago and found some bars of silver in the bay on the northern side of the island."

"Well, our main target is the galleon," I said. "We already have the information on it and it's much more valuable than Drake's silver."

Andrés sat back on his chair, and ran his fingers slowly through his hair.

"I'm after another treasure," he said luringly. "Why don't you forget this galleon and come with me. I have found the mountains where the Inca treasure was hidden from the Spaniards when Francisco Pizarro held Atahualpa for ransom. It's a hundred times more valuable than what's on your galleon."

Andrés jumped up and disappeared into another room to shuffle through drawers and papers. He came back with a map of Ecuador and a well-worn copy of an old letter.

"In the 1930's," Andrés began, "an English gentleman explorer came here and spent years searching for the Inca treasure. He actually found the cave where the treasure was stashed and he wrote to a friend of his in England to say that he had seen the treasure and that there was more gold than ten thousand men could carry out. But he dared not recover any of it for he knew rogues were watching him. He would return to England, he wrote, and form a proper expedition capable of recovering the gold. But no one ever heard from him again. I have a copy of the letter he wrote to his friend right here in my hands. The letter describes exactly where to start from and how to find the cave."

I tried to grasp what Andrés was telling me - *more gold than ten thousand men could carry.*

"Every November for thirty-three years I've trekked into those mountains," Andres went on. "The clouds and fog only clear during November. During the rest of the year you can't see six inches in front of you. Men and pack animals on my trips have fallen into ravines and been lost because they couldn't see where their next step would be. The going is so rough I don't know if I can make it any more, and now I think my son will be the one to recover the treasure. He accompanied me on the last several visits. We are closer to the cave than you are to your galleon. Join us."

I was speechless, confused. I surely hadn't expected someone to be selling me on lost treasure. I had been ready for a yes or no, not a "forget the whole thing and come with us." Pancho, looked as stunned as I was.

"You see, I'm investing my money in my own treasure hunt," Andrés finally said. "I wanted to hear what you had to say because I was hoping you had developed some new device to help you find treasure, something I could use on my project."

"Our equipment is geared for underwater work. I'm not sure it's adaptable," I told him hesitantly. "Look, I think we need some time to consider this."

"I understand." Andrés lowered his eyes and nodded his head. "In the mean time let me put you in touch with Presley. He can tell you more about Isla de La Plata."

Presley was a portly man with a crewcut, a friendly, in-the-know kind of guy. If what you were interested in had to do with archaeology or treasure in Ecuador, Presley already knew about it. He was the director of an ongoing dig in the coastal town of Salango and he was building a museum to house the ceramics and relics his people were finding from the Valdivia civilization, which had flourished on the coast of Ecuador from 1500 B.C. to 500 A.D. Connected with the Smithsonian Institute and the Central Bank of Ecuador, he'd taught anthropology in the U.S. and Europe. Although he was Ecuadorian, he spoke American slang as well as any gringo I ever knew.

"So you're a treasure hunter," Presley said frankly, appraising me the first time we met. "But you don't have that wild and crazy look in your eyes. You look normal."

"I am normal," I assured him. "Some people who look for treasure are sane."

"None that I've ever met," said Presley. "Especially not in Ecuador. Andrés tells me you've got Isla de La Plata under concession."

"He tells me that you know where Drake's silver is," I countered. "Do you really?"

"Yeah, I can take you there."

"You know *exactly* where it's at? You can pinpoint the location? No searching around? You can take us right to the spot?" I asked.

"It'll be like shootin' fish in a barrel," Presley smiled.

"And you actually saw a silver bar with your own eyes?" I asked, trying to remember what Andrés had told me.

"I saw one silver bar," Presley said, holding up a single finger. "This guy from New York had a ninety-foot barge out there with a clam bucket on it and he was digging up the bottom. He spent a month out there and then he ran out of money. Never brought the rest of it up."

"How much is there?"

"Well, it's not the whole forty-five tons. An expedition from some British museum was here in the 1950s and dug up fifteen tons of it. I've got all the information right here. In fact, I made copies for you."

"I won't spend more than two weeks there."

"I understand. You're going at this like a level-headed businessperson. Are you sure you're a treasure hunter?"

"Let's say I'm a treasure *huntress*, I do it with *finesse*."

Presley chuckled, "I believe you will. Here, take these copies with you."

Sir Francis Drake and his men, according to Presley's papers, had ransacked the port town of Callao, Peru, where the Spaniards loaded onto vessels all the gold and silver they had stolen from the mines in Peru and Bolivia, to transport it to Panama. Drake learned then, that two weeks earlier, the yearly shipment of treasure had left for Panama on a galleon named the *Concepción*. He immediately set sail to capture it. His vessel, the *Golden Hinde*, was faster and more maneuverable than the loaded galleon and overtook her within a few days. As the captured treasure was loaded onto the *Golden Hinde*, Drake realized that his ship was sitting too low in the water, that its seams were cracking and leaking, and that he'd never make it back to England. In the gentlemanly manner Drake was famous for, he invited the Spanish captain for dinner and inquired as to the best place along the South Sea coast for repairing a vessel.

The sly Spanish captain told Drake of an island at 1 degree 17 minutes south latitude that had a steeply inclining beach, fresh water, and many wild goats to eat. It was a natural paradise, he said.

Drake found the island and anchored in a calm bay on the northerly, leeward side, but quickly discovered that the island had neither fresh water nor goats. The place was desolate. But the *Golden Hinde* was badly in need of repair and too heavy to be dragged up on shore. So, the legend goes, Drake scooped up bowlfuls of silver and divided a good amount of it among his men before tossing the rest of it overboard to lighten his ship. The crew successfully patched the ship and continued northward to what is now Drake's Bay above San Francisco, looking for a northwest passage back to the Atlantic Ocean. Finding none, Drake sailed west across the Pacific, eventually arriving back in England a rich and famous man.

The question has always been, was the island Drake stopped at actually Isla de La Plata, or could it have been the Cocos Islands at 1 degree 17 minutes *north* latitude, as was written in other accounts?

Ecuadorians like to believe it was Isla de La Plata, and I was beginning to believe so as well. Of course, it didn't matter much. I still hadn't raised one penny for the expedition. I'd found out the hard way that rich Ecuadorians don't invest in risky ventures. They like things they can see, like bananas and shrimps and fishmeal. I had even gone so far as to talk to a spokesperson for the head of the Ecuadorian Mafia, but the percentage they wanted was way too high. It was looking like, contract or no contract, my fund raising efforts had failed.

I had to sell a gold necklace I'd brought with me for enough money to buy a plane ticket back to Guayaquil. At Amelia's apartment building, I sat on the roof, brooding over the six months of our contract time that I'd already wasted and counting the cash I had left. Exactly $47.16. This was another one of those treasure-hunting low points. I felt defeated. I was lonely. I missed Kevin. I wanted to go home. Sometimes the only thing that kept me going was knowing I at least had a place to sleep and food to eat.

I walked for hours along the river front street in Guayaquil. Poor people tugged at my sleeve begging money, holding out scrawny hands. Under the trees in the narrow strip of park that lined the river, more poor people washed in the public water fountain and squatted to defecate in the mud along the river's edge. Men spat on the sidewalk. Trucks and buses belched black diesel smoke into the air. It was all getting me down. I was tired of the bullshit excuses, the wasted days, the heat, the mosquitoes, and the stink of urine everywhere. It seemed ridiculous to believe I was going to find a multimillion dollar treasure when I was sitting in the park, broke and completely out of ideas. Ugly, prehistoric-looking iguanas rustled in the trees above me and suddenly, as if on cue, a big, stinky splotch of yogurt-like iguana shit landed on top of my head, and I felt the tears roll down my cheeks.

Don Quixote once said it was madness, "To see life as it *is*, and not as it *should be*." John's books were telling me that if you stop *believing* a certain thing will happen, you shut off the power and it will never happen. If you go back to believing that your situation is only what you see in front of you, there's no way out, no way to change it. Well, *hell with that! I'll find a way to change this situation.*

I started imagining myself, ten years from now, looking back at this wasted time. In retrospect, a few months wouldn't seem

233

like very long. I had to keep believing I could do this expedition. I had to shake off this depressing mood, believe good fortune was just around the corner. I took a deep breath, dried my eyes, scraped off the iguana shit, and walked the ten blocks back to Amelia's apartment.

"Margarita, I have an appointment with Señor Roca!" Julieta shouted the moment I walked through the door. "Tomorrow morning. You see, I accomplish things."

As sure as iguana shit falls, I thought to myself as I smiled back at her.

Señor Roca owned the only treasure hunting vessel in Ecuador. The vessel hadn't been used in years and was now tied to two pilings, rocking gently in the river current, faded, rusted, and neglected. But we needed a boat for our expedition and, rusted or not, this one was available.

"So you think you know where some treasure is?" Señor Roca asked me from his chair at the head of the conference table in his office. "You know, you're not the first one who's thought that."

"Perhaps not." I folded my hands together on the table.

"What makes you think I'd be interested?"

"Well, you own a vessel that's completely equipped for treasure hunting. At one time you must have been very interested in that type of activity."

"I keep that boat now just for pleasure trips. My son uses it. It's more trouble than it's worth," said Señor Roca.

"Then why don't you lease it to me?" I said quickly.

"Have you got a legitimate contract to work in Ecuador?"

"Right here," I answered, handing him a copy. He read it carefully.

"This only gives you the right to search for something, not to salvage it. The Ministry of Defense issues all salvage contracts."

"I'll get the salvage contract when I need it," I said, silently cursing Pancho's lawyer for not telling us this fact. "All right. When you come back with a signed salvage contract, I'll lease the boat to you. Would you like some advice?" Señor Roca added as I was about to leave.

"Of course," I said.

"Never talk to the press. Let the Navy do all the talking for you. And get yourself an apartment with some girls. If you don't keep your crew happy, they'll cause you a lot of problems."

I disregarded the advice about the girls. I already knew the problems they caused. I had more important things to worry about. It seems I had to get another contract now from the Ministry of Defense. I was right back at square one.

Chapter Seventeen

For seven weeks I lived on nothing but bananas and bread. That was all I could afford. I was sleeping on Marieana's couch again, waiting for the Minister of Defense to grant us a shipwreck salvage contract. We had let the contract with the Ministry of Geology and Mines expire and requested a combined exploration and recovery contract from the Ministry of Defense. With some additional help from Hugo's family the request was approved. The contract itself would take another six months to be signed, so I returned to California to entice some investors.

There's an old saying, 'You can't catch a fish unless you put your hook in the water'. It's a line I used alot when I was raising funds for the expedition. It's simple, logical, and it eases you into the part of the presentation where you ask for the money. You can't be shy when you ask for the money, especially when you're selling a treasure hunt. I mean, let's face it, you're asking people to consider their money gone when they give it to you. You're not offering any guarantees that a wreck will be found, or that once found it can be salvaged, or that once salvaged, the government will give you any part of the treasure. You're offering a risky fishing trip using a very expensive hook. But thank goodness, unlike Ecuadorians, Americans are risk takers.

Of all the speculative activities I could think of, wildcat oil drilling was the closest to treasure hunting. You either make big bucks or you come up dry. To keep their investors involved after they'd invested their money, oil companies sent samples of the soil they were drilling through, to their investors. I decided to keep my investors interested by sending them coded messages. After all, the Ecuadorian mail service was not always reliable, and we sure didn't want our information falling into unknown hands. So when you invested with me, you got a copy of...the code book.

Code 22
E Calm and clear
C Perfect working conditions
U Water visibility good
A Water visibility impaired
D Rain storms or rough seas intermittently stopping
   work
O Bad weather has stopped work completely
R All's well

Code 33
E Pirate interference
C Sharks in the area
U Injury on board
A Contact our lawyer immediately

D Government protection requested

O Minor equipment breakdown - still on site

R Major equipment breakdown - returned to port

Code 44

E Still searching - nothing found yet

C Nothing found on first site - moving to second site

U Finding evidence of ship - unidentified

A Finding evidence of ship - target wreck

D Finding modern debris

O Finding coral-encrusted objects - unidentifiable

R Have delivered recovered items to the Central Bank

Code 55

E Finding ballast rock

C Finding cannon or cannon balls

U Finding iron ship's rigging

A Finding Spanish anchors

D Finding pottery shard

O Finding wood sections

R Finding non-precious artifacts

Code 66

E Recovering gold bullion

C Recovering gold coins

U Recovering silver bullion

A Recovering silver coins

D Recovering jewelry or chains

O Recovering valuable artifacts

R Recovering raw gem stones

It took me five months to raise $250,000 for the expedition. I formed another limited partnership and this time named it *Oceanus Ecuador*. Some of my partners from the Bahamian expedition reinvested with me. They figured that with so much experience behind me I'd know what I was doing this time. At the first partnership meeting the investors started chanting 66E... 66E... 66E.

It was the middle of February 1986, when Kevin and I finally arrived in Ecuador with six professional divers and thirteen giant wooden crates of diving equipment. We were bubbling with enthusiasm, anxious to get on the boat and be on our way.

We hit the first kink in our plans when Señor Roca changed his mind about leasing his boat to me. "Too much to worry about if you lease it," he said. "But I'll sell it to you, as is, for a $100,000."

I felt like I'd jumped off the starting line and ran smack dab into a brick wall. We didn't have an extra hundred thousand to purchase the vessel and there were no other boats in Ecuador suitable for the job. So I borrowed the money from my parents and broke the first cardinal rule of treasure hunting: Never hunt for treasure on borrowed money.

The crew and I checked out the vessel before I bought it. It was floating, my basic requirement, and it was bone dry inside. It had an indoor bathroom and an outhouse which hung over the side of the railing. No plumbing problems that way. There were eight bunks, and a full galley with stove, refrigerator, TV and stereo system. She had been built as a fishing boat in Louisiana in 1957 and still retained her 50's styling. Other than a few bullet strafing marks on her exterior she hadn't been changed. In the cargo hold, we found anchors, rope, buoys, metal baskets, an outboard motor, spare parts, and a welding machine, everything we needed. The only problem was we couldn't start the engines or generators, there were too many missing parts.

That evening, at our economy hotel, with the sloping floors, I found a moment alone in which to contemplate the prospect of buying a used boat that wouldn't start. The only word that screamed in my mind was, yes. I bought the boat the next day. Her name was *Hooker's Holiday*.

The second kink in our plans came when we drydocked the *Hooker's Holiday* and found that the vessel's bottom was full of holes. Apparently, the boat had been sitting in the mud at low tide for so long, that dried mud had filled all the holes. We had to weld seventeen sheets of new metal to the hull to solve the problem. We also had to crack off a slab of concrete that had been laid over the back deck to hide some rotting metal. Rust had to be removed, engines had to be overhauled, in short, fifteen drydock workers, four engine mechanics, and our crew of six divers spent two months making that vessel seaworthy.

All the while we were in dry dock, it was the hottest time of the year in Guayaquil. The sun scorched our skin like fire, the humidity made us irritable, and our bodies were constantly covered with mosquito bites. After the first week, the crew started getting severe stomach cramps and diarrhea. Parasites were growing in their intestines from the food and water we were consuming. As the weeks wore on, they got amoebas in their blood and worms in their poop. We told ourselves it would all be worth it when we found the treasure.

By mid-April we were ready to launch the vessel. The Archbishop of Guayaquil came to bless the boat and our crew.

Everyone in the shipyard stopped pounding and welding to listen to the Archbishop's blessing and watch him throw holy water on the hull. I realized we were doing the same thing the Spaniards had done centuries before, getting a church blessing before we went to sea.

At high tide the drydock ways were greased with pig fat and six Ecuadorians, using the equivalent of a telephone pole, began ramming the wooden frame that held our vessel in place. They pounded and pounded until the frame slipped backwards a couple of inches, then they scattered like rats, yelling *"Afuera!"* (Get out!)

As if released from the top of a roller coaster, the boat whooshed backwards into the brown Guayas River. Line handlers pulled it around to the outside of some pilings, and we began ferrying back and forth to shore in small metal boats with broken oars. Diesel, oil, food, diving gear, equipment, and all personal belongings were loaded on board as the final adjustments were made to the ship's main engines and generators.

Ecuador's Oceanographic Institute assigned one person to our expedition as an observer and the Department of Merchant Marines assigned one diver. Our zarpe (permission to leave the port) was issued with a total of ten persons aboard for our initial voyage: Captain Cooke; Engineer Toone; Lead Diver Marc; Crew Divers Kevin, Achilles, and Lawrence; our archaeologist friend, Presley; the two observers; and me.

The expedition was officially underway the day we started up the engines and headed down the Guayas River, away from Guayaquil. I was so proud of myself. I stood on the bow with my eyes closed, letting the hot breeze brush my cheeks as we glided down the river. I felt triumphant and powerful, like nothing could stop me. I was as free as the Frigate birds soaring through the air high above me, with their red throats and long, slender tail feathers. I was as strong as the engines vibrating the deck under my feet. And I was as happy as a kid on a field trip.

In the wheelhouse, Captain Cooke had charts spread all over the place and binoculars hanging around his neck as he searched for the buoys that marked the shallow spots. Dense green mangrove forests lined the banks of the wide, flat, river like a primitive jungle barrier. Skinny brown men sat like carved statues on small wooden boxes atop balsa rafts as they floated downstream with the current. Six hours after embarking, we passed Isla Puna, a huge green island that marks the end of the river and the beginning of the Pacific Ocean.

As the afternoon sun hung bloated on the horizon, the boat started bucking and rocking in the rough ocean waves. The swells were hitting us broadside as we traveled northwest towards Punta Santa Elena, the westernmost tip of Ecuador. I headed for my bunk. There were enough capable men on board, they didn't need me throwing up all over the place. At nightfall we passed an area called Mar Bravo, a turbulent coastline full of reefs. By 10 p.m. we'd rounded the point and dropped anchor in an immense calm bay to spend the night.

At sunrise we were traveling due north again, heading directly toward Isla de La Plata and Sir Francis Drake's treasure. That's why Presley was on board with us.

We were running with the swells now, smoothly gliding over the royal blue water. A wet mist hung in the air like a delicate veil and gradually, the soft gray outline of a gigantic rock appeared in the distance. The whole crew was on the bow mumbling about how it looked like a ghost island floating in the air. We approached it cautiously, Captain Cooke keeping us well away from the shoreline. We motored around to the north side, where a small cove was tucked behind a steep mountain slope. Presley was already in the wheelhouse directing the captain where to anchor.

"Well, here we are," Presley remarked proudly.

"Okay, where's the spot?" I asked. The cove was a mile wide.

"This is it!" Presley said pointing out the wheelhouse window at the water.

"You mean right in front of us?" I questioned.

"I mean this cove," Presley answered, sounding perturbed. The captain leaned against the wheel and rolled his eyeballs.

"But you told me you knew the *exact* spot!" I moaned.

"I do. It's in this bay somewhere."

"Presley, that's not an exact spot!"

"Well, hell, I wasn't diving with the people. I was on the barge. They worked this whole center section of the cove. Can't you go down with your metal detectors and find it?"

Now the divers were filling up the wheelhouse, their brows furrowed at what they were hearing.

"What about the silver bar, Presley?" Marc asked. "You actually held it in your hands, right?"

"Actually, it was a polaroid photograph," Presley confessed. Everybody groaned. "But it was definitely a rectangular silver bar. And this is definitely the place where Sir Francis Drake threw the silver overboard."

We'd been suckered again. Poor Presley didn't understand our disappointment - but then he'd never searched for something buried under water and mud. It just wasn't as easy as he had presumed. It wasn't like shootin' fish in a barrel.

We dove all over the cove, finding nothing but a modern 500-pound anchor and some square-cornered rocks that Presley claimed were English cobblestones.

In the evenings, as we ate barbecued fish, Presley told us tales about the island. Pirates used to anchor in the cove and send a lookout to the top of the mountain, he said. When a northbound ship came by, the lookout would yell down into the cove and the pirates would sail out, taking the ship by surprise.

At the end of two weeks we pulled up anchor and headed for Manta Bay to start our search along the mainland for our Spanish galleon. We had much more reliable information for that treasure site. When we arrived in Manta, I sent the investors the following coded message:

22E, C, U, R   44C

After checking in with the Port Captain, I got out my treasure map and we cruised along a fifteen-mile stretch of coastline that matched the drawing on our treasure map. The city of Manta was the small village on the map, the point with the rock beside it was off in the distance to the west, the mountain Monticristi stood tall behind the city, and somewhere in the bay next to the rock our shipwreck was waiting. Now, I remembered what treasure hunting was all about. It gave me goosebumps, or chicken skin, as the Ecuadorians say.

Our first task was deciding where to start our search. I recalled the accounts I had read by the two survivors of the sinking. One said, "The ship had been lost midway between

Manta and Cabo San Lorenzo." The other said, "The ship pounded out its bottom on some rocks a league more or less to the west of the village." Now, a Spanish league was four miles, measured by the pace of a horse or the distance a horse could walk in an hour. Our treasure map was a British map that had been copied from a Spanish map, and the scale of leagues were already marked off in three miles. But was that land miles or nautical miles? In the dictionary a league could be as long as five miles. To be thorough we would have to search from 2 1/2 to 5 miles to the west of Manta.

The number of small bays along the coast was another factor. Not all the points on the old map still existed today. In fact, a large one, Punta Murcielago, had fallen off into the ocean scarcely twenty years before. Then there was the compass rose drawn at the top of the old map. Had it been placed precisely where it was on purpose? By the scale on the map, the compass rose was exactly ten miles off shore to the north. We motored our boat out to that distance and looked back at the coast to see how things lined up. The location of the wreck was supposed to bisect the angle made by a line to Cabo San Lorenzo and a line to Manta. But did the sailors in 1590 know about magnetic north and true north? Did they know about the four-degree difference at this latitude? Maybe the position of the compass rose didn't have anything at all to do with the location of the wreck?

The greatest source of confusion was the fact that there were really two bays that could be construed as being next to the point with a rock. A small cove about three-quarters of a mile across was immediately next to the rock, and a much larger bay about three miles across started where the first cove ended. The bay on the old map was extremely large, but then nothing on the map was to scale. Was the area of the wreck enlarged compared to the rest of the coastline? Or was the rendering absolutely precise, which would mean that it represented the cove? But maybe the smaller cove hadn't even existed four hundred years ago. It could have been formed by a landslide in recent history.

To make matters worse, the Spaniards were known for drawing their maps one league off to conceal their wrecks from others. Was this such a map? Another puzzle cropped up when a local fisherman told us that gold coins washed up on the beach after severe storms, not west of Manta but to the east. So where was the wreck?

I called the crew together on the bow and spread out the old map and our current nautical chart before us. I wanted their opinions. Two men felt the wreck was in the cove, two felt it was in the bigger bay, one thought we should go home until we had more information, and the other didn't care where we started, he just wanted to dig. I decided to be scientific about the whole thing. We would start in the cove next to the rock and work east. If we didn't find the wreck there, we would know it was in the larger bay.

During the next week, we set up the magnetometer and started a systematic search. The magnetometer wasn't working quite right, but it was giving us higher metallic readings in one particular area, so we decided to blast some holes. At the bottom of all the holes, ten feet deep, we found round, smooth river rocks. "Ballast rocks!" the crew was shouting. "We've found the wreck!"

Not true, it turned out. We dug more holes and found round, smooth river rock at the bottom of each one. They were coming from a river at the center of the cove. We worked another whole month from sunrise to sunset and found nothing but whale bones, stone anchors, and modern garbage. "Nothing but junk," the divers kept telling me. The Ecuadorian observers on board gave up watching us. They spent most of their time sleeping, or looking at our Playboy magazines.

As the money ran out and disappointment increased, I kept studying the chart and reading the narrative again and again. We must be missing something. We were working all around a rock reef that the chart referred to as the Plazel, the wreck *had* to be here. Then Presley made a suggestion.

"You should call Greg Gino," Presley urged me. "He knows this whole coastline. I bet he could help." So the next time we were in port in Manta, I waited the half hour in line at the public telephone company and called Mr. Gino in New York. I sure wasn't ready for what he told me.

"I know you're looking for the Plazel wreck," Gino said to me over the phone. I was awestruck, disbelieving, and pissed off all in the same instant. How did he know about the Plazel? I decided to act dumb.

"What's a plazel?" I asked innocently.

"Don't play dumb with me," he retorted. "You're after the galleon in front of Manta that's got thirty million on it. It wrecked on the plazel."

"I'm working off Cabo San Lorenzo. I don't know what you're talking about," I insisted.

"I can help you. I have some information I think you'd be interested in."

"What makes you so sure?"

"Because I've got the same map you do."

"I don't think so," I said. But I was thinking, Oh, shit, now I've got to deal with a rival treasure hunter. Thanks, Presley.

"Let me show you. I'll be down there on the next flight."

"Suit yourself. You can ask at the yacht club when we'll be in port again. I really should be going."

"I'll see you in two days," he said before I hung up.

The fact that Gino even *knew* the word plazel, made it imperative that I meet him. I had to study the enemy. He showed up two days later and we met at his mother-in-law's house, three blocks from the yacht club. In the living room, as we looked at each other distrustfully, Greg Gino handed me an 8-by-10 black-and-white photograph of an old chart showing the same coastline as the chart I had - with one big difference. Where mine said "a ship in which was a prodigious treasure," his said "In this ship was thirty million royals and 37 pieces of ordnance. And on the same rocks hath been lost many more ships."

Then Greg handed me two more photographs of older maps showing the same area before the galleon had sunk. Now I was fascinated. The ship I was looking for had forty-two cannon, Gino's had thirty-seven cannon. The narrative on his chart was cleaner, more organized, easier to read. Mine had a compass rose; his didn't. Mine had a scale of leagues; his didn't. His was either a later version of the same chart, showing the same shipwreck, or a different chart showing a second shipwreck in the same place.

"I have the chart in color too," Greg said, breaking the silence. "You know, there's nothing in the cove you're working in right now."

"Who *are* you?" I suddenly asked, wondering if it was wise to continue talking to him.

"I'm a specialist in satellite technology. I've found a way to detect gold ionization on the earth's surface using land-sat photographs taken from space. I've got charts of shipwrecks along the entire coast of Ecuador. I can tell you right where the gold's at."

"Then what do you need me for?"

"You've got the ship, the crew, and the contract. For $10,000 and ten percent I'll pinpoint the wrecks for you. What do you say?"

"I've gotta think about this for awhile," I said. I glanced about the room and noticed a computer and peripheral equipment set up on the dining room table.

"Listen, there have been others looking for this wreck." Greg continued. "A guy named Don Spacher was here a couple of years ago dragging a magnetometer all over this place. Mel Fisher's son was even here checking the place out. And back in the fifties, Lieutenant Harry Reisberg was here searching for it. They all failed. They didn't understand the amount of sediment buildup in this area. I've done geological studies of the entire coast. This is a major earthquake zone, it's right in line with the Galápagos Islands. There are sometimes as many as two hundred tremors a day through here, small ones, of course, too small to feel. I've also completed electromagnetic spectroscopy surveys of this region."

"Spectro-what?"

"Spectroscopy. I've studied the ocean plants for mineral content. Plants or shells growing over a concentration of iron, let's say, would have a different mineral composition from plants or shells that were not over an area of buried metal. I also know that you won't find any cannons or iron objects because of equatorial countercurrents. The cold Humbolt current and the warm Niño current from Panama converge on each other right in front of this coast. The constant warming and cooling of the water does not allow iron to stabilize. Any iron objects down there would decay completely. Are you following me?"

"Of course, go ahead," I said, wondering if he was a genius or another kook.

"Have you ever seen something like this before?" Greg asked, holding out a coral-encrusted object.

"Yeah, hundreds of them. It's a spike, one of the large square nails that held the galleons together."

"I found it not far from here on one of my survey dives. I've also found gold and silver." Greg handed me a color photograph of some small broken pieces of gold jewelry and four silver coins. On one of the coins was a barely visible Spanish cross. I was starting to believe this guy.

"If you've got so much information, why don't you raise some money and go after the wrecks yourself?" I asked him, leery eyed.

"I've got too much other stuff going on. I've got a deal with a French mining company to recover gold from the rivers in the Amazon. There's tons of it there. I can't concentrate on salvage work like you can. I'll even sweeten the deal. I'll include copies of all the wreck charts I have for Ecuador. It would take you years to accumulate the data I've collected. Now, what do you say?"

"I don't know," I stalled. "What do you know about magnetometers? Mine's not functioning very well?"

"A straight mag won't work here. Too much mineralization in the surrounding rocks. You need a dual differential gradient magnetic anomaly detector. I've constructed one. I could bring it here from New York if you wanted to work with me. Believe me, I can save you a lot of time and money. Think about it."

I did think about it, constantly. The diving conditions were worsening every day. The currents, which changed 180 degrees from morning to afternoon, had increased to four knots. Underwater visibility had dropped to three feet. The bottom sediment we were digging in was like a mud-sand ooze. As we dug deeper, we came upon scattered layers of hard, compacted shells that had to be loosened with a high-pressure water jet before they could be sucked out of the way with the airlift. The holes bottomed out, meaning we hit bedrock, at eighteen to twenty feet deep. Past ten feet, the divers were working in total blackness, doing everything by feel. If a diver shut off the airlift, he was buried up to his knees in silt in seconds. The rocks at the bottom of the holes varied from refrigerator-size boulders to basketball-size river rock to penny-size pebbles. The coded message I sent to the investors simply said:

44E.

By the middle of July, I had to face the cold, harsh truth that we were out of money, our contract was about to expire, we were heading into the bad weather season and we hadn't found our shipwreck. It was a treasure hunter's worst nightmare. This is the point at which most people give up, but not me. I still believed someone would take me right to the treasure. I spent the last $10,000 of the partnership money to buy Greg Gino's information. It showed gold ionization circles in the larger bay closer to Manta.

Chapter Eighteen

We brought the *Hooker's Holiday* from Manta back to Guayaquil and tied her up to the pilings. Kevin had to stay on board to guard all our gear while the rest of the crew went home to the United States and I went to Quito to negotiate another contract with the government. Although guard duty was boring Kevin accepted the task, knowing it was his contribution to the expedition. From the time he was a teenager reading adventure books from the library, he'd always wanted to have a salvage boat, so looking after the *Hooker's Holiday* didn't feel like work to him, it felt like a dream fulfilled. My negotiations in Quito dragged on for weeks, proving the validity of the saying that the only thing slower than a two-hundred-year-old Galápagos tortoise, is the Ecuadorian bureaucracy.

In September I left Kevin in Ecuador and flew home to California to raise more money. By November I still had no new contract and no new investors. I was heading into gloom and despair until Bob Marx, our historical researcher, called. He'd been in the Philippines searching for deep-water shipwrecks and was just passing through San Francisco on his way back to Florida. He was calling from the airport, so I dashed over to pick him up.

"What have you found so far?" was his first question.

"Nothing." I hung my head in shame.

"The wreck is there, darlin'. You just have to do more research."

"I've already gone through all the books I know about. Let me in on some of your research secrets. Give me a hint," I begged.

"All right, when we get to your house," he agreed. "So how many of your crew have you slept with?"

"None!" I shouted embarrassed and offended. "I never mess around with crew members."

"Why? That's half the fun of treasure hunting. I always go for the captain's daughter myself. Look, I'm gonna build a replica of a Manilla galleon and sail it from the Philippines to San Francisco. You want to come along as my concubine?"

"Do I have to cook?"

"No."

"I'll consider it."

At my house I dragged out all the books I had about wrecksites, underwater archaeology, and treasure hunting. One, written by the successful adventurer Lieutenant Harry Reisberg, made reference to the Manta Bay wreck in Ecuador.

"What's this? Did you miss it?" Bob pointed to the book.

"Read further." I insisted, "Reisberg calls it Manta Bay, but the verbal directions he gives for getting there don't point anywhere near Manta Bay. In fact, they point three hundred miles south of Manta Bay."

"Wait a minute." Bob stopped, "It says here that Al Mikalow was with Harry. I know Al. He lives here in the Bay Area. Let's go talk to him."

We headed down to the wharf area of Oakland, among the rusty boats and drydocks, and found Al in his office. Bob and he reminisced awhile, swapping current adventures as we strolled around the grounds. Behind the office, where Al piled his junk and defunct dive gear, Bob saw four black, narrow-barreled cannons hidden under some broken pallets.

"What the hell are these, Al?" Bob asked, pulling off the pallets.

"Oh, me and Harry dug those up in the Exumas back in the sixties. They're worthless." Al said, apparently trying to hide something. But Bob wouldn't let up.

"These are sixteenth century, Al. I've been all over the Exumas, and there are no sixteenth century wrecks there. Where did you really find them?"

"I told ya. The Exumas. Who the hell cares? They're rusted away to nothin' anyhow." Al sounded a bit perturbed.

Bob brushed off his hands and jumped down off the pallets, giving me a wink as we followed Al around front and said goodbye.

"Now, this is research," Bob said as we drove back to my house. First thing he did when we got home was call Al's wife.

"Rose, its Bob Marx. How ya been, sweetie? Listen, I was just down at Al's office and I forgot to tell him about the Explorers Club meeting in San Francisco next month. It's on the 17th. You both should come. I'm the guest speaker."

"Oh, we'd love to come," Rose bubbled. I was listening on the extension phone. "How've you been, Bob? Still chasing all over the world?"

"Till they bury me or the sharks eat me. I've been in the Philippines getting shot at by the communist guerillas. They hate my white ass down there."

"Oh, you're incorrigible."

"Say, Al and I were crawling around some of the junk he has in back of the office and I found four old cannons. Do you remember where he got those from?"

"Those ugly old things? My goodness, he had those shipped up from South America back in the late fifties when he was down there with Harry. I think they were in Ecuador. Why do you ask?"

"Just curious. Why didn't he do something with them?"

"Nobody wanted them. All the markings were rusted off. I don't know why he's kept them around so long."

"Well I gotta go, I'm on the afternoon flight to Florida."

"You take care, Bob. We'll see you next month." Click.

"Okay, I got you started," Bob said. "Now, tomorrow you go see Al and tell him you know the cannons are from Ecuador. The rest is up to you."

"So that's how you do your research."

"Yep. That's how I got the edge on all those bookworm archaeologists. Now, let's get to the airport. My flight's in an hour."

I had all my charts and documents with me when I visited Al the next day. I leveled with him right from the start, told him I was after one of Bob's wrecks in Ecuador, told him I was working in Manta Bay and that I knew his cannons were from Ecuador. Al led me into one of his back rooms where a seven-foot-tall gray safe stood behind the door.

"Hell, I'm not plannin' to go back to Ecuador," Al said, pulling stacks of papers out of the safe. Maybe some of this stuff will help you out. Bob's been a friend of mine for a long time. If he sent you here, he must trust you."

"Did you find a wreck in Ecuador?" I asked while he sat at his desk and rummaged through the papers.

"Found those cannons and about sixteen hundred silver coins. Back in those days, nobody messed around with permits. You spent about a month on a wrecksite and moved on. Harry's the one who had all the historical data."

"Was the wreck in Manta Bay?"

"Hell, yes. I got the chart here somewhere. You know, Harry gave me this stuff just before he died. On his death bed he said, 'Al, if you ever want to hit it *big*, go back to Manta Bay.' I just never got back there."

My whole body was twitching. This was too good to be true. Al was going to give me the exact spot where he and Harry had found the wreck. It was hard to keep a giant grin off my face. Suddenly Al found a rolled up chart. He spread it out on the desk.

"This is it," he said. I got up out of my chair to see better. Al's finger pointed at a penciled X along the southern coast of Ecuador. I was confused.

"That's not Manta Bay," I told him. "Manta Bay is up here in the north. Are you sure you got the names right?"

"Sure I'm sure. That's exactly where we found the wreck."

"Well that's not Manta Bay, Al," I said as I got out my charts to show him.

"Well, I'll be a son-of-a-bitch," said Al when he realized we were talking about two different places. "All these years I thought Harry wanted me to go back to the wreck. Now I don't know if he meant I'd hit it big at the wreck, or at Manta Bay!"

Was I any better off after talking to Al? I don't know. I sure wasn't any closer to the treasure, and I still didn't have any money in the bank. I was using my own funds to keep everything going and I was running low. I'd talked to venture capital firms, private funding groups, even philanthropic organizations. The answer was the same everywhere: not interested. I was at my desk thumbing through a Fortune magazine that listed all the millionaires in the United States when the phone rang.

"Oceanus Ecuador," I answered like a secretary.

"Is this Margaret Brandeis?" the male voice asked, "*The* Margaret Brandeis?"

"Yes it is. May I ask who you are?"

"Philip Piper. You don't know me, but I've been following your activities for a long time. I know all about your project in Ecuador and I can help you raise money."

"Really."

"Yes, I'll be in San Francisco tomorrow. I'll meet you for lunch at that seafood restaurant at the foot of Market Street."

As I usually did when I was to meet an unknown person in a public place, I wore a nice dress and a funky gray cowboy hat. The odds of two fools dressing like that are astronomical. Philip had no problem recognizing me.

We took a table in the far corner, ordered two glasses of wine, and set down our respective piles of documents. He had described himself as a short Tom Selleck over the phone, pointed eyebrows, square jaw and a bushy mustache. He was neat, businesslike, but definitely not a stickler for details. Above all, he was energetic, you could feel it in the air around him. I could tell that he was determined to be my buddy before lunch was over. Like a smiling insurance salesman, he opened his battered leather briefcase. I drank the rest of my wine.

"I know some of your friends in Santa Barbara," Philip said as he rearranged the pens in the briefcase pockets. "Several of them went to the Bahamas with you." He showed me a stack of newspaper clippings about our expedition and our capture by the Colombian navy.

"What brings you to me now?" I inquired.

258

"I've always wanted to be involved first hand in a treasure hunt. Until now I was too busy with other projects. At the present I'm affiliated with a mortgage and loan brokerage house, but my real specialty is financial consulting. I don't have money myself to invest in your project, but I have time. And I know the people with enough bucks to finance your entire expedition."

"And what do you want?" was my next question. Nobody ever helps out on a treasure hunt unless they've got a piece of the action.

"Naturally a small percentage for the time I put in," Philip replied. "But most of all I want to come aboard the ship. I'll do anything. I used to be a commercial diver in the North Sea. I have all my gear. I'll do anything you say, any job that needs to be done."

Maybe it was his boyish enthusiasm when he talked about being on the ship. Or maybe it was his seemingly harmless, spunky nature. Or maybe I was just getting tired of searching for money by myself. All I know is, a week later, for the first time in my treasure hunting career, I made a deal with a "professional" money finder.

Philip went right to work setting up appointments for me with some of the richest people in Santa Barbara. I lived out of a suitcase stashed in the trunk of my car, sleeping in the front car seat, or on somebody's couch, or on Captain Cooke's sailboat. I knew where all the public restrooms were. I ate three meals a day at local delicatessens. Most of the money I had left went to pay for gasoline and Philip's phone bills. As the weeks wore on, I traveled all over southern California meeting bankers, real estate moguls, rock and roll promoters, corporate executives, drug dealers, horse breeders, retired millionaires, car builders, a man selling the biggest pearl in the world, a relative of Fletcher Christian, whose family had come from

Pitcairn Island, bar owners, smugglers, other professional money finders, and Philip's friends.

I spent four months working with Philip, and although he did know a lot of people, there were few, as Philip put it, with the proclivity for investing in treasure hunts. Where I had been very careful in the past, only allowing the news of our expedition to travel by word of mouth, Philip's strategy was, throw enough mud on the wall and some of it will stick. He wanted to hold seminars, advertise in the *Wall Street Journal*, and set up a booth in Las Vegas. He was not a "professional" money finder, he was a loud speaker, and I was the product he was selling. He got angry when I objected to bulk mail flyers and television spots.

Soon he started objecting to the way I gave the presentations, butting in when he felt I wasn't emphasizing the right points. After some meetings we'd spend half an hour in the car yelling at each other. Philip wanted to sell the fewest units at the highest price. I just wanted to sell any units, at whatever price I could, to get back to Ecuador. What I thought was a mutual goal was turning out to be a conflict of interests.

"Philip, you've got to stop chasing the big fish and concentrate on smaller, attainable amounts," I suggested one day as we were driving back up to the San Francisco area.

"Margee, we're on a roll now, can't you see it?" he protested.

"What I see is a lot of big talk about big money and no cash in the bank."

"Hey, it's a lot tougher than I thought selling a treasure hunt. I'm doing the best I can, so get off my case."

"When I met you, you said you had people ready to invest, not that you had to *sell* the project. The working season in Ecuador will be over by July. I have to get back there to check out Greg Gino's gold ionization sites. One of them is in forty feet of water,

260

the other in a hundred feet of water. Working them will take some time."

"Remember, you promised I could come aboard the ship as a crew member."

"I never said as a crew member. I have all the divers I need. I said you could come aboard, that's all."

"Oh, you're just like all the others. You walk over people. You let me do all the work and then you take the money and forget all about me. I can cause bad things to happen to you, you know. Just by thinking it. I've done it before."

"What are you talking about?" I demanded, shocked by his words.

"There's an angelic struggle on this planet right now, and we're the players. You've got to choose between good and evil. Frankly, I've found there's more power on the evil side. And I can use it against you. I can make you get in a car accident or fall down some stairs and break your leg."

"So you've already chosen the evil side, huh?"

"I will if you try to squeeze me out of this deal. You couldn't have raised any money without me."

"Philip, I've raised plenty of money, and long before I ever met you."

"And I thought we were friends," Philip said. He crossed his arms and stared blankly out the front window as if he were a thousand miles away. We drove the rest of the way in silence.

It was now the end of April 1987. A whole year had passed since that joyful trip down the Guayas River and out into the ocean. I'd come to realize that treasure hunting was thirty percent raising money, sixty percent getting permission papers, and only ten percent actually searching for the treasure. After I redirected Philip's efforts towards smaller investment amounts, we managed to raise $150,000 which I considered enough to return to Ecuador.

As a parting gesture of appreciation I took Philip to meet Bob Marx at the Annual Underwater Archaeology Conference where Bob was having a battle with several government agencies about excavating a wreck in California. We were seated with representatives from the National Parks Department, the Army Corp of Engineers, and the National Oceanic and Atmospheric Administration. Philip greeted them all by saying, "So how does it feel to be sucking off the tit of government?"

Bob went into shock. He sent me over to the white courtesy phone to have him paged so he could make a gracious exit.

"Margee, how do you find these guys?" he asked me, with genuine concern.

"I don't find them, they find me!" I'd said. "I guess I just have a malfunctioning shit detector."

"What?" Bob looked at me strangely.

"Never mind," I'd told him.

The Abandoned Shipwreck Act was being passed by the United States Congress and treasure hunters were furious. The marine archaeologists had won the legal battle, little realizing that they had just closed the doors to any cooperation from the people who find most of the shipwrecks. From now on nobody would report anything they found and the big money would turn to the deepwater shipwrecks outside U.S. jurisdiction. The U.S. treasure hunting world was collapsing and I wanted to run. I had to get away, somewhere inaccessible, somewhere like the bow of the *Hooker's Holiday* gliding down the Guayas River.

Chapter Nineteen

Back on the *Hooker's Holiday* - what a relief! I'd escaped again from the civilized world, it was getting too weird for me. When I had gotten off the plane in Guayaquil, it felt more like home than California. I'd grown accustomed to the heat, the smells, the dust, the poverty, and I was speaking Spanish so well people asked me if I was Ecuadorian. I even swung my hands around wildly when I spoke. In two days we had loaded the *Hooker* with provisions, revved up the engines, and motored down the Guayas River again on our way to fortune and glory.

As I sat on the bow of the boat, mesmerized by the jungle-like landscape floating by me, I turned my attention to new treasure hunting techniques.

Of the two gold ionization circles that Greg Gino had shown me, I decided to investigate the shallower one first. The crew was all jazzed by the high-tech wizardry, but when we arrived at the site, it took only one dive for them all to come up complaining that the bottom was solid rock. There was no shipwreck. It was flat hardpan in every direction. They tried to chip away at the hard, compacted clay/mud substance with their diver's knives, but twelve inches into the stuff it just got harder. They started laughing at my modern technological wonders, and Greg Gino wasn't around to defend me. He was back in New York, probably selling his satellite surveys to some other sucker.

I called Greg on the phone, told him there was no evidence of shipwrecks under his gold ionization circle, then I called him a fraud. He admitted that he hadn't been completely honest with me. It seems that satellite pictures only record the top of the ocean, they don't penetrate the water to the ocean floor. His explanation for our failure was that the gold ions were seeping up through the water to be detected on the surface but that the strong current in the area was carrying them downstream by the time they got to the top. To arrive at the gold deposit, we would have to calculate the rate of movement downstream and backtrack along the current. The problem was, he didn't know the rate or direction of the current on the day the satellite photos were taken. I'd been hoodwinked again.

I tried dowsing next. This was another suggestion from my archaeology friend, Presley, only this time, he had seen the dowsing work with his own eyes. I paid the airplane ticket for a highly respected man from the American Dowsing Association to come to our site. His several hand-held rods and plumbs spun around wildly every time our vessel passed over two different spots. The first was smack-dab in the middle of Greg Gino's gold ionization circle, in solid rock, and the second spot was in the center of the bay. We dug a twenty-foot-deep hole at the second spot and our probe sank another twelve feet without hitting any treasure. We'd come up empty-handed again.

While we were trying all these different methods to locate the treasure, shipboard life began to take shape aboard the *Hooker*. The atmosphere was a kind of loose respectability, as if we were engaged in a serious family business. I, however, noticed some dicey aspects to being the only woman living with nine men on an eighty-foot boat.

First of all, you see alot of naked, male butts. I always averted my eyes if I was about to see a frontal view. Second, you see alot of naked girl pictures taped up on walls, in the outhouse, and on the underside of top bunks. You also find x-rated magazines hidden everywhere you can imagine, full-color magazines like *Hustler*, *Penthouse*, and *Lust at Sea*.

The use of swear words is also an important issue. A female expedition leader has to learn how to swear with gusto, with fuckin' gut-level intensity. A wimpy swear word is worse than none at all. And you can't look embarrassed, no matter what words you hear.

You don't dare wear makeup, short shorts, skirts, fingernail polish, curlers, lipstick, jewelry, perfume, or nightgowns, and you never go braless. You have to take your cuts, bruises, mosquito bites, sunburns, and bashed fingers like a man, with no whining. Men hate whiners. And you'd better know what to do when somebody throws you a rope, or you'll piss everybody off. You'll be branded a useless twit and expected to remain out of sight in the galley.

Above all, you learn to keep your mouth shut when something's going wrong. Men don't need to be reminded that they've screwed up. You never rush into the middle of something going wrong, unless they call you. By then the situation is so bad they don't care who knows they messed up.

The only way to get any respect on a boat full of men is to earn it. You have to know the names of all the tools. You have to know how to shut off any machine on board. You have to know the difference between lube oil, hydraulic oil, diesel oil, outboard oil, and waste oil. In the case of divers, you have to know the function of the anchor line, the down line, the load line, the com line, the tag line, the CP line, and the messenger line. God help you if you touch the wrong one.

Inevitably, you'll be faced with a boatload of horny men. The subject usually comes up at the gripe session around the breakfast table, after we've been out at sea for ten or twelve days.

"Margee, I'm tired of beatin' my meat," one of them would say. "Don't you think we should go into port for awhile?"

We had one real horn-dog on board. If he didn't get off the boat at least once a week, he was the most irritable man you ever met, snapping at everybody, bitching about everything. I made it a policy to go into port every Friday night. It seems that Señor Roca's advice about keeping an apartment and some women had been accurate.

The last topic was liquor. Here I put my foot down, no liquor on board. That was another reason the crew had to get off the boat on Friday nights.

All and all, living with nine men, especially professional divers, was unpretentious. The work the divers did was serious, dangerous. There was no time for games or false fronts; there were no business suits to hide behind. The divers didn't have to talk about how good they were because they proved themselves every day. And if someone couldn't cut it, they were replaced. Granted, there were always personality conflicts aboard, but they never got in the way of the work. And after work, the men retreated to their bunks, the only six by two foot space on the boat that was truly theirs. By 9 p.m. everybody was asleep.

Kevin and I had adapted our marriage to shipboard life again, making love without making noise. We had our own cabin with a door this time and we had fun sneaking moments to be alone together. As usual, Kevin melded in with the crew. He was my spy and confidant. He became the cook and I became a combination of mom and the boss.

Of course, it would be dishonest to suggest that everything was always peaches and cream. We had our tense moments too, especially after several weeks of nonstop work. Patience wears a little thin, tempers get short, and accusations start flying when frustration reaches a certain level.

"Margee, you don't *do* anything around here," one of the divers complained one day, while I was washing dishes. True, I didn't dive everyday or hump the airlift around on the bottom of the ocean. I didn't do the "manly" stuff. But I did see that everything ran smoothly. I made sure that there was always water, oil, diesel, food, spare parts, permits, visas, money, sheets, towels, medicine, government observers, logistical support, mechanics, communication, and the right paperwork whenever we needed it. But that wasn't *work* to the divers. They figured diving was the most important aspect of shipwreck salvage.

The one incident that convinced them that I was a valuable crew member occurred on the day we were anchored on a rock pinnacle two miles offshore, in a strong current. Everybody was in the water inspecting the submerged rock outcropping and the surrounding area. Only the two Ecuadorian observers and I remained on board.

When a vessel is anchored in sand and large waves strike its bow, the vessel is lifted up momentarily and the tension is released by the anchor dragging a short distance in the sand. But when the anchor is hooked on a solid piece of rock and a large wave tries to lift the vessel, something else has to give. In this case, when a series of larger than normal waves started lifting the bow, our anchor chain broke, and suddenly our vessel was adrift. I was on the bow when it happened. I watched the chain drop out of sight into the water. The boat was out of control. We were caught in a five-knot current on our way to Colombia. It was panic time!

The waves immediately pushed the boat parallel to the oncoming swells and we started rolling mercilessly, forty-five degrees to either side. Dishes and pots in the galley went crashing to the floor. Three gallons of soup that had been cooking on the stove spilled all over the place. Things were banging against the metal bulkheads, echoing throughout the boat like a junkyard in an earthquake. I ran to the stern deck and found the two observers clinging white-handed to a metal pole with ghastly fear in their faces. What to do? What to do? I ran back to the bow and saw a diver's head pop out of the water a quarter mile behind us. Shit, I've got to do something!

I clawed my way to the engine room, getting bashed and bruised as I was thrown around by the rolling vessel. Just as I made it to the stairs, the bilge alarm went off like an ambulence siren. Oh, God, we're taking on water - *we're sinking!* The divers are stranded two miles off shore. They'll never be able to swim against the current. They'll *drown*! I screamed in Spanish at the observers to get into the Zodiac and pick up the divers, but they wouldn't let go of the pole. I ran back, and forcefully peeled their hands away, then shoved them to the edge of the boat where the Zodiac was bouncing wildly, as it was drug by a rope tied to the *Hooker*.

"Vaya, ahorita!" (Go right now!) I screamed at them, pointing to the bobbing diver's heads now a mile behind us in the water.

I descended the engine room stairs, grasping at anything to keep my balance. I slipped on the last two steps and fell to the metal floor that was now covered in grease and oil. I crawled on my stomach like an alligator to the handles of the low-pressure air system that started the engines. *Varoom* ... the port engine started up. There was no time to check oil pressures, it didn't matter. If we didn't get to the harbor before we sank it was all over anyway. I crawled across the engine room floor to the starboard side. *Varoom...* the diesel engine responded. Now all I had to do was drive this eighty-five ton, wallowing mass of steel, something I'd never done before.

I made it back up the stairs, noticing that the Zodiac was gone. Then I slipped and slid my way through the galley. Everything was on the floor, sloshing back and forth, in a mini-sea of noodle soup. I felt things break under my feet as I dashed for the wheelhouse, my heart thumping in my chest like a pile-driver.

My hands were on the throttles, one forward, the other in reverse. I'd seen the captain do it a hundred times. I circled the wheel around as far as it would go, counting desperate minutes as the vessel pounded into the swells and ever so slowly swung around to face the oncoming waves. My hands were shaking uncontrollably and sweat was dripping down my face.

"You're doing great!" Captain Cooke shouted as he raced to the bow, still in his dripping wetsuit. He had been the first one to be picked up by the Zodiac. He readied the spare anchor we kept on the bow, connecting it to some thick rope we had for emergencies, before he hurried back to the wheelhouse. As the rolling subsided, still dripping wet, he took over the wheel.

We spent two hours traversing the area searching for our lost anchor. All the divers were back on board. They told me they had known something was drastically wrong when they heard the engines start up, but I had saved the day. I even got an embarrassed apology from the diver who had said I never *did* anything.

It turned out the boat hadn't really been sinking. It had just rolled over so far that the small amount of water in the bilge had swished up the sides, enough to activate the alarm. I was still a heroine though. I had saved the boat and all the divers.

Since Greg Gino's satellite technology didn't show us the shipwreck we tried visual inspection dives. We started at the end of the bay and worked towards the center. Each diver had a compass heading to follow as he swam out a thousand feet from the boat; then he turned and followed a different heading back. This non-technical, embarrassingly simple procedure yielded our first evidence of a shipwreck. It was pottery shard - thick, red, ridged, Spanish olive jar, pottery shard and it was very old. Kevin found the first of two pieces we recovered. It didn't look anything like the indigenous pottery made on the Ecuadorian coast. I'd seen enough Spanish olive jars from other shipwrecks to know that this was from the type of ship we were looking for. We delivered the pottery to the port captain, and that's when the local newspapers got a whiff of what we were doing.

The first article came out under this giant headline: RAPE, PILLAGE AND PLUNDER OF OUR ARCHAEOLOGICAL RICHES! It said that an American vessel captained by archaeologist Margaret Brandeis had spent the last ten years cruising the coast of Ecuador and "who knows what riches they have stolen from our waters?" The head of exterior relations in

Quito said we were looking for manganese nodules. The Central Bank spokesmen claimed they didn't know anything about it. The Minister of Defense was hauled in front of the National Congress to explain what was going on. The Director of the Cultural Heritage Institute demanded a complete investigation of our project and interviewed the port captain, the Oceanographic Institute, the Merchant Marines Office, and all the observers who had been aboard our boat. Our monthly reports were reviewed and our work vessel was inspected. At the end of the investigation, four lawyers declared that our contract was perfectly legal and enforceable and that we had complied with all regulations and stipulations therein. At that point, I ran out of money, and for the second time we took the *Hooker's Holiday* back to Guayaquil and sent the crew home to the United States with no treasure to show for our efforts.

❦

Sometime around Chrismas 1987, I got a call from one of my partners. He told me about a man who had just won the International Inventors Award for a device that locates buried gold. He said he'd met the inventor personally and seen demonstrations of the device, which could both locate gold anywhere within a ten-mile radius and determine the gold's quality and purity. Yeah, sure, was my first response. I called Bob Marx to ask if he'd heard of the thing and all he said was, "What are you smoking, Margee?"

I contacted the investors anyway and they all wanted to try the new devise. They chipped in enough money to make a third attempt at locating our Ecuadorian shipwreck. I called Captain Cooke, hired a new lead diver named Chester who put together a fresh crew and we all flew to Ecuador. In the space of three weeks we were back on the *Hooker's Holiday*, anchored in the Manta harbor.

When the inventor arrived, I took him straight from the airport to the beach before he had a chance to talk to anybody. He got out his gizmo, which looked like something Flash Gordon would have used to zap aliens, and connected all the wires and clips and meters to two twelve-volt car batteries. Then he stood at the water's edge, holding the device out in front of him, and made passes back and forth from left to right.

"Gold's the deadest metal on the earth," he told me over his shoulder. "You gotta wake it up. Right now I'm agitating any gold molecules that are in the area. I'm making them jump around like boiling water. Next, I'll just turn my machine on reverse and it'll register the location of any agitation."

"Interesting," I said. I was busy looking around us for curious onlookers who might be watching. "How long did it take you to invent this machine?"

"I've got fifteen years into developing this baby," he said proudly. "It's a combination of three different kinds of technology. I had to... wait. Look at this!"

"What is it?" I shouted. The curlicue antenna seemed to be stuck on some distant point on the horizon. No matter which way the inventor tried to swivel the device around, the antenna always pointed to the same spot.

"Well, gal, you've got yourself a big one here!" he said triumphantly. "There's several tons of gold out there. Let's go down the beach so we can shoot it again and triangulate the position."

I felt that old tingling again, the thrill of discovery. The excitement felt like bumble bees buzzing through my body.

Instantly I was a believer in this inventor's contraption. We moved down the beach to a place I could identify on our map and we penciled in the two headings on which the device was pointing. The lines crossed in the middle of the bay about a mile offshore.

Early the next morning, we took the inventor out in our rubber boat and asked him to find the target again. He dropped a buoy, and we brought the *Hooker's Holiday* around to the site and anchored right over it.

"By my calculations," the inventor said, as he climbed out of the rubber boat, "your target is buried thirty-two feet under the sediment."

"THIRTY-TWO FEET?!" the divers gasped in unison.

"Give or take a foot," he added. "You boys got a problem with that?"

"It'll just take some time," Chester said. "We've only got a six inch diameter airlift. And to have any room at the bottom of the hole we'll have to start it about twenty feet in diameter at the top."

"Well, let's get going," the inventor urged. "That buoy is over the largest concentration of gold. There's also a huge amount of silver scattered randomly around the area, but you dig here and you'll hit the gold for sure."

The first week of digging went pretty fast. Everyone was in high spirits and there was plenty of natural light filtering into the hole. By the second week there weren't as many smiles on the divers' faces and all the digging was shrouded in darkness. During the third week I was giving short pep talks at the morning gripe sessions around the breakfast table and the divers were looking at the digging as just another job. At the end of the fourth week there were visible signs of fear, fatigue, and skepticism.

"If there's gold at the bottom of this hole, I'll stick a dinosaur bone up my butt!" Captain Cooke remarked at the crew meeting one morning.

"Listen, Margee, there's old divers and there's bold divers. But there's no old, bold divers. Understand?" Chester added.

"I didn't sign up on this job to be diving in pitch black holes, upside down, with my legs wrapped around a six-inch Loch Ness monster," another diver griped. "And those damn poisonous sea snakes are hanging onto the walls of the hole every morning. And you yourself told us there's no antidote for the poison."

"And what about the cave-ins?" someone else broke in. "The rocks and silt are falling right back down the hole on my head. If I turn off the fucking airlift for a second I get buried up to my knees in muck. It's scary."

Chester tilted his chair back, clasped his hands behind his head, and addressed his divers. "I want to make it very plain here that you're all risking your life by going down into that hole. We're digging upside down, head first, in total darkness, and if there is even a small cave-in of this soft sediment, you're a gonner. I've been trapped before and I know what it's like. The type of face masks we're using would probably get pushed to the side and you wouldn't be able to breathe. If we were working for some big company and getting paid lots of money, I still wouldn't make you go down in that hole."

"You don't mean hole, you mean mine shaft," griped Captain Cooke. "We're losing at least an hour every morning because the stupid fishermen around here keep stealing our buoys at night. And you said there would be clear water, Margee. Even out of the hole the visibility is only twelve inches. We might as well be closing our eyes down there. We have to do everything by feel."

I held up my hands to call an end to the discussion.

"There seems to be only two things we all agree on," I said, looking around the table at six weary divers. "One, we haven't passed a pile of gold on the way down this hole, and, two, the only way to find out if this inventor and his gold-finding gadget are for real, is to keep digging. Now, you're all paid to the end of the month. We've spent $480,000 to get this far, and this is probably the best shot any of you will have at finding an enormous treasure. There isn't enough time or money to bring in big equipment, and I don't want to stop without at least going to the depth the inventor told us. However, I'm not the one who has to go down in that hole and dig, so ultimately the decision to quit or keep digging is yours."

We were five feet from knowing if we'd found the treasure. Here we were gathered around the galley table, anchored right beside the hole, and each diver had to decide for himself if finding the gold was worth his life. Kevin spoke up first.

"I vote we keep digging."

"Yeah, let's keep digging," Another said.

"For myself, I'll keep going," Chester voted.

"I'm in, too," the others added.

All eyes turned to Captain Cooke.

"I up the bet to two dinosaur bones, but I'll keep digging," he grumbled. Then he added, "But I'll probably be the first one to leave."

The next day the captain came up after his dive to say we'd hit solid rock bottom. The water jet wouldn't cut it, his chisel couldn't chip it, and the airlift was useless. Another diver went down with an axe and hacked off a chunk of it. Besides being black and extremely hard, the sample was a completely different

275

type of sediment from what we had been digging through. We still had three feet to go to the inventor's depth.

Defeat was in everybody's face as the crew milled around the back deck. The captain was grateful he was still alive and had already started packing his bags. The inventor was telling us the hard layer was a crust, caused by the chemical reaction between gold and the mud sediment. I was searching my brain, wondering what to do next, when Chester came up with an idea. We could try boring through the sediment with an air-driven coring drill, like the ones the mining industry uses to bore dynamiting holes in rock. We decided to try it.

"I'm on natural bottom," the diver reported through our underwater communication system the day we tried the pneumatic drill. We were all hanging around the communication speaker like expectant fathers in a hospital waiting room.

"Roger," Chester answered.

"It's really clear down here today. I'm descending into the hole."

"Roge-o"

"Okay, I'm at the bottom of the hole. Lower down the pneumatic drill."

"We're lowering away."

Kevin slowly fed out the line as the drill disappeared below the blue-green waves. Several minutes of silence passed with nothing but the sound of the diver breathing.

"Slack off on the line. I've got the drill in position," the diver reported. "I'm ready to start drilling."

"We're all set, up here."

An immense rumbling started and a huge mushroom of white swirling air bubbles rose toward the surface like an underwater geyser. For a hundred feet around our boat the bubbles exploded on the surface as if the sea had come to a boil. A garbled message came through the speaker as a hundred pounds of air pressure rushed by the diver's face.

"Say again!" Chester said worriedly. "Message unclear. Say again!"

"Shshshsh, blubblub, I say I'm down two feet into the black stuff," the diver reported as the air bubbles subsided.

"Any change?"

"None. I'll keep drilling."

"Roger."

The white bubbling started up again accompanied by a rumbling, as if thousands of horses were stampeding. Five more intense minutes passed by, then the answer came.

I broke through!" the diver shouted excitedly. "At three feet exactly, I broke through into something soft. I'm pulling up a sample now."

"What is it?" Chester asked. All of us were leaning toward the speaker, wondering what the soft stuff was. We were all sure it was gold. It *had* to be gold. The anticipation felt like a firecracker ready to explode as we waited for the diver's joyous reply.

"Aw, shit!" The diver's voice blasted through the speaker, "It's gumbo!"

I looked around at the crew's discouraged faces and sagging shoulders as they backed away from the com-set and shook their heads.

"What's gumbo?" I demanded.

"It's a diver's term we use in the oil drilling industry," Chester explained. "It's a gooey gray substance kind of like silly putty that sticks to everything. It gums up the drill bit in seconds and you can't drill any further. If that's what's down there, we're finished."

Well, it was gumbo, and yes, we were finished. Bad weather was approaching again and none of the crew wanted to continue digging with the equipment we had on hand. Our third attempt to find the shipwreck, and the gold, had failed.

Chapter Twenty

The day I got home from Ecuador, I found a bright yellow booklet with a red ribbon around it, sitting on my doorstep. I knew John, my seeking-the-answers friend had sent it. The text was written as an instruction handbook, the kind that tells you how to build a shelf or fix the plumbing. In a very concise, descriptive manner, this book explained how to make things and events manifest in your physical environment. It referred to Buddha and Jesus as Superbeings and explained how they were in tune with their divine center, or God-self. How their consciousness anticipates every possible need in the physical world, chooses divine fulfillment, accepts it, and through acceptance expresses the conviction of having it. And it is through this knowledge of *have,* that the superbeings image fulfillment as a present reality. Jesus could instantly bring forth ideas into visibility.

This is what the booklet said:

In our spiritual research, we discovered that an individual's consciousness is in reality an individualized Energy Field -

With the understanding that what can be seen in the mind's eye is a NOW experience, the activity of the law (spiritual mind action) is automatically called into play, and the invisible substance begins to take shape as the particular form, situation or experience desired.

In the spiritual treatment of the manifestation process, please keep in mind that the secret of success is in the sequence, because each step sets the stage in consciousness for the one that follows.

1) INTUNEMENT: Tuning into that Presence and Power of God within you

2) CHOICE: Choose (focus your thoughts on) things, circumstances, situations or experiences that you deeply desire

3) ACCEPTANCE: Mentally, and, with your feeling nature, accept what you have chosen

4) HAVE: Shift from a sense of need, to a sense of already having what you chose

5) VISUALIZATION: Controlled mental picturing of what you chose

6) LOVE: Love what you visualize

7) SPOKEN WORD: Saying "IT IS DONE" proves your faith and acknowledges the action of the God-Force

8) SURRENDER: Allowing the God-Force to take and complete the manifestation process

9) GRATITUDE: Being thankful that your needs are fulfilled, before they are visible
10) ACTION: Make some definite move. Position yourself to receive what you chose

Through this particular spiritual treatment, you are duplicating the automatic activity of Superbeing Consciousness in a step-by-step process.[3]

By now I was starting to understand that there was more to manifesting what you want, than just positive thinking. There's a big difference between, thinking positively that some particular thing will happen in the future, and *believing*, without any doubt, that you already *have* the thing, in the present moment.

Apparently, masters and gurus and religious cults and divine teachers are unnecessary. You don't have to practice rituals, breathe a certain way, say certain mantras, or pay a single penny. All you have to do is *know*, that by your thoughts, and according to your beliefs, you possess the power to create anything. I found that throughout history many people have tried to tell the human race this very same thing:

"All things will be at once according to your mind and according to the mind of God"
Epictetus, first century A.D.[4]

"Man is made by his belief. As he believes, so he is."
Bhagavad - Gita[4]

"All that we are is the result of what we have thought."
Dhammapada[4]

"A man becomes what he thinks."
                                        Gandhi[4]

"All things are possible to one who believes."
                                Saint Bernard of Clairvaux[4]

"Be careful what you believe, you will get it."
                                Ralph Waldo Emerson[4]

"As a man thinketh in his heart, so is he."
                                        James Allen[5]

"Did you ever see the episode of Star Trek in which they beamed down on this planet and were forced to go to the gunfight at the O.K. Corral? Spock said, 'If you believe the bullets are real, they'll kill you!' Well, that shit is true."
                                        Eddie Murphy[6]

OK, I thought to myself, maybe there is some common theme in all these books John was sending me, but I didn't have time right now to follow steps. I just kept believing someone would show me right where the treasure was hiding.

❦

Back in the diving industry, rumors about me were running wild. Some said I had already found the treasure. Some said I was all washed up. A friend told me he had heard people talking in a bar in Houston about the thirty-foot-deep holes I was digging. A German archaeological magazine wrote an article about me, and I received letters from several people wanting to invest in our project. I ignored all of it. I was only interested in one thing - why there had been gumbo, and not gold, at the bottom of that hole.

"It doesn't work," I told the partner who had found the inventor in the first place.

"But the device has found gold in other locations. I've got letters from witnesses," he insisted.

"There was no gold at the bottom of the hole. What more proof do you need?" I asked coldly.

"Listen, I've discussed the whole thing with the inventor," my partner went on. "The depth of the water must be causing a deflection. He says to move the excavation sixty feet to the southwest and you'll hit the gold."

By October 1988, when the weather had calmed, we were all back in Ecuador at the site. Chester had spent the whole summer designing, constructing, and testing a core drill he had built from scratch. The rig sat on a four-hundred-pound metal skid that we could slide along the ocean floor. The whole thing was driven by eighteen thousand pounds of hydraulic oil pressure. The core drill itself was five inches in diameter and was built to allow a one-inch diameter tube to be lowered inside it, so when we hit something solid, we could manually retrieve a one inch plug sample. We had also constructed a tubular metal detector that we could lower into any hole we cored, to see if there were metallic readings in the walls of the hole.

We set up a base line on the ocean floor with cable and began a series of core holes to the southwest of our excavation. As the weeks went by, we cored more than thirty holes and found nothing but mud and rock, but one day in December, something happened I thought best to keep secret.

Too much news of what we were doing had been leaking out and I didn't want the rest of the world to know what had

283

happened. Besides, I was kind of embarrassed about the way it had come about. Only the crew knew, and I swore I'd cut their balls off if they told anybody.

I was on land the day it happened, buying food and hydraulic couplings. The *Hooker* had gone out to the site to work. At four o'clock, Kevin and the rubber Zodiac were waiting for me at the dock.

"Well, don't you want to hear what happened today?" Kevin asked, obviously anxious. We loaded the supplies and he headed the Zodiac back out of the harbor toward the boat.

"Okay, what happened today?" I said to humor him.

"We found gold flakes!!"

"Are you serious??" I squealed, tingling all over.

"Swear to God! We found gold flakes! The diver was reaming out the hole so we could lower the metal detector, and all of a sudden he was shouting over the com-set that gold flakes were coming out of the hole and flying all around him!"

"That's fantastic!" I yelled, wanting to bounce up and down on the Zodiac's rubber pontoons. A mixture of relief and elation rushed through me like a raging river before I asked for proof.

"So you've got the flakes on board, right?"

"Well... not exactly." Kevin hung his head down. "We sorta lost 'em."

"You *what?*"

"They sorta blew out the door."

I groaned.

"The diver only collected four or five flakes," Kevin went on, "because the current carried them away so fast. He brought them up in a pill bottle and we picked them out of the sediment and put them on a paper towel. Then I think someone who didn't know what was happening, turned on the fan in the galley, and the next minute, they were gone."

The paper towel and magnifying glass were still on the galley table when I got on board the *Hooker*. Chester came down the steps from the wheelhouse with a 'what can I tell ya' shrug and a lopsided grin.

"I was underwater," Chester said, to clear himself. "I can't believe they left the flakes laying on the table. I gotta tell you, though, yesterday when I was drilling at that same depth, I hit something strange. I reported over the com-set that I was probably drilling right through a bar of gold. But I'm not coming to any conclusions yet. Remember, this could be just some brass shavings from the brazing rod that holds the carbide tips onto the drill head. Brass is the same color as gold."

One of the other divers passed me on the back deck, leaned toward my ear, and said, "I checked. There was no brass missing from the drill head."

"We'll know for sure tomorrow," said Chester, rubbing his hands together as we motored the *Hooker* back into port to get a good night's rest in the calm harbor water.

At six in the morning, just as we were heading back out to the site, the port captain showed up in his nice white uniform to deliver a letter from the Ministry of Defense. The government had suspended our contract.

It seems that this was the day on which the one-year extension of our permits began, and the Director of the Cultural Heritage Department was now claiming that our contract was invalid.

The *Hooker* stayed in port while I flew to Quito to see the Minister, but it didn't do any good. My choice was to either continue with a contested contract or suspend operations until things were set straight. Of course, I didn't mention anything about the gold flakes. Anybody who knew we'd found something would try to get rid of us and dig up the treasure himself. No, the best thing was to play it cool and find out what was really going on first. Besides, I couldn't prove we'd found anything anyway. Our evidence had blown away.

For the fourth time, we brought the *Hooker* back to Guayaquil, and sent the crew home to the United States. Kevin and I stayed on board the boat while we waited for the Ecuadorian government to clarify our contract.

Waiting, waiting, waiting. We heard one excuse after another about why they needed more time to settle the problem with our contract. In the midst of the bureaucratic battle we learned that the Director of the Cultural Heritage Department had secretly signed an agreement with other treasure hunters for the entire coast of Ecuador and he was trying to get rid of me because I had one hundred miles of coastline in my contract.

Television news programs denounced the Director for his illegal action. Newspapers showed pictures of the Director in his futile attempts at denying everything. Colored articles depicted our lease site and the methods we had used to locate the shipwreck. Columnists wrote stories on both sides of the issue, some saying treasure hunters were thieves, others praising us for having the guts to undertake such a risky endeavor. TV talk shows interviewed local archaeologists who condemned me without ever reviewing the facts. Then the lawyers got involved and declared that the Director had no authority to write agreements on behalf of the government of Ecuador.

After weeks of controversy, the Director was asked to resign, but he refused to go. Behind the scenes, the Director's uncle, a personal secretary to the President, was fighting to keep the Director at his post. It was a political struggle now, even family against family. Who had more power? Who was willing to use it for the sake of treasure hunting? Who was getting paid? Who had the final decision? Who would lose his job?

Week after week, I kept badgering the officials, complaining that we were losing money every day we wasted in Guayaquil. Our lawyer reminded the officials of all our contractual rights. I was sincerely trying to cooperate with the government, but I was losing my patience. The heat was getting to me. Fungus was starting to grow on my stomach from the constant humidity. A whole year passed by since the day the government suspended our contract, and even for Ecuadorian time, that was sufficient. I had reached my limit. I was fuming mad.

I had been told that it was the new Commander General of the Navy who was stalling all the paperwork for reinstating our salvage contract, so before I returned to California, I sat down at the typewriter and wrote him a typical gringo-style letter.

I pointed out that the Ecuadorian government was cheating us by delaying our contract so long. I told him we had three years of work and over a million dollars invested in our project. I told him if we didn't have the contract within two weeks, the investors were going to sell the exact coordinates of the shipwreck to other treasure hunters who would come with underwater robots and take the treasure without giving Ecuador anything. Of course, I was just bluffing about the robots.

Chapter Twenty One

At midnight on New Year's Eve 1989, I was thirty thousand feet over Mexico City, flying back to Ecuador to make my personal apologies to the Commander General of the Ecuadorian Navy.

The commander had considered the letter I had written him, an international, political insult and had ordered my boat seized, my crew deported and me put in jail.

My Ecuadorian partner, Pancho, had been called to the Navy office to explain about the letter and since he didn't know anything about it, the matter had been postponed until I could be summoned. Being the gentleman that he was, Pancho had not wanted to discuss details over the telephone with me. He would wait for my arrival in Ecuador. Kevin on the other hand, being the understanding husband that he was, told me to "get my butt down there immediately."

As the plane landed in Guayaquil, a voice in my head started chanting "It's the beginning of the end Margee Brandeis, the beginning of the end." I wondered if I would be arrested at the immigration counter, or as I exited the airport.

To my surprise, only Pancho was waiting for me outside the customs gate. We kissed cheeks while the scurrying luggage boys fought over my suitcases and the tip, then we grabbed the first taxi for the trip to Julieta's house. It was hot, sultry and muggy. Dark, gray, rain clouds hung thick and low in the sky. I was already soaked in sweat.

The taxicab bounced and jolted through the pot-holed streets of Guayaquil while the driver cursed at other drivers for cutting him off. Noise and dust were swirling inside the taxi like hypnotic dancers, whirling everything into a blur. I leaned my forehead against the back seat window, remembering the bureaucratic quagmire that had driven me to write my scathing letter to the commander of the Navy.

"Your letter was in the newspaper." Pancho said sharply, waking me out of my daydreaming. The taxi was stopped at a red light, revving its engine to keep it from stalling. "The headlines called it a buccaneer style letter. A veiled threat directed at the Commander General of the Navy."

"Oops. That's not good, is it?" I replied. Pancho ignored the comment.

"They're calling you La Bucanera (the female buccaneer)." Pancho went on, obviously irritated. "Margie, why didn't you tell me about the letter before you sent it? This isn't the United States. You can't do things like that. Especially when Julieta and I are responsible in front of our government for all your actions. You have put us in a very bad position. We might lose the contract completely."

"They can't do that!" I huffed, sitting forward on the taxi seat to dry the sweat on my back. "You said we have acquired rights under Ecuadorian law. They can't just cancel the contract."

"Margie, we have the law on our side, yes, but we have to be careful not to make enemies who could delay the reinstatement of the contract."

"Well, I had to stir things up a bit." I said, trying to defend myself. "Nothing was happening, everybody was just pushing the papers around."

"Margie, you said the Ministry of Defense had no intention of completing the contract. You accused the commander of cheating."

"I didn't mean him. I meant the government was cheating."

"That's not what the letter said."

"So my Spanish isn't that good. I was just bluffing anyway."

Pancho was genuinely mad at me for the first time in our relationship. I suddenly realized I had put the treasure hunt in real jeopardy.

"Let's not beat the bush around," Pancho said. "You have to make a personal apology to the commander or we will never get the contract."

"That's beat around the bush, Pancho. And I will apologize. I'll do whatever you say."

"And no more bluffing!" Pancho said sternly.

"No more bluffing." I agreed.

The taxi dropped us off in front of Amelia's apartment building. I dreaded going upstairs. Pancho's reprimand was docile compared to what Julieta could unleash at me. She was pacing like a caged panther when we entered the living room.

"Diós mio, Margarita! Qué pasa?" Julieta said disdainfully, putting her hands on her hips. "What's the matter with you? Why did you insult the commander?" She stopped pacing and glared at me, waiting for an answer.

291

"It was never my intention to insult him." I said honestly holding my hands up like someone was pointing a gun at me. "I'll never do it again. I promise."

"Ay! Margarita!"

"Maybe we can convince the commander that Margie does not know how to write in Spanish and the letter is an unfortunate mistake," said Pancho reassuringly. "Can you take her to see the commander yourself, Julieta?"

"I can call my cousin." Julieta sighed. "He went to school with the commander. He can explain the situation for us. But Margarita still has to apologize in person."

"Oh, I will, I will," I jumped in. "I'll do exactly what you tell me to do. And I'll never write another letter as long as I live."

"No more letters!" Pancho repeated forcefully.

"No more letters!" I conceded, holding up the three-fingered Girl Scout sign. Then I wiggled the three fingers and added, "but you gotta admit - my letter sure lit the fire under some bureaucratic butts."

Our serious partner meeting ended in laughter but I knew I had pushed things too far. Julieta and her little black telephone book would have to save me. Knowing when to retreat should be written into every handbook for aspiring treasure hunters.

We left Amelia's apartment, lugging all my suitcases back downstairs to stuff them into another taxi for the ride to the boat.

A taxi ride in Ecuador is a mini-adventure in itself because you never know what part of the car will be missing. Floorboards often had holes clear through to the road, or door handles only existed on the outside of the car. Once in awhile you got one with no brakes or an engine that sounded as if it only had one speed. Missing windows were commonplace, especially in Guayaquil where the heat made them a useless commodity anyway. Shocks were too expensive to replace, windshields were non-existent even if you wanted to replace them and steering linkages were as precious as diamonds.

The taxi we had flagged down for our excursion to the boat seemed to be missing this last item, the steering linkage. The driver, or "chofer" as they are called, made six complete turns of the steering wheel before the taxi changed direction and we turned onto the waterfront street where I saw the *Hooker's Holiday* floating listlessly beside her pilings in the river.

The firemen from the fireboats that were moored in front of the *Hooker*, were the first ones to see me as the taxi rolled to a stop. The fireboat siren started wailing to get Kevin's attention and four short, dark-skinned firemen in blue tee shirts ran down the dock to greet me as Pancho and I yanked my suitcases out of the trunk and plunked them down on the curb.

"OYE Margarita, La Bucanera! La Bucanera!" the firemen were shouting as they came closer. The whole waterfront came instantly alive. Even the beggars looked happy to see me, smiling and waving at me as if I was a homecoming queen.

"Hey Bucanera!" Kevin shouted from the dock. He had tied off his rubber dinghy to the 80-year old fireboat and was maneuvering his way past the crab fishermen, and buckets to get out to the street.

"I'll be going, Margie." Pancho said hurriedly as he got back into the taxi. "I'll see you after your meeting with the commander."

"Hasta luego." I grinned, just before Kevin grabbed me and hugged me. Car horns were blaring, kids were running, ice-cream ,vendors were ringing their bells. Gosh it was good to be home.

"You'll have to climb over the fireboats to get down to the dinghy." Kevin was saying as he held my hand and led me through the maze of dock dwellers. "The floating platform got washed away," he said. "Don't step in the fish guts."

"Where's the ramp?" I questioned, when I got to the end of the dock and stared thirty feet straight down at the muddy brown river swirling past. The dock was perched high above the river, on spindly, manglar tree trunks with only a four inch wide plank bridging the eight foot gap between the end of the dock and the two fireboats.

"Just don't look down." Kevin advised me as he sprinted across the plank.

"Right," I said, looking down at the broken off pilings jutting upward from the river bed like a torture pit

"Margee you can do it. Don't be a sissy." Kevin goaded me on.

"Oooooh, I don't know," I whined as I slid one foot along the plank. "Isn't there another way?"

"Come on. I do it twice a day."

"Why?"

"Because, I spend so much time in the hammock, that if I didn't make myself get off the boat, I'd turn into a sloth."

Kevin knew I was keeping him talking so I didn't have to walk the plank. It was only eight feet from the end of the dock to the fireboat, but that wasn't what was scaring me. It was the fact that the other end of the plank was moving, sliding back and forth as it rested on the top handrail on the roof of the fireboat. There was nothing to hold onto as you crossed. You had to trust your balance.

"Come on now." Kevin continued. "Stand up straight, deep breath. Just do it."

Like Butch Cassidy and the Sundance Kid yelling their fool heads off as they jumped off a cliff, I held out both arms for balance and ran across the plank, screaming all the way. At the other side I threw caution to the wind and jumped off the plank, landing with a thud on the roof of the fireboat's wheelhouse. A roar of laughter and clapping rose up from the firemen and a crowd of pedestrians that had gathered along the river front to watch the spectacle.

"La Bucanera, La Bucanera!" the firemen were cheering again.

I curtsied to the crowd and the firemen and scurried down the vertical ladder to the main deck of the fireboat. The railings, and now my hands, were covered in grease. I had to crawl over the railings of the small fireboat to get to the larger, old fireboat as they bashed together in the rocking swells of the river. Then I had to hang from the railing of the old fireboat to jump down into our rubber dinghy waiting in the river. Who needs an aerobics class, I thought, as I landed amongst my suitcases, on the aluminum floor of the dinghy. The front of my clothes was now stained with diesel fuel because the firemen always wiped the boats down with diesel to make the paint look shiny.

"Welcome back, sweetie," greeted Kevin as he started the outboard motor and we puttered out into the river towards the *Hooker's Holiday*. "You'll get used to the plank. In a couple days you'll be doing it with your eyes closed."

"Sure." I said, doubtfully.

Once onboard the *Hooker* I walked around the back deck, nostalgically touching the workbench, the winches and the engine room door. I peered down the side to see the blue outhouse still hanging off the starboard rail. Plastic tarps covered the compressors, polypropylene ropes held the spare anchors in place, and coiled around some overhead air hoses was the unmistakable tail of a monkey. "Breeeep," it chirped, almost like a bird. Then it iran along the air hose, waving it's tail in the air for balance and disappeared behind the smoke stack.

"That's Hairball." Kevin remarked as he dragged my suitcases into the galley. "It's a marmoset. Look at the white fur above his eyes. Isn't it cool?"

"This is something right out of the jungle, isn't it?"

"Initially yes." Kevin admitted, "But I got it at the mercado. It was either Hairball, or a baby crocodile. Hairball eats less."

I followed Kevin into the galley and sat on the vinyl bench seat behind the galley table. Kevin slid into a chair across from me and we held hands stretched across the table.

"I really missed you." he said gazing solemnly into my eyes. "I mean I *really* missed you."

"I missed you too. This isn't fun anymore, is it?" I said grimly.

"Not when they threaten to throw you in jail."

"Do you want to quit?"

"Do you?"

"I asked you first."

"Oh no. You're not gonna pin the end of this project on me."

"Why not? You're the reason we started it."

"I might have thrown the ball, but you're the one who caught it and ran with it. This is your project now, babe."

"So do you want to quit and go back to selling scuba gear?"

"Do you think you can get out of this mess with the commander of the Navy, without losing the contract?"

"Probably," I said semi-confidently.

"Then I'll hang in there a little longer. I'm growing fond of rice and beans. Hey. I love you."

"I love you too." I smiled, squeezing his hands till it hurt. "You know you're my best friend, don't you?"

"Only because I cook for you." Kevin smirked, getting up from the table, stretching his fingers to get the blood circulating again after I released my grip. "Are you hungry?"

"Yeah. Where's that monkey?" I said, looking under the table.

Kevin and I eased back into a relaxed routine on the boat. The galley table being the natural center of activity, we used it for card playing, story telling, eating, chart drawing and monkey business. Hairball ate his bananas there while we read books or newspapers.

In one old book I was reading, printed in 1855, I came upon the true meaning of the term 'buccaneer.' It seems I had more in common with these unjustly treated pioneers than I cared to admit. The book said this about buccaneers:

The name Buccaneer, which originally signified one who dried or smoked flesh in the manner of the Indians, was given to the first French settlers of St. Domingo, who hunted wild boars and cattle, in order to sell the hides and flesh to their more settled neighbors. They lived in huts built on patches of cleared ground, just sufficiently large to admit the drying of skins. These spots were named Boucans, and the huts, which were commonly only temporary, Ajoupas, terms borrowed from the native Indians. With the more regular Spanish settlers on the same island they were continually at war, and therefore concealment was, in some degree, necessary: the motives of the Spaniards for this persecution being jealousy of the presence of all other Europeans.

The tennants of the Boucans, having neither women nor children, congregated in parties, each keeping a servant, who, being some adventurer from Europe, was obliged to bind himself for three years to an older Boucaneer, in order to gain a footing in the community; more a companion, however, than a servant, the fruits of their labors were enjoyed in common; and, in cases of death, the domestic regularly succeeded to the property of his master. In process of time some, tired of this occupation, settled as planters in the little island of Tortuga, situated at a short distance from the north side of St. Domingo, to which they were, by degrees, driven by the repeated massacres of the Spaniards. Others commenced free-booters by sea, amply revenging upon that nation the injuries sustained by their companions on land. Success continually added to their confidence and to their numbers. They seldom at first, acted together, but in parties of from fifty to two hundred men each, embarked in small boats, ill adapted either to war or security from the elements, and would attack the largest vessels, overpowering them by a desperate bravery which nothing could withstand. Thus they fought their way to riches and power. Thus far, they became knonwn, as pirates.[7]

On June 8, 1990, after I apologized to the commander of the Navy, all the turmoil of the bureaucratic battle was ended by the signing of Presidential Decree number 1571. It declared that three Ministers had the power to sign salvage contracts on behalf of the country of Ecuador. The Director of Cultural Heritage was silenced, and promptly resigned. The Decree cleared the way for our contract to be reinstated, but of course, nothing happens that easily in Ecuador.

A three-month teacher strike took priority when the third Minister returned from his ordeal in Congress. A cholera epidemic busied all other branches of government. We stayed on the *Hooker* most of the time to avoid contact with people or mosquitoes carrying viruses.

The hot, rainy season returned again, the sixth one we had endured on this treasure quest. Dengue fever was rampant in Guayaquil along with several cases of malaria, whose victims sought care at the tropical disease clinic five blocks from our boat.

If anyone had asked me how to characterize our host country, I would have said: Ecuador is a place where you ALWAYS check your shoes for cockroaches and you ALWAYS look a gift-horse in the mouth. In the lethargic heat of January 1991, I had forgotten that second part.

On one sweltering hot, moldy, mid-day afternoon, when the sun was straight overhead and the air hung still and heavy in a colorless sky, Greg Gino came walking back into my life.

I was sitting in the bow of a twenty-foot dug-out canoe we had purchased after our rubber dinghy had developed too many leaks. I'd been waiting in the sun, bobbing up and down in the river, for two hours with the canoe chain-locked to a floating platform that the firemen had constructed to support their latrine. The smell was unbearable but I couldn't leave because Kevin had the only key to the chain padlock. I was spitting mad and cursing Kevin under my breath when this pudgy, gray-haired gringo came sauntering down the dock, pointing at the *Hooker's Holiday* and asking for Margarita.

"Hello, Greg." I said, matter-of-factly. "What brings you down to the bowels of Guayaquil?"

"Well hello, Margaret," Greg said, looking around to see where my voice was coming from. His eyes looked lower and lower until they focused on me in my canoe. "I thought you were long gone years ago," he added, seeming surprised.

"No. I'm still here, tied to the friggin' pilings, still fighting with the governmen," I summarized.

"I thought your contract was canceled." Greg said inquisitively.

"It was just suspended, not canceled," I corrected him. "Now the damn lawyers can't agree on the wording of the new contract."

"Well, I can help you with that." Greg beamed. "I've got lots of contacts in Quito."

"Let's see," I said, looking skyward. "The last time you said you were going to help me, I waited two months in Manta for you to show up with your gradient magnetometer."

"You're still sore about that, huh? Why don't you let me make it up to you? If you've got legal problems I can set you up with a friend of mine in the Attorney General's office. This lawyer can get you out of any mess." Then he leaned over to rest his elbows on the dock railing. "I can get you that contract in two weeks with my connections in Quito. Let me know if you want my help. Be seeing ya around."

Greg Gino was gone by the time Kevin showed up with a coil of rope slung over his shoulder and two cans of paint swinging in each hand. I told Kevin about Greg's visit as we paddled the canoe back to the *Hooker*.

Kevin couldn't believe I was even thinking about hooking up with Gino after he had left us hanging in Manta four years ago,

300

and we had never found any treasure with Gino's fancy satellite technology. 'The guy's a liar' Kevin kept saying, 'You can't trust him.'

Many times I should have listened to Kevin's intuitive advice, but like all the other times, I didn't. Pancho and Julieta weren't making any progress with the government so I made a deal with Greg Gino to get me the new contract, agreeing to pay him two percent of the treasure if he were successful.

At first, my working relationship with Greg Gino seemed normal. He had a decent office on the respectable side of Quito in a building that was occupied by other mining companies. He had used his satellite technology to locate a gold mine in the Amazon jungle. Pictures of excavation equipment stationed along a riverbank were taped to the office walls.

Greg made contact with the lawyer at the Attorney General's office who wasted no time in reviewing my documents and coming up with a plan of attack. The lawyer would write a final version of the contract and have it approved by the Attorney General. That way, the lawyers at the ministerial level were not responsible for the wording of the contract.

Greg's "two weeks" stretched into three months by the time the final version of the contract was formally typed on legal paper with the signature and seal of the Attorney General filling the whole last page. Then it was delivered to the Ministers.

The Ministers pushed it around on their desks for another two months until it was decided that a meeting should be convened to properly approve the document. The underlying problem was that ours was the first contract under the new Presidential Decree and nobody wanted to be the first to sign it.

Easter Holy Week came and went. The dry season settled in accompanied by the winds that signaled the end of the calm weather at our wrecksite. We'd missed the whole working season again. Kevin was discouraged. Pancho and Julieta blamed me for the endless delay. And Greg Gino was spending more time at his mine in the jungle than in Quito. In July, when I couldn't figure out why everything had come to a halt, I met the witch.

Chapter Twenty Two

Marieana, my quick-thinking, level-headed, dear friend from Romania, whom I always trusted, who had seen me through the most impoverished times of my life, had insisted I come to Quito to meet a man from Chile. Marieana was doing well these days. She had a job as an architect and lived in a small, three-bedroom house with her new boyfriend, Hector. I had no reason to suspect anything strange when she had asked me to come to Quito to meet her Chilean house guest.

I arrived at about seven o'clock in the evening, dressed warmly for the chilly Quito nights. I kept my jacket on as I sat on one of the overstuffed couches, rubbing my hands together to keep them warm.

"Can I get you some hot tea?" Marieana asked as she bent over and kissed me on the cheek.

"Yes please," I said energetically. "I'd forgotten how cold it is here at night. How's Hector?"

"I'm fine," Hector said as he came through the kitchen door carrying two cups of steaming hot tea. Before we could talk any further there was a knock at the door.

"Adelante," Marieana said with a big smile as she opened the door and a medium-built man with dark, wide eyes walked in. He was a little hesitant as he came inside, shaking Hector's hand and then glancing at me with a familiar look that seemed to ease his tenseness. He nodded politely then sat down on the couch opposite me.

"Manuel doesn't speak any English," Marieana said as she sat down beside me. "I'll translate for you if there is anything you don't understand."

I continued smiling at Manuel while out of the side of my mouth I said to Marieana, "What's this all about?"

"Remember all those nights we used to stay up late talking about the universe and powers of the mind, and you told me all the theories about how the mind uses energy to create what you are thinking?"

"Yes," I said slowly, still smiling at Manuel.

"Manuel has developed those powers since he was a child," Marieana continued. "He came to Ecuador three years ago looking for a blond, North American woman who had an important project that would make her very famous. It's you he's looking for, I'm sure of it."

"Don't do this to me," I said through clenched teeth. "I promised Kevin I wouldn't get mixed up with anymore weirdoes."

"He's not a weirdo. He's a brujo. A male witch. But he prefers to be called a para-psychologist."

Both Hector and Manuel were staring at me anxiously. I noticed that Manuel was wearing blue jeans and a tee shirt. He looked ordinary enough, someone you see on the street any time of the day. But his eyes, they were very dark. I couldn't see any pupils. He was smoking a cigarette, nervously tapping the ashes in the ashtray he was holding in his other hand. I smiled again and kept talking to Marieana.

"You know how many of these psychics I've tried, Marieana. Most of them were frauds. They never did what they said they could do."

"Manuel can," Marieana said with a determined, unyielding look on her face. "They tested him at the University of Santiago in Chile. He cured sick people. He dissolved a brain tumor in a nine-year-old boy. Just hear what he has to say. I haven't told him anything about your project. I just told him I had a North American friend that has blond hair."

"Wait til Kevin hears this one." I said to myself, shaking my head.

To my amazement, Manuel spoke very precisely, using medical terms and drawings to explain about his mental abilities. He said everyone is born with clairvoyant or precognitive or telepathic abilities, but since we don't train our children how to use them, by puberty they go dormant.

He was raised by his grandmother in a remote village in southern Chile where the mountains are filled with copper ore and one can find lots of artifacts from ancient civilizations. He had always had visions of future events and began keeping a systematic record of them during his teen years. It was his life's ambition to bring these abilities out in the open where they could be studied scientifically, not leave them shrouded in mystery, associated with witchcraft and sorcery.

He said he had traced the path of energy through the brain and knew that modern medicine had it all wrong. They were building their medical research based on incorrect assumptions about the energy flow. He said when we are in tune with the energy field of which the universe is made, we activate the part of our mind that contains all these abilities. He said the ancients had all these abilities because they practiced them and perfected them. But when they saw the arrival of the Spaniards in their world, they destroyed or hid all the tablets on which they had written the procedures. They even destroyed their own buildings and cities so the white man would not find the information or search further. The white man was not ready for this knowledge. They had not evolved enough, mentally or socially, to handle the powers without destroying themselves and most of the world.

Then he told me how, in his mind, he could magnify viruses millions of times larger than electron microscopes and that once he located the viruses in a body he could direct the body's energy flow to attack and kill them. He brought out a suitcase from one of the bedrooms and showed me case studies of several such experiments he had done at the university. Then he showed me cassette tapes on which he had documented all the verbal sessions he had conducted in groups with other people he had taught how to develop the skills. He insisted on playing one of the tapes, dated eight years ago. Marieana translated to me what the rapid voices on the tape were saying, because the Chilean dialect was difficult for me to follow.

"First they are being directed by Manuel to focus their thoughts on nothin," Marieana said with her ear to the cassette player, squinting to listen more intently. "Now two of them are saying they see a young blond woman, standing in North America and then standing on a blue boat somewhere between Columbia and Chile.... Another voice said I see her going underwater.... I see Manuel with her, standing on a beach, another said.... Manuel just asked if they knew what

306

year it is ... it's eight to ten years from now a voice said. Manuel is sitting on a beach with the woman, talking to her, the same voice said, the woman has a cloud around her. She has a problem, a heavy problem." There was a long silence then the first voice spoke again and Marieana sat up and looked at me with a stunned expression. "They are saying there are treasures all around the woman. Immense treasures." Then the tape was scratchy and Marieana could not make out the rest of the conversation. Manuel turned the tape off and laid the player on the floor.

"You are that woman," Manuel said to me in Spanish "I recognize you."

"Ah, just a minute here," I smiled disbelievingly. "You could have made that tape yesterday for all I know. Marieana, what do you expect me to do? Believe everything this guy says?" I stood up to stretch and the three of them thought I was going to leave.

"No, no, no." they shrieked in unison.

"There's more," Marieana pleaded, grabbing my hand to stop me from leaving.

"Silencio!" Manuel said in a commanding voice. "Margarita, quieres dar un paseo?"

He was asking me to go for a walk. I was thinking he might zap my brain into submission once he got me alone. Then I thought, you're wigging-out, Margaret. Get a grip. I agreed to a walk, but only down the street in front of the house. Manuel nodded in agreement.

I borrowed one of Marieana's thicker coats and a pair of gloves. It was now eleven o'clock at night. The street lights bathed us in a pink-amber glow as Manuel and I walked down the middle of the street, side by side, conversing in Spanish.

307

"You are not here by accident." he said calmly. "All the events in your life have prepared you to make a great discovery here in Ecuador. You were selected for this task. Do not reject the information I bring to you."

"I'm sorry," I said, trying to sound earnest. "I don't mean to offend you, but ..."

"You had a dream many years ago," Manuel interrupted me. "You dreamt you were going through a black hole on the bottom of the ocean and at the bottom of the hole, you were suddenly in a room full of gold objects stacked from the floor to the ceiling."

"How did you know that?"

"The memory is still very vivid in your mind."

"So you can read minds too?"

"Yes. So could you if you practiced. Margaret, I'm not here to perform tricks for you. I'm forty-five years old and have spent my entire life examining the functions of our minds. I have proved that psychic abilities are natural, that we can move objects with our minds, even kill people with a thought. You are extremely psychic but you suppress it with fear. You want to probe these ideas but the people around you keep you grounded in physical beliefs and concerns. I have seen us together in many visions, not just here in Ecuador but in the future."

"Look, I'm not worried about the future. I have enough to think about in the present."

"That is exactly why I am here. The future is changing. You are not in the pictures with the treasure anymore. There is a man on the boat now. A broad-shouldered gringo with clear eyes. He has gray hair but it is so close to his head it looks like he is almost bald. He is your worst enemy."

"You're describing Greg Gino," I chuckled, "and you're totally wrong. Greg has been helping me for the last six months to get my contract."

"No. He has only been helping you to get a contract written. It will not be signed. He wants you to go away. He wants to take over your project. One of your crew has agreed to work with him if you do not get the contract."

"Who?" I demanded.

"I can't see that clearly yet. I must work with the other two people I brought from Chile. They are waiting in a hotel around the corner."

"Oh, I see. You've got this whole thing planned."

"Margaret, if you choose not to believe me, I will return to Chile and not bother you again. It's your choice. We should go back to the house now. Marieana and Hector are worried about us."

It was midnight when I went to Marieana's back bedroom. Manuel had gone to the hotel to be with his friends. I didn't tell Marieana anything when we returned to the house. I was too unsettled. Manuel had been very accurate about many things. What if he was correct about Greg Gino? I had heard too much to sort it all out. My head was hurting. I was grateful when my eyes closed and my mind shut down for the night.

"We were worried about you two last night," Marieana said at the breakfast table the next morning. "You were out there for an hour. Manuel called to say he would be here tonight at ten o'clock for your decision. What does he mean?"

"I'm supposed to decide whether or not to believe him," I answered as I buttered my toast.

"You do believe him, don't you?"

"Let's say I'm curious. I don't totally believe him but the things he said last night really shocked me."

At ten o'clock that night Manuel appeared with two young men named Pablo and Juan. It was explained to me that it was more efficient for Manuel to guide the minds of his assistants while he stayed conscious and collected the data. It was also easier for them to work at night when people's minds are less active and usually less cluttered.

We returned to the hotel where the two young men laid down on a pair of twin beds and closed their eyes. Manuel spoke softly to them, guiding them into a deep state of meditation. I sat in a chair on the side of the room, apprehensive about witnessing my first mind reading session.

The assistants looked very peaceful, their hands were alongside their bodies, their shoes were off and they seemed to be barely breathing. Manuel stood between them, holding one arm up, palm skyward. The other arm he aimed towards Juan's head, his fingers pointing straight. Manuel said he was directing more energy to Juan.

In the next moment Manuel struck Juan's shoulder and Juan went instantly limp. Nothing on his body moved. Even his eyelids didn't twitch. He looked dead. Then Manuel did the same thing to Pablo, a swift slap to the shoulder and the body went limp. During the entire next hour those two bodies did not move at all except for a slight mechanical jerk of a hand when Manuel asked them to answer a question.

Manuel told them to start with the mind of the clear-eyed gringo, find out what he is planning to do with the contract, then move your hand when you are finished. A few minutes passed, then Pablo's hand jerked, then Juan's. The process continued with Manuel telling them to travel to a mind that Greg, the

310

gringo, was thinking about and collect information. Then we waited for the assistant's hand to jerk before we went on. I kept track of at least eight jumps we made from one mind to the next mind, all based on whether or not the mind was involved with my contract.

An hour later Manuel clapped his hands three times and the assistants opened their eyes. They seemed stiff, brittle, as if they hadn't used their limbs in years. Slowly they arched their necks, stretched and twisted until they sat up on the edge of the beds and nodded to Manuel.

They spoke very rapidly, describing to Manuel the thoughts they had seen in each mind they explored. Manuel asked questions, they answered. It was as though the assistants could not access the information until Manuel asked the question. Then they spoke freely, like a tape recorder. I heard enough of the conversation to know they had contacted the main people responsible for writing the contract and that there was a deliberate delay taking place, a delay controlled by the gringo.

"Go to the lawyer who wrote the contract," Manuel told me after the assistants had left the room. "Tell him you know that the gringo is delaying the contract. Tell him you will give the same amount of money the gringo offered. Ask him for the names of the others that the gringo has promised to pay."

"Why is Greg delaying the contract?" I asked. "And how much money has been offered?"

"Twenty thousand dollars to the first lawyer, smaller amounts to the others. While you are being delayed, the gringo is obtaining another contract for your area from a different part of the government. He has visions of using your boat and your crew to dig up your treasure. He knows what shipwreck you seek."

"That part is true," I said. "He has a map exactly like mine."

"If you continue to work with the gringo," Manuel went on, "you will lose everything."

Any doubts I had about Manuel were obliterated the following day when I met with the first lawyer. Not only did the lawyer confess what Greg had done, he even called Greg to prove it. I watched him dial Greg's phone number, then I picked up the extension phone to listen in on the conversation.

"Señor Gino," the lawyer said as soon as Greg answered. "I need the money you promised me."

"What money?" Greg demanded in an ill-tempered tone. I recognized Greg's voice immediately.

"The twenty thousand for writing Margarita's contract," the lawyer explained.

"Eso era para el retraso... (that was for the delay)" Greg said with obvious disputation.

My jaw dropped to the floor. I stared at the telephone receiver in my hand as if it were an alien contraption. I had heard it with my own ears, Greg was paying to hold back my contract.

From that point on I distanced myself from Greg. I went to each of the others he had made a deal with and offered to pay the same amount if my contract was signed immediately. In two weeks time the contract was signed and officially delivered to us with all the blue stamps and seals and recording numbers.

At Greg's house, the day after I received the contract, I called him a liar and a cheat. I told him I was on the extension phone when the lawyer had called him and I knew of his deceit. Greg denied everything but his words were without conviction. He knew it, and I knew it. He stormed out of the living room and came back with a paper saying we were no longer partners and that he was giving me back my two percent. He had already signed the document and thrust it at me like a dissatisfied teacher returning an unacceptable page of homework.

"We can't do business together if you don't trust me." Greg proclaimed.

"You're absolutely right," I replied, snatching the paper from his hand to check the signature. Then I stomped out of his house shouting, "Adios Greg."

I never saw him again.

PART THREE

Some luck lies in not getting what you thought you wanted
but getting what you have, which once you have it,
you may be smart enough to see,
it is what you would have wanted had you known.

Garrison Keillor

Chapter Twenty Three

By January of 1992, I had raised more money based on our new contract and was ready to go back to work in Manta. Three unproductive years had passed since the morning in the Manta harbor when the Port Captain had come out to tell us our contract was suspended. Three depressingly long years since we were up at dawn preparing to head back out to the site where the gold flakes had been discovered, and lost, in the space of one hour. Three dismal years since the electrifying moment when we believed we had found the treasure, only to be dragged away before we could dig it up.

My investors had rekindled their hopes of becoming overnight millionaires but my dive crew had scattered to the far corners of the world in search of jobs; none of them were available. I was so anxious to get back to the site that I made a hasty deal with a commercial diving company in New York to provide me with a crew and underwater excavation equipment. They sent me a forty foot cargo container filled with twenty-four thousand pounds of compressors, diving chambers, dive gear, winches, pumps and hoses, and a crew composed of five cocky divers from England and Ireland. Overzealousness is to blame for the preposterous events that resulted from this disastrous combination of men and machinery. On top of that, I had to learn English the way the English speak it.

The final ingredient I needed for a complete recovery team, was a captain. While Kevin and I had fought the paperwork wars in Ecuador, Captain Cooke had gotten married and taken a day-job close to home. His new wife was not about to let him skip the country in search of dubious fortunes.

As I racked my brain, trying to think of someone crazy enough to go on a treasure hunt, Captain Glenn Miller came to mind. I wasn't actually thinking of Glenn, that cantankerous old coot, I was thinking of his son, Zachary.

Glenn had died in a helicopter crash shortly after I left him at the dock in Florida, at the end of the Bahamian expedition. Other than a condolence letter, I had not communicated with Zachary in ten years. I figured the Bahamas was ancient history by now and Zach wasn't the kind to hold grudges. When I finally found him in Santa Barbara, sitting in front of a computer screen writing magazine articles, he was a pale, overweight, reclusive shadow of his former fun-loving self. All I did was mention the shipwreck in Ecuador and he started packing.

With all the pieces put back together again we headed back to Ecuador, eventually anchoring in Manta with high expectations, and a mild, but evident, uneasiness among the crew. Had I taken control at that time, acknowledging the stress lines forming between my inharmonious band of divers, I might have altered the outcome, but I was too busy to notice and missed the opportunity.

The first diver quit the same day we arrived in Manta. It was too hot for him. The second problem arose when we unloaded the cargo container and realized the equipment was all second-hand, used junk that had probably been sitting for years in the back lot of the New York diving company. The third complication involved the renting of a wooden fishing boat called the *Lucciola*, to carry all the gear that had arrived by container. And the fourth bit of bad luck revealed itself as the El Niño weather phenomenon.

Extreme high tides bashed the boats around whenever we tried to anchor them side by side, or tie up to the docks to receive water and fuel. We were forced to lash the boats together, cramming twenty tires between their hulls to keep the *Hooker's* metal rub rails from tearing the *Lucciola* apart.

Heavy rains inundated the coast of Ecuador, cutting off roads and communication to the outside world. Visibility underwater was reduced to three inches making the divers cranky and irritable. Flooded streets in Manta delayed us for days when we came into port for provisions. Within the first three weeks everybody was miserable and not very receptive to the idea that I had brought Manuel and his assistants aboard to help us salvage the sunken treasures.

"She's off 'er bloody rocker." A British diver spouted off one night at the galley table after dinner had been cleared away.

"Right you are, mate," Another concurred. "She told us she found gold the last time she was 'ere. We don't need no stinkin' fortune tellers."

"Listen lads," the first diver spoke again. "I'll bet ten quid there's no treasure 'ere at all. We might as well find a pub in town and 'ave ourselves a nice vacation."

"I didn't come 'ere for no bloomin' vacation!" a diver named Steve growled, pounding his fist on the table. "Why don't ya give the blokes a chance. They might tell us something."

"We've already been 'ere a fortnight." Les, the first diver said. "All we've done is bust our balls humpin' equipment around, and bury ourselves divin' in a mud 'ole. I say we get Maggy up 'ere for a lit'l chat." The others nodded in agreement.

"Oh Maggy, darlin'," Les called downstairs. "Might we 'ave a word with ya luv?"

I warily entered the galley followed by Kevin, Zach and Charlie, who formed the American contingent of our multinational crew. They were not going to miss any battles between the Yanks and the Brits.

When the British divers had taken over the diving control systems on the back deck and changed everything to their liking, Charlie had adapted quite easily, having spent a good portion of his diving career working in the North Sea. He knew how tempers could fly on those oil platforms north of the United Kingdom and had strategically leaned himself against the bulkhead, close to the galley door. Kevin, Zach and I pulled our chairs right up to the table and faced our limey friends eye to eye.

"What's on your mind?" I asked them in general, looking around the table with a pleasant smile. Les, the biggest and loudest of the group, hiked up his drooping swim trunks and spoke up first.

"We 'eard you were bringin' some psychologicals on board. Are you 'avin' some doubts about the 'ole we're diggin', Maggy?"

"Not doubts exactly." I responded, attempting to sound intellectual. "I simply have a scientific curiosity regarding the abilities of some para-psychologists from Chile. They proved to me in Quito that they have some extraordinary talents that could be applied to what we are doing here on the ocean floor, that's all."

Jerry was the next diver to speak. He was a timid sort with fragile hands that seemed out of place on a diving rig. He owned a pub in Manchester. His inexperience had shown from the first day we started work. "I'm a lit'l curious meself," Jerry said, "What can they do?"

"They say they can see under the sediment," I explained. "They say they can take us right to the shipwreck."

"I thought you already found the shipwreck," Les said a bit tiffed.

"We *think* we found the shipwreck," I clarified.

"What about the gold flakes?" said Les.

"Yeah, what about the gold flakes?" Lou repeated, raising the volume of the discussion. Lou was from Ireland, full of spite, eager to jump into a fight just for the sport of it. He wore baggy shorts, and galoshes with metal reinforced toes, to be on the safe side he told me. He was a jokester when the beer bottle was out, a capable hand at work time and a belligerent asshole when he didn't get his way when he thought he should.

"Don't get too pushy," Jerry said gently.

"Aw piss off Jerry," Lou said back to him.

"We weren't able to test the flakes," I said loudly to settle everybody down. "They were metallic and gold in color. We're here now to dig down and find out if it is the shipwreck. At the same time I'd like to experiment with the para-psychologists. If there are more wrecks around here and they can locate them, it would save us a lot of searching."

"That's reasonable," said Steve, from the corner of the room. Steve had assumed the role of lead diver. He was the silent, lethal type that watched his adversaries for weaknesses before he struck. His rugged face and tight body matched his commanding air right down to the military tattoo burned into his left forearm.

"Bloody Hell, it's reasonable," Lou spoke again. "We're wasting our time."

"Back off, Lou," Les ordered. "Maggy's the boss 'ere. Why don't you get yourself a girly magazine and go to bed."

"Ahhh. The girls are too skinny in these American books." Lou cooled his temper.

"Right you are," Les grinned. "I likes fat girls meself. They're more appreciative."

I learned that evening that British dive crews were run by force. When I left the galley, Kevin and Zach followed me. Charlie, having a better feel for foreign diplomacy, had slipped out the galley door, meeting up with us down in the crew's quarters.

"I don't like Steve," Kevin sneered.

"Why?" I asked. "He wasn't the jerk, Lou was."

"He's wrecking all our equipment," Kevin said. "He never puts anything away. And he never helps out with any of the chores on the boat, he just sits there like he's some king or something."

"He's not your worst problem Margee," Charlie added. "That Lou is a fighter."

"We better watch Les," Zach said. "He's bigger than all of us."

"What's going on here?" I snapped. "The war with England was over two hundred years ago. We're supposed to be civilized."

"The British don't forget," Charlie said prophetically.

We all went to bed then, but I had the feeling this was just the beginning of a deteriorating alliance.

The next day I brought Manuel and his Chilean assistants out to the *Hooker* in our twenty-five foot fiberglass launch. They had been staying at an apartment I rented in town. The dive crew was hard at work digging in the muck, blasting out an alluvial fan of sediment from the airlift. The Chileans climbed on board and immediately sat down on the port side of the boat facing the burst of sediment. After a few minutes with their eyes closed, they reported to Manuel and Manuel reported to me.

"There is nothing in this hole you are digging. There is nothing around here for two hundred meters in any direction," Manuel said, circling his arm around in a sweeping motion. I was thankful none of the British divers understood Spanish.

"Are you saying there are no shipwrecks around here?" I asked timidly.

"There are two wrecks in this bay. One of them is right over there." Manuel pointed to the northeast, about a thousand meters from our current position. "Do you always dig square holes?"

"No." I looked at him with surprise. "We dig round holes."

"Pablo says you are digging a square hole and your diver is digging much deeper on the south side of the hole."

I walked over to Steve our lead diver who was on the communication set, talking to the diver down below. The sounds of compressors and gurgling bubbles made it hard to hear.

"How deep are we?" I asked, with my hands cupped around my mouth. It was a usual thing for me to check on our progress throughout the day.

"Les is down approximately ten feet," he answered shouting into the wind. "But 'e's down further on the south side. "'E says it's softer there."

"And what shape is the hole?" I shouted above the roar of diesel engines.

"We made it square this time. With this bad visibility it's easier to keep track of where you are with flat walls instead of curved ones. What does Manuel say?"

I switched off the communication set before I leaned closer to Steve's ear and told him the bad news. Steve nodded in acknowledgment and went back to checking air gauges. I led Manuel and his two assistants into the galley, away from the loud noises on the back deck, and offered them some tea.

"If you move your boat now, to the other location, you will recover the treasure within a week," Manuel said as he squeezed a lemon over his cup of tea.

"How do you know?" I asked him, still reluctant to accept everything he told me, even if he had been consistently right so far.

"Reading minds is hard," he said, smiling, "Finding shipwrecks, that's easy."

"And what about your assistants?" I asked further. "What are they getting out of all this?"

"They have agreed to use whatever money you give us to build my institute. They will study at the institute and be paid a salary."

"Ah huh. And what are you expecting me to pay you for showing me the wrecks?"

"Ten percent."

At that moment Steve came storming into the galley with his hands clenched into fists.

"We've reached bedrock Margaret, and there is no gold, nor any shipwreck. Everybody's pissed. And you better send Jerry 'ome." Steve growled, "'E never should've been sent on this job. 'E's an idiot. 'E's not even a diver."

"Excuse me," I said to Manuel, turning my back to him and leading Steve outside by the arm. "All right, what's the problem?" I shouted at the divers who were all standing around the back deck with their arms crossed over their chests. Les had come up from his dive. Sea water was dripping off his wetsuit while he disconnected the hoses that were attached to his dive helmet. Charlie, Zach and Kevin were on one side of the deck and the rest of the crew was on the other side.

"They're destroying our equipment," Kevin said, pointing to a bent capstan on the stern of the boat. "They've ripped it right out of the deck."

"It's too small," Lou remarked, "It can't take the strain."

"Not when you try to lift a three hundred pound anchor with it," Zach stated as he pointed at the crane. "That's what the crane is for. Those capstans are only used for mooring lines."

"And they lost my pair of fins," Charlie said, obviously upset.

"Kevin, could you bring up some more fins," I asked.

"Why should we?" Kevin said smugly, "Why didn't they bring their own fins?"

"That gear is always supplied on a dive job," Steve yelled. "The only thing a diver brings is 'ees wetsuit."

"You mean none of you brought your personal gear?" I asked in disbelief. The British side of the deck all shook their heads no.

"That's standard in the North Sea," Charlie advised me. "They do everything different there."

"We do it RIGHT!" Lou shouted. "You Yanks do everything backwards. Your dive panel was all screwed up when we got 'ere."

"Irrelevant!" Steve bellowed. "The worst problem 'ere is Jerry. 'E hasn't got a clue about what 'e's doing. Someone's gonna get 'urt."

We all turned our attention to Jerry who was sitting in a folding chair with one pale-white, skinny leg crossed over the other. He had a shy, forlorn look on his face.

"I've never dove before," he said meekly. "I usually monitor air pressures on an offshore job."

Now Kevin and Zach and Charlie shook their heads negatively.

"Send 'im some," Steve said.

"I can't afford to," I shouted back at Steve. "It cost too much money to get you all here. I can't afford to replace him. That's the end of this discussion! Dismantle that stern capstan and put it in the launch. I'll take it in to get repaired. Charlie, please go down to the compressor room and bring up my pair of fins for these guys. I want this hole enlarged to make sure we haven't missed anything. Now get back to work!"

Everybody grumbled as they shuffled to their positions on the deck, and prepared the next diver to go in the water. I realized nobody was on my side, not even Kevin. When the capstan was lowered into the launch and the extra gas cans were filled, I started up the launch's outboard motor and drove Manuel and his assistants back to the Manta harbor.

When I returned about two hours later I went straight to my cabin without talking to anybody. I was only lying on my bunk for a few minutes when I jumped up at the sound of someone banging on my cabin door, shouting. *"Margee, get out here right now!"*

"What is it?" I shrieked as I swung the door open to see Charlie, literally shaking, with a look of horror on his face.

"Steve punched Jerry in the face!" Charlie ranted. "Knocked him right to the deck. There's blood everywhere."

I raced up the stairs, ran through the galley and shot out to the back deck. Les was straining to hold Steve back against the stern crane while Lou and Zach were picking Jerry up off the deck. A blood-soaked rag was covering Jerry's swollen face.

" 'E almost killed the diver!" Steve yelled as he fought to free himself from Les's strangle hold on him.

" 'E just got mixed up," Lou said in Jerry's defense.

" 'E's a bloody lunatic!" Jerry spat out, jabbing his finger in the air at Steve. " 'E oughta be locked up!"

"Take Jerry down to my cabin," I barked harshly. "And lock the door." Then I blasted out an order that everyone could hear. "There'll be NO MORE VIOLENCE on this boat! Les, don't you let Steve loose until he's cooled off."

"Aye, aye, Maggy. Anything you say, luv."

Down in my cabin Jerry was stretched out on the bed, holding a cold compress to his left eye. When he pulled the compress away to show me his face, I saw the one inch gash on his upper cheek still oozing blood out of a golf-ball sized lump that had formed on the black and blue skin. His eye was swollen shut. It looked terribly painful.

"He needs stitches," Charlie said, rinsing out the compress in a bowl of cold water and handing it back to Jerry. Kevin and Zach were watching from the doorway.

"Do you think you can make the trip back to Manta in the launch?" I asked Jerry.

"I think so," Jerry replied weakly. "But I'll not go past Steve on the back deck. And I'm not comin' back."

"I'll arrange a flight home for you tomorrow," I said. "For now, you guys sneak Jerry out through the wheelhouse door and take him to the doctor in Manta. I'll keep Steve occupied on the back deck."

"I'm going home too," Charlie said. "I'll probably be the next one Steve hits."

I didn't say anything, just lowered my head and left the makeshift infirmary on my way to the back deck to deal with Steve. As I passed through the crew's quarters I saw Lou stuffing his clothes in his duffel bag.

"I'm leaving," said Lou in disgust. "You can't control Steve."

Again I said nothing, just continued up the stairs on my journey to meet Steve the bully. Les and Steve were having a calm conversation as I approached them on the back deck. Steve was wrapping duct tape around one of the compressor hoses. Les was grinning as usual. All the engines had been shut down, the quiet felt strange, unfamiliar, like entering a forest from a bustling metropolis. The only thought that flashed through my mind was 'I wonder if Steve hits girls too.'

"'E 'ad it comin' to 'im," Steve said before I could speak.

"So what did he do that warranted getting smashed in the face?" I said with my hands on my hips, trying to look powerful and unafraid.

"I told 'im to take up the slack on the dive 'ose and instead, he paid out more 'ose on top of the diver. Could'a killed the diver. You think I like punching people?"

"I don't know," I shrugged. "I don't know you. Maybe you're one of those guys that gets his kicks beating people up."

"Not Steve, Maggy," Les spoke first. "That's just 'ow Steve runs a dive job."

"You mean he's done it before?"

"At least once a job," Les said, unbothered by it. "Let's the lads know who's in charge. No squabblin' see."

"Well that's not how things are run on this boat, get it?" I glared at both of them. "Half the crew is packing to leave."

328

"Tell 'em to stay," Steve said "I'm the troublemaker, I'll leave."

"I don't want anyone to leave," I said quickly. "I just want your promise there'll be no more violence. We've still got excavating to do."

"On what?" Les asked. "There's no galleon down there."

"I have another location in mind," I smiled. Inside I was thinking those gold flakes must have been brass shavings after all.

Just then the launch sped away from the starboard side of the boat with Kevin at the wheel and Charlie propping Jerry up to keep him from falling over.

"We're taking the *Hooker* into port now," I dictated. "You boys haul in the stern lines and I'll get Zach to start up the main engines."

I left the two of them standing there awkwardly, without giving them a chance to say more. I preferred to end a discussion with me having the upper hand, one of my own techniques for letting the lads know who's in charge.

After all the tempestuous dust had settled, only Jerry left the boat for good. The other divers waited around to see what I might have up my sleeve as far as another location for the shipwreck.

In two days time we returned to the work site. Zach expertly pulled the *Hooker* alongside of the *Lucciola* and the two boats were lashed together again to ride out the still rough seas caused by the El Niño. When the engines were shut down and the stern anchors pulled taught, we gathered on the back deck to discuss the plan for locating the shipwreck by mental means.

First the Chileans would go up to the tuna tower, fifty feet above the main deck of the boat. There they would do their mental thing to localize the shipwreck and direct us to it.

I went up to the tuna tower with them to observe the process first hand. With one assistant standing behind the other, they closed their eyes for several minutes, turning slightly as if focusing in on a distant noise. Then they pointed to the northeast. By hand held radio, I sent out the launch and relayed the message to drop a buoy when the Chileans said the launch was right over the shipwreck. Once the buoy was set they all nodded in agreement that that was the spot.

The following morning we anchored beside the buoy, cranked up all the diesel engines to begin a massive excavation.

By the end of the next day the divers reached bedrock and found nothing. Les was getting a good laugh out of the situation, saying "Maggy's fortune tellers are knackered!"

"Blimy, 'ow could we 'ave missed the shipwreck?" Les exclaimed, grasping his forehead with one hand and his chest with the other. "We must've miscalculated. Well, kiss me britches."

"We should make you kiss the Blarney Stone in Ireland," Charlie joked.

"Lads," Lou shouted with a dreadful seriousness, "Don't *ever* kiss the Blarney Stone. Me brother pisses on it every time 'e gets drunk."

I left the galley in an uproar of laughter. None of them were taking our expedition seriously. I was starting to think I wasn't taking it seriously either. What if the investors knew I was digging holes where psychics were pointing? I needed to think on my own level, to arrive at my own conclusions about mental capabilities. I went to my cabin without eating and fell asleep with my clothes still on.

By the time I dragged myself up to the galley in the morning, the divers were already working stowing away equipment. Kevin had already cleared breakfast away and Zach was at the galley table, tinkering with some throttle levers he was trying to tighten.

"I suppose you want something to eat now," Kevin said in a snitty tone.

"I am pretty hungry," I said, rubbing the sleep out of my eyes.

"Then why don't you get up with the rest of us," Kevin griped.

"Forget it then. I'll get my own breakfast," I snapped back.

"Fine! And clean up your mess when you're finished."

"Yes sir!"

"Now don't start fighting you two," Zach said as referee. "The last thing we need is another battle on this boat."

Kevin left the galley and I ignored him. I had more important things to attend to. The three Chileans had arrived in the launch and I asked them to accompany me to the bow where I always held my serious meetings.

"What's going on here?" I blasted at them in Spanish. "Are you playing with me?"

"I don't know what's wrong," Manuel shrugged.

"I'll tell you what's wrong," Pablo spoke for the first time. "Juan and I are not going to show you where the wreck is. We've decided we want our share of the treasure for ourselves, not for Manuel's stupid institute!"

"But we all agreed," Manuel said back, effectively cutting me out of the discussion by turning away from me. "We agreed we would all work together at the institute."

"We've decided we don't want to spend the rest of our lives learning what you know. We want to know now," Pablo said. Juan, the shorter one, stood close at his side, nodding affirmatively. "We want you to teach us how to read minds by ourselves, or we will never show Margarita where the shipwreck is."

"You greedy little bastards," I butted in, unable to hold my tongue. "You've been deliberately making us waste time and money digging useless holes."

"Margarita, please!" Manuel raised his voice.

"Don't Margarita m,." I shot at Manuel. "I thought you had some control over these two. Now I see you're at their mercy. Maybe you should teach them what they want to know so we can get on with the expedition."

"I can not," Manuel said coldly. "They are not mature enough to handle the ability. They will only bring destruction upon themselves and those around them."

"So that's it?" I huffed with my hands on my hips. "You're going to let them destroy me instead? Can't you see the wreck yourself?"

"No," Manuel admitted shamefully. "I must use their minds to locate it. I cannot direct my own mind if I am in trance."

"Well that's just great," I said, throwing my hands up in the air. "And you two would rather get nothing than show me where the wreck is?"

Pablo and Juan stood firmly in place with their arms crossed and said "Yes!"

I gave up. I wasn't going to beg them or force them. Manuel had failed me even though he had proved his superiority with mind powers. Greed overcomes all. I called the divers together on the back deck, thanked them for putting up with my crazy idea and told them we were heading back into port.

Before the sun set we were anchored in the Manta harbor. The Chileans were taken to shore in the launch and Kevin was busy as usual preparing dinner. When everything on the boat was cleaned and stowed away I invited the crew ashore for a few beers to ease the tension. Les was the first one in the launch and had the outboard motor humming before I could blink. We took the table at the far end of the patio under the Yacht Club awning and ordered Pilsner beer in the brown bottles.

It wasn't long before we were comrades again, slapping each other's back, making fun of American and British accents. When they were all real happy I asked for suggestions on the best way to continue searching for the wreck. Another round of beers were delivered to the table and I lost count of how many we had drunk so far. To my surprise, they lowered their voices, huddled together and came up with some well thought out plans for detecting shipwreck anomalies.

The best idea was Steve's. He promised to return to England and arrange to send me a pinger sub-bottom profiler that sent high-frequency sound waves to the ocean floor in a forty-foot-wide spread. The profiler was designed for shallow-water, high-resolution reconnaissance.

When we all returned to the boat halfway between tipsy and drunken stupor, we were three hours late. A cold, crusty dinner was sitting on the galley table. Kevin was nowhere in sight. The crew sat down to eat the dinner anyway but I, knowing I was in trouble, headed for my cabin to make my apologies to the chef.

"Hi sweetie," I said cheerfully, "hiccup. 'Scuse me."

"Dinner was ready at seven o'clock," Kevin said, rolling over on the bunk to look at me in disgust. "Dinner is *always* ready at seven o'clock. Where were you?"

"You know I took the crew out for a beer." I stiffened. "I'm sorry we were late. It's no big deal."

"Yes it is a big deal. What the hell did I spend two hours making dinner for if you weren't going to eat it. You could've sent someone back in the launch to tell me you'd be late. Or maybe invite me to have a beer with you. But no. You left me stranded on this boat while you all had a good time."

"Hey, they're up there eating your dinner right now. And I'm sorry I forgot about you. I assumed you were busy here."

"That's right. I'm always busy and you always forget about me."

"Keep it down. They'll hear us fighting."

"I don't give a shit if they hear us. I'm tired of being left out of all the meetings. Of having to keep the whole boat running. Of cooking for seven people. Of always being in the background."

"Geeze you're sounding like a bitchy housewife."

"So what if I am!"

"You've got an attitude problem Kevin. You chose to be in the background and let me deal with all the people and problems. And I'm not going to have a screaming match while the whole crew listens. If you wanna fight, we'll go to the apartment and fight!"

"That suits me just fine. Let's go!"

This was really serious. The both of us stomped up the stairs, our faces taught with anger. I told the crew that Kevin and I would spend the night at the apartment and nothing more.

Neither of us said a word the whole ride to shore. We still said nothing the entire walk to the apartment. We passed the door where the Chileans were staying and continued in silence up to the second level that was empty. When the door was closed behind us we each took opposite ends of the room like duelists and faced each other with crossed arms.

"OK," I said first. "What else do you want to bitch about?"

"Don't you see what's happening?" Kevin pleaded "Our roles are completely reversed. I'm at home cooking and cleaning like the woman and you're out there making a name for yourself like a man.

You're so obsessed with succeeding in this shipwreck salvage you've forgotten who you are."

"Well I am the one who got all the pieces together and raised all the money to do this in the first place. You think I should just stand back and let you take over? You think you deserve to be out in front taking all the glory when I made it happen?"

"Listen to yourself! You even talk like a man."

"I've practically had to become one to deal in a man's world. They don't give me any slack out there. If I look weak or don't swear as much as they do, they take advantage of me. I have to keep the investors happy, the divers happy, the government happy, Pancho and Julieta happy and you happy. Nobody pats me on the back when I do a good job. They just gripe at me when things are going bad. I'm supposed to have a solution to every problem and an alternate plan for anything that happens. You think I'm having fun playing this role?"

"You think I'm having fun playing a woman's role? Do you ever notice that the floors are always swept? That you never run out of spare parts? That the laundry is clean every week? That the food tastes good? No! You just expect it."

"Look, we've been married for sixteen years and it's been an abnormal relationship since we sold the ranch. Why are you bringing all this up now, in the middle of the expedition?"

"Because we're not finding anything, you're off believing in hair-brained psychics, and I'm sick and tired of putting our personal relationship second to this damn treasure hunt!"

"So what are you saying?"

"I'm saying it's time to decide which is more important; us or the treasure!"

"Are you giving me an ultimatum? Are you making me choose between you and the expedition?"

"Yes. Which is it going to be?"

In one of the most cold-hearted acts I've ever committed in my whole life, I tore off a blank sheet of paper from the desk notepad, held it out to Kevin as I slowly walked towards him, and said, "Sign off your two percent."

He was stunned. I was scared. The whole scene seemed unreal, like we were actors on a stage. A part of me was crying at the thought of losing him. Another part of me was calling him a deserter for walking out on me. Another part was chastising me for being so callous to choose cold metals over a warm love. And the last part, the male part, was saying don't back down, don't let this detail ruin your chance to be the first woman ever to recover a Spanish galleon.

A long silence was broken when Kevin cleared his throat and said, "So you choose the treasure over me."

"I don't choose it," I moaned. "I'm stuck with it. You could walk away right now, with no responsibilities to anybody. I can't. I have to answer to the people whose money I've spent. I borrowed from my parents to buy the boat. I have lawyers and accountants and partners to deal with. To do what we've done, I had to commit my life to using all my efforts to recover the shipwreck. I can't just walk away."

"You're not leaving any room for me."

"On the outside no. But on the inside, I love you. If you leave, I'll have to stay here and finish what I started. Please don't leave ... I don't want to do this without you."

My eyes were swelling with tears.

"I love you too," he whispered in my ear, as we grabbed each other and held on tight. "It's just so hard always being in your shadow."

"I'm sorry," I pouted, tears streaming down my cheeks. "I'll try to be more considerate. See, I am still the woman. I'm the one who's crying."

"That's not a good test these day," Kevin sniveled. "I'm crying too."

Then I saw his tears glistening in the moonlight and squeezed him harder. We made love in slow motion, tender caresses soothing the pain and stress and bruised egos. It didn't matter which gender we were. The yin and yang worked in either direction.

In the morning we were refreshed and rejuvenated and the whole crew noticed when we got back to the *Hooker*. Kevin made a splendid breakfast and I spelled out the plans for the day's workload, but something had changed. A tiny crack had developed, deep down inside, though on the surface everything seemed the same.

We brought the *Lucciola* back into port, stripped off all her diving equipment and loaded it back in the forty foot cargo container. While that was being done I packed up the Chileans and put them on a plane back to Chile.

When the equipment was cleared by customs, I sent it all back to New York on the first container vessel leaving Manta. The letter I faxed to the owner of the diving company simply said, 'Here's your junk back.'

Then I took the British divers back to Guayaquil on the bus that dropped us off at the entrance to the international airport. I paid the excess baggage fees and arranged for their flights that would take them back across the Atlantic ocean and out of my sight. We all shook hands at the departure gate, making empty promises to see each other again someday soon. That's when Steve lingered behind the rest to give me his parting message.

"This isn't over, Margaret," he said with sincerity. "I'll call you at the apartment when I've found the right sub-bottom profiler."

"I'll be waiting," I said in jest, not for a moment thinking it would ever happen. The only person I could count on was myself. I had quit putting my trust in others. They were only along for the ride.

Back in Manta, I gave Charlie and Zach extra spending money if they would stay on the boat while Kevin and I took a couple of days off. We never left town. We just stayed at the apartment, lounging on the balcony.

"You really believed in Manuel, didn't you?" Kevin asked when the conversation turned to metaphysics.

"Yes, I did." I answered truthfully. "He has a real power."

"You talked with him alot. Did he teach you anything?"

"He explained to me the nature of the universe. Do you want to hear what he said?"

"Sure, why not?"

Kevin fluffed up the pillow behind his back and nestled into the lounge chair for what he expected to be a long dissertation. I took a sip of my cola, then stared at him, grasping all his attention.

"Manuel said that enlightenment is just realizations: the realization that we are all pieces of the creative energy of the Universe: the realization that our true nature is not mortal, its energy: and the realization that the physical body was created from the elements of the planet Earth, so we could house our individual focal points of energy, on the physical plane."

"He said the body was necessary so we could receive information from the five senses and learn how to create and manipulate physical matter, through our thought processes."

"He said that when we realize these facts, everything changes for us. We see that life is an illusion. That the obtaining of goals or achievements or material possessions or status or relationships, are all pastimes, and by themselves, mean nothing."

"He said that understanding who we are and what we are a part of, is the only thing that matters. Because with that understanding, comes happiness, the end of searching for answers, and no fear of death. In fact, we would have no fear of anything because we would control the world around us, with our thoughts and beliefs."

"He said that after this 'realization' occurs to you, (which comes in an instant but must be remembered daily) you also see that nothing has changed. There are still people, cars, jobs, trees, televisions, money, success, failure, accidents, power struggles, famine, hate; all the things that were there before your 'realization.' But now you understand that these things are all created by the people of this planet, through their individual thought processes."

"Now you understand that your life is the way it is because of your beliefs about it. And now you understand that you can change it all by changing your thoughts and beliefs. We just have to remember, that the belief must come first - materialization follows."

"And what does God have to do with all this?" Kevin asked.

"Manuel said that God, or Dios, or the Source, or the Great Spirit, the One, the Is, the Force, the Godhead, the Unified Field, whatever you want to call it, is an energy field, a thinking energy field. And everything that exists, is made of the same stuff: Energy. Energy that is manipulated by thought."

"He said that evolution is the gestation period during which mankind masters the maintaining of the physical body and finally becomes self-aware through enlightenment."

"He said we are now nearing the end of the gestation period. It is time to realize the truth of our existence on a planetary scale."

"He said that each of us must choose. Choose to remain in the darkness of ignorance, believing we are separate entities controlled by fate and circumstances, or, awaken from the ignorance by understanding we are pieces of God-energy, able to change anything to our liking at will with our thoughts. There is no middle ground. No space between ignorance and knowledge. Knowledge reveals the state of grace, the Kingdom of Heaven, the attainment of Nirvana, the Oneness with Creation."

"He said each of us feels the urge to survive, because each of us has a task to perform, a desire to do something. As you fulfill your desires, using the power of thoughts and beliefs, you are completing the task for which you were created and furthering the evolutionary process."

"Manuel said that all obstacles we encounter are there to test the thoroughness of our understanding of this reality. And all the questions we have, are there to train us how to receive the answers from within. And all fears we have are there to remind us that we have not yet reached perfection."

"He said that each of us will reach perfection, or else be swept away; be dissolved back into the energy flow to be used for further creation."

"He said that enlightenment is followed by teaching, passing on the information to others."

"So what do you think?" I asked Kevin as he sat there, rhythmically tapping his fingers on the armrests of the chair.

"That's great. That's nice. A little wordy, but good."

"Is that all you can say?" I droned looking at him quizzically.

"Well," he said, folding his hands across his stomach. "I tend to live by an old Arab saying."

"What's that?"

"Trust in Allah, but tie your camel tight."

Chapter Twenty Four

Swinging lazily in the hammock on the back deck of the *Hooker* as she lay at anchor in the Manta harbor, I gazed at the wooden fishing boats anchored all around me as they swayed side to side in the mild swells that rolled into the harbor from the north. The wind on this fine, balmy day was gusting from the west mostly, except when it shifted to the south, or southwest. When it did, all the boats gracefully pivoted on their anchor lines, gradually realigning themselves so their bows sliced directly into the oncoming breeze.

Not all the boats moved at the same time. The bigger ones took longer to adjust, their weight and bulk requiring more air pressure against their superstructures to blow them into line. For this reason you always watched the small boats in a harbor when you came in to anchor. The small boats will tell you which direction the wind is coming from so you can anchor correctly. If treasure hunting had simple guidelines like anchoring, my life would have been a lot less complicated.

I was alone on the boat for a few days. The captain, Kevin and crew had all jumped ship to go sightseeing in different parts of Ecuador while I guarded the boat, waiting for new equipment to arrive. The rhythmic ocean swells kept the hammock swinging like a slow-moving pendulum while my mind contemplated the twisted, blustery, unproductive path I had taken so far to find sunken treasure. Without guidelines, I had been blown around by the conflicting winds of crooks and competitors and soothsayers, when all I wanted to do was anchor correctly ... over a wrecksite.

Sipping Colombian rum on ice, toes wiggling to the salsa music on the radio, I continued to swing away the afternoon in my hammock. No arguments to settle, no decisions to make, no breakdowns to fix. Just a quiet, peaceful day, temperature 88° in the shade.

Once in awhile a canoe would row by hauling fishermen out to their boats, or a school of silver flying-fish would spring out of the water, staying airborne above the surface for several seconds before submerging again beneath the waves. Lining the far shore of the harbor, a grove of tall palm trees bent and tossed in the shifting breeze. Days like these were the second best thing about treasure hunting, but they were few and far between, and I was determined to enjoy this one before the winds of change blew me onto another course.

In two days time a pinger-type sub-bottom profiler would arrive from England, sent by Steve, the fist-wielding British diver whose last words to me at the airport were, "This isn't over yet." Steve had decided I needed a more scientific search method. He had used his savings to rent a state-of-the-art profiler normally operated by big commercial diving companies searching for oil pipelines. The profiler would come with a technician and a helper who were to assemble and monitor the device during a thirty-day survey. So I had nothing to worry about. Modern technology would succeed where gizmos and wizards had failed. I rolled over in the hammock and took another sip of rum.

When the fancy sub-bottom profiler, and the two technicians, finally arrived from England, I was in Guayaquil to receive them. Right from the start the two men were bickering at each other. They also disagreed with me on how to conduct the survey. However, being professionals, we bit our lips and made the best of things.

The sensor end of the profiler was a canary-yellow, fiberglass canister the size of a roasting pot for cooking turkeys. Its manageable size was deceiving because it weighed over 100 pounds and required two people to move it. On board the *Hooker* it was mounted to a two-inch diameter metal pole and lowered ten inches into the water, just outside the wheelhouse door. The metal pole was then bolted to the hull of the boat.

The recording end of the profiler was set up in the wheelhouse and consisted of wires, amplifiers and a chart machine that drew a black and white rendition of everything buried in the ocean sediments. The profiler's sound waves penetrated fifty feet into the bottom, all the way to bedrock. As soon as the thing was working, we headed the *Hooker* back out to the bay where we knew the galleon had been lost on some rocks. Up to this point, we had never found the rocks, even after a week of visual survey dives. The natural bottom of the bay was flat terrain like a desert.

Zach, our captain, used the global positioning system to make straight runs, parallel to the beach. Two divers were using the launch to place bright orange buoys across the width of the bay. Once Zach drove the *Hooker* by a buoy, the launch crew picked up the buoy and moved it fifty feet further offshore. At the end of a run Zach would turn the boat around in a wide loop, line up with the buoys in their new position, and traverse back across the bay.

Back and forth. Back and forth. Boring work, especially when nothing is showing up on the chart recorder. Back and forth for six days. From sun-up to sun-down. Back and forth. Over one hundred passes to cover a distance of one mile from shore. And then… something happened. Something big and dark registered on the chart recorder. Something that altered the sound waves that were bouncing off it. Everybody scrambled to the wheelhouse to see what it was.

"It's the treasure!" I grinned, clapping my hands with delight.

"We don't know what it is yet." The technician cautioned.

"It's the treasure all right." I repeated. "It's screaming up at us, 'here I am, here I am.'"

"Don't get so excited Margee," Charlie warned me, "Stay calm."

"It's probably geologic," the technician stated apathetically.

"What's that mean?" I asked, swallowing hard.

"It means it's a rock," Charlie said.

"Let's go over it again," I insisted, giving a nod to Zach.

"Oh, no you don't." shouted the technician's helper as he came through the wheelhouse door. "We stick to the survey course till we're finished. Then we go back and mark the targets."

"We'll lose it if we don't mark it now," I replied.

"We have the latitude and longitude coordinates." the helper pressed. "We can get back to the target later."

"The hell with coordinates," I sneered. "This positioning system is only good to within three hundred feet. I've been out here long enough to know we may *never* get back to it. Mark it now."

"I knew this was going to happen," the helper said looking to the ceiling. "Non-technical personnel never understand the proper procedure for a successful survey. You don't stop in the middle to mark targets. You're wasting time and money. You might never finish the survey."

"Where's your priorities, man?" I pleaded, "The objective is not to finish the survey, the objective is to find something. Non-treasure hunting personnel never understand that. Now excuse me."

I brushed the helper aside and picked-up the radio mike. Holding the transmit button down, I told the guys in the launch to leave the buoys in position and return to the *Hooker*.

"This will certainly go in my report to Steve." the helper said stiffly, bending down to murmur something to the technician. The rest of the wheelhouse was silent.

"Report whatever you want." I said without interest. "Just please relocate that target and let one of the divers go down and drive a couple of stakes into the bottom. Then I'm sure I can get back to it."

The rest of the survey was a tug of war between my philosophy and the technician's, but the job got done and the technicians and equipment returned to England.

As soon as we could, we positioned the *Hooker* over the area where the big, dark images had appeared on the chart recorder. The divers dug a huge hole and encountered a solid, hard-clay structure at about eight feet under the sediment. They excavated down one side of the structure until it met bedrock. Then Charlie dove down into the hole to take a look around.

"There's something down here," Charlie radioed through the diver communication system. "Wait a minute. I think I got a hold of it."

347

Like an anxious football team huddling around the quarterback, we all crouched around the communication speaker again. Adrenaline was suddenly surging through us like fire racing up a trail of gasoline. We were zapped into a state of alert. Our breathing was shallow and rapid.

"What is it?" we radioed back expectantly, impatiently.

"It's heavy. And squishy." Charlie answered, breathing strenuously, as water gurgled around his diving helmet. "It's about three feet long. I think it's... yeah, it's a piece of wood!"

It was wood all right. A smooth-sided, half-round hunk of spongy hardwood that was later carbon-dated to be slightly over 400 years old.

The hard-clay structure we'd uncovered was actually a broad rock formation. Several formations were scattered over an area of a quarter mile. Four hundred years ago the sediment layer was lower, so the tops of the formations would have been sticking up out of the sediment, looking like a scattered group of rocks.

Rocks! That's it! The rocks where the galleon had struck bottom and started to crack up. We'd finally found something. We'd found the rocks that showed on the old treasure map! Oh the joy of discovery. We were all smiling like lottery winners when Charlie came out of the water.

"It's a piece of wood from the shipwreck!" Charlie shouted as he peeled off his wetsuit and hosed himself down with fresh water. "It's gotta be. Look at all the wormholes in it."

We all inspected the wood carefully, passing it back and forth amongst ourselves as if it was a new toy that we all wanted to play with. The rest of the wreck couldn't be very far away.

Everyone started talking about being rich and what they would buy first. Zach and Kevin had narrowed it down to the three L's: Lexus, Laser-disk and Large-screen TV. I let the crew thoroughly savor the moment before I told them we were out of money again.

That single piece of wood kept me going for the next two years. Actually, the wood, and Aly Bruner.

Kevin and I had found Aly on the front page of the Life-Styles section of the Sunday newspaper back in 1985. In the picture he sat behind an ornate desk with his Cheshire-cat grin, surrounded by jewelry, furs and Victorian antiques, as if he could sell you something just by looking at you. The article told how Aly, from humble beginnings, had become a self-made millionaire as a wheeler-dealer in the diamonds and antiques business. But Kevin recognized Aly as an old student from scuba school classes.

"Now here's someone who would invest in a treasure hunt," Kevin commented as he held up Aly's picture from the newspaper. "This guy's crazy."

The next morning we were in Aly's office.

"I like to shock people," Aly said as he played with a dozen large diamonds he had spread on a black velvet pad on the desk in front of him. He gave me the impression of a prowler, always on the lookout for an undervalued piece of history, or a perfectly cut gem. He was six-foot five with large round eyes and blue hair tightly-wound in dread-locks, curling to his shoulders.

When I told him about our expedition to recover Spanish treasure, he called his secretary in to make out a check for ten thousand dollars. Over the years Aly became my largest investor and best friend. We were in the hunt together, to the bitter end, whatever it took. I braving the South American government and treacherous ocean; he steadfastly supporting me with money, advice and a shoulder to lean on.

"Just bring up one coin and I can get you millions for the expedition." Aly kept telling me.

"I'm trying, I'm trying," I kept saying.

As the years went by, it got harder and harder to find investors. The wood I had found was nice, but it didn't prove I had a wreck with treasure on it.

Now it was 1994, and I was desperate for cash to keep things going. We had tried another new technology that colorized the readings from the sub-bottom profiler according to the density of the objects it passed over. We had several good targets to dig on, but no money to get to Ecuador to do the digging.

The recession of the early 90's had taken its toll on spendable cash. All the gamblers had vanished like a passing fad. Even Aly couldn't find us a buyer. None of the people who had promised money came through, painfully reminding me, that verbal commitments for money, have as much substance as a fart in a tornado.

Of all the potential investors I came across, none were more devastating to my psychological foundations than the guy from New York.

For eight months I dealt with a guy named Joe, from an international finance company that placed large investments in a variety of projects. After I'd satisfied all his inquiries and complied with all his demands, he had agreed to invest two million dollars to complete our entire project. I spent all the cash I had left to pay for legal fees and when the documents were ready to close the deal, I flew to New York to meet Joe. When I got to his office, it was completely empty. Joe had disappeared.

On the plane coming back from New York I covered my face with my hands and cried softly. From my window seat, looking down over the central plains, I admitted to myself that I had failed. I was forty thousand dollars in debt with zero income. Worst of all, Kevin was stuck on the boat in Ecuador, tied to the pilings, eating boiled cabbage and beans.

At home that night I stared at myself in the bathroom mirror, trying to see if some exterior part of me had changed - some visible scars marking my failure. I felt empty, exhausted. All I saw were the wrinkles around my eyes that had deepened from squinting so much in the sun.

For hours I oscillated between sulking at the foot of my bed and staring myself down in the mirror. I realized that all I had were stories to tell and a few artifacts gathering dust.

With the last credit card I had I finally flew back to Guayaquil to spend Christmas with Kevin. He hated Ecuador now; hated staying on the boat; hated the endless waiting; hated the pills he was taking to kill the amoebas in his intestines. But he wouldn't quit unless I did. He wouldn't have it on his conscience that he gave up before I did.

Dense, sagging clouds hung over Guayaquil the day after Christmas, turning the river to pearl gray as it swirled past the pilings and ropes that held the *Hooker* in place. I stood at the railing and watched Kevin stroll down the dock, a backpack slung over his shoulder. He wanted a few days off the boat; said it was my turn to be guard. I watched as he got in a taxi and drove out of sight, leaving me alone to contemplate our future.

I felt sick to my stomach. A headache started throbbing at my temples, inching its way up to the top of my head. I was dizzy, feverish, weak at the knees. I had to grab the railing to steady myself. My body jerked in spasms, vomit raged up through my throat and spewed out over the railing into the river. I was shaking now, searching for someplace to sit down. What was wrong with me?

Carefully I eased myself around the engine room door and sat on the bench seat on the back deck, trying to breath calmly. Just as I wiped my mouth in my shirt sleeve I felt a hot stinger of acid-tasting liquid jut up from the pit of my stomach again and I dashed for the railing. Again and again I vomited over the side of the boat. This must be food poisoning from breakfast I was thinking as I gasped for air. It'll pass.

Twenty minutes later I was at the railing again. The purging process continued into the evening, leaving my body weaker and more dehydrated. I slept fitfully that night and in the morning I drank only water. A few minutes later I vomited the water so I just lay in my bunk, all day long, without eating. The next day I was so weak I could hardly walk. I knew something was terribly wrong as I leaned against the walls to keep from falling to my knees.

Outside, on the back deck, I knew I had to make it to shore to get help. My breathing was shallow, I couldn't yell. I had difficulty lifting my arms high enough to climb over the railing and lower myself into the rubber dinghy. It was hard to concentrate. What illness did I have? What could make me this sick? Maybe it's cholera, that horrid disease that makes you shit and puke yourself to death in a matter of days. I was afraid, thinking I'd waited too long. I might be beyond treatment. I'll die before Kevin returns.

I fell to the floorboards of the dinghy and lay there awhile before finding enough strength to pull the cord on the outboard motor. I knew I couldn't swim. The firemen on the red fireboat two hundred feet away, were watching me uneasily, sensing something was wrong. They saw me stagger and fall as I limply pulled again on the starter cord. They had no small boat to rescue me. I'd have to make it ashore myself.

Finally, in a supreme effort that sapped all my strength, I pulled the cord with both hands and the motor revved up in a billow of blue smoke. I slouched on the floorboards with my head hung low, fighting the dizziness. I crashed into the dock beside the fireboat and was lifted to land by the firemen all talking at once.

"La clinica," I whispered breathlessly just before I doubled over in pain. With two of the firemen under each arm, I was dragged to the clinic five blocks from the boat, then I passed out.

❦

"She's forty percent dehydrated," the doctor said, adjusting the solution bags on the metal stand next to my bed. "We'll have to restore her body fluids before we can fight the infection."

"What's wrong with her?" Julieta asked in distress, clutching the metal rail at the foot of the bed.

"We don't know yet," was the reply. "It could be just intestinal intoxication but we're treating her for everything, malaria, typhoid and yellow fever. I need more needles and this list of medication quickly."

"Julieta," I moaned, still delirious. "Tell them to use new needles, I can afford new needles."

"AY, Margarita, qué te pasa?" Julieta said, patting my foot, astonished that I was talking. "Don't worry, this is a good doc…"

I didn't hear the rest, I passed out again.

Hours later I woke up, still in my clothes, alone on a bare, foam mattress, in a room no bigger than a jail cell. My right arm was strapped to the metal bed frame and two needles were dripping fluids into the back of my hand. The tiny cement room was barren except for a chair and a plain wooden table at my bedside covered with needle wrappers and medication bottles. I stared at the cracks in the ceiling. I was alive.

My next thought was, why am I here? Not in the sense of my current condition, but in the larger sense, the big picture. Why was I still here in Ecuador? All I'd managed to do was spend people's money with nothing but some old wood to show for it. Nothing to really prove there was any treasure at all. So why was I still here? Was I hanging on because I was too ashamed to quit? Was this a case of destructive obsession? Was it all just for Kevin?

In that moment, in that instant of humility, I let go. I released my attachment to the goal. I had been so wound up in forcing my discovery of treasure, that I had forgotten one of the most important steps in fulfilling any desire: Relinquish your attachment to the goal.

It was Dr. Deepak Chopra who explained that there is a precise mechanism through which all desires can be manifest. That it is a four step process based on the understanding that the source of all material reality is God, which is pure energy, pure self. And that the self is not in the realm of conscious thought, it's in the gap between our thoughts, the place where we quiet our minds and enter into a higher mental state of being.

Dr. Chopra says the gap is the window, the corridor, the transformational vortex through which the personal psyche communicates with the cosmic psyche, meaning God. And that in the gap you have the potential to organize and orchestrate the details required, to effect any outcome.

So the first step in manifesting your desires, is to slip into the gap between thoughts. Get in tune with the energy field on a direct wavelength.

Second, have a clear intention of your goal, in the gap. Make a clear picture of what you want, then make an irrevocable decision to go for it, a decision not countermanded by any other conflicting thoughts or desires or activities.

Third, you relinquish your attachment to the goal, because chasing the goal, or getting attached to it, stops the goal from materializing.

And fourth, you let the universe handle the details. You must only be alert for the opportunities that the universe presents you.[8]

In other words, what you direct your mind to think about, after you have shut out the noises of the world and are in direct communication with the energy field, causes the universe to bring before you all the people, things and circumstances you need, to create what it is you are thinking about. You simply have to look for the pieces as you encounter them in your life.

And why does this four step process work? Because it is the nature of physical reality to respond to thought.

Physical reality is what we experience as events or matter. Physicists tell us that all matter is made up of atoms. That atoms are made up of sub-atomic particles. And that sub-atomic particles are impulses of energy and information. So the atom, which is the basic unit of matter, is not a solid entity, it is energy and information.

Thoughts are also impulses of energy and information. So thoughts and sub-atomic particles (matter) are made of the same stuff: Energy and information.

A sub-atomic particle is literally created by you and me by the mere act of putting our attention on it. This is proven by quantum field theorists whose unified field theory defines the universe as "a field of all possibilities" made up of sub-atomic particles, which they call "probability amplitudes" (impulses of energy and information). They say that the universe is a huge limitless void of probability amplitudes and that whether or not a probability amplitude passes from energy form, into physical form, depends on whether or not we are putting our attention on it. It is attention that transforms a certain probability amplitude, into material existence. So ultimately, whatever we experience in our life is the result of our attention (what we think about).

Therefore, if we direct our attention (our thoughts), we can choose which events or matter we want to come into material existence. And, if we improve the quality of our thoughts (meaning how we think, and under what circumstances we spend time thinking), we improve the exactness and speed that sub-atomic particles are transformed into physical reality. In other words, physical reality responds to thought.

Suddenly my body relaxed. Something inside me breathed a sigh of relief, a release of conflict, a recognition of truth. I finally understood that our minds are little factories that take our thoughts and automatically form them into physical reality. Just like our lungs automatically breathe and our hearts automatically beat.

I knew what I had to do next. I had to kick off the training wheels. I had to put the theories into practice. I had to take the leap of faith.

Chapter Twenty Five

When you finally give in to it. When you finally stop doubting the fact that your thoughts create what you experience. When you finally put your faith in the process and start purposefully using your thoughts to produce outcomes you desire, you discover a prodigious treasure... that as you believe, so it is with you.

After I was released from the clinic in Guayaquil I started looking at the treasure hunt from a whole different perspective; from the point of view that matter and events are caused by thought.

Whatever I needed, I simply thought about it in the way the books described and watched for it to appear. Of course I always needed money, but instead of chasing every investor I heard about and worrying over the bills, I created the attitude that I always had money whenever I needed it.

Every time I felt myself getting nervous and anxious about money, I sought out a quiet room, calmed myself with deep breaths, slipped into the state of mind that I was part of the creative energy of the universe and pictured in my mind, what I wanted to happen in my life.

I mentally created scenes in precise details down to the color and feel of objects. I envisioned the object in my hands, touched it with my fingers, felt the texture of it. Then I imagined the internal feeling of having the object in my possessio possession0y possession, the *knowing* that it was already mine. A smile would appear on my face as I mentally felt the joy of having what I wanted and I held onto that feeling as long as I could. Then I continued with my day's activities, trusting that the universe would place the desired object in my path.

There were no overnight miracles. As with anything we learn to do, it takes time, and practice. And the more we practice something, the more proficient we become. Although it was never instantaneous, eventually, I always received what I thought about. Sometimes it was days later, sometimes it was weeks. I found I could not plan how or when an object would come to me, but as long as I kept looking for it with the knowing attitude that it would appear, it always did.

I found that smaller, inanimate objects were quicker to appear in my life than larger desires that involved other people. I also found that the more I trusted the manifestation process, the more anger and fear disappeared from my life. I was happier. Life's problems didn't bother me as much. I saw that everybody's life is exactly what they think it is, and everybody gets exactly what they think they will get.

So I thought about investors handing me checks and it happened. In the spring of 1996 we returned to Manta with our salvage boat and all the divers. But this time I started thinking about finding the shipwreck the way the books described.

That's when the local Ecuadorian divers started showing me where they had been finding pottery.

They sighted off hills and trees, a dead-reckoning method of marking a spot. All of them took us to the same area.

We brought the *Hooker* to the area and dove around ourselves in all directions, then sucked the sediment away with our air-lift to check the pockets and crevices in the ocean floor. We found large, broken pieces of red clay pottery scattered all over the bottom. The pottery matched my pictures of sixteenth century Spanish olive jars. Even after all these years I still felt the surge of excitement, the thrilling rush of adrenaline at finding a piece of history.

That season we recovered over three hundred fragments of Spanish pottery and one jar almost totally intact. We had found a debris field, the first sign that we were closing in on the site of a shipwreck. However, pottery can float a long way so we still needed our survey equipment to detect the bulk of the wreck.

At the end of the season we photographed and inventoried the pottery fragments and turned them over to the Port Captain of Manta, who sent them to the Central Bank Museum to await the division process. Our contracts with the Ecuadorian government had always said we would receive half of everything we recovered.

On a bright Tuesday morning in the middle of June, I stood beside my Ecuadorian partner, Pancho, as I stared down at all the pottery we had laid out on the floor of the Central Bank Museum. The Port Captain was there in his crisp white uniform as was the Director of the museum, a red-headed lady in a blue dress whose only desire was to get the division completed so the pottery could be moved.

The last people to show up were the representatives of the Cultural Heritage Institute. There were three of them. They were an hour late. They took one look at the pottery on the floor and said, "This is all cultural heritage of Ecuador, we're taking all of it."

The relative decorum that had presided during the first few minutes of the meeting turned to restrained antagonism, then outright attack. I gritted my teeth and showed the contract. The three representatives ignored it. The yelling lasted an hour before the Port Captain decided the meeting was over and the division was impossible to accomplish until some higher authority settled the controversy. We ended up with nothing.

Over the months that followed we wrote letters, met with lawyers, and I was interviewed on television and in newspapers again. We called in every favor we had, but we still ended up with nothing.

I should have quit then. I should have packed up my marbles and moved on, found a different career, one that didn't depend on government bureaucrats. But I didn't. The pottery had fueled the quest and the manifestation process had made me feel indestructible, like I had a magic wand capable of dissolving all obstacles in my path.

Even though all of the anomalies that our scientific surveys had detected, had turned out to be rocks, I still couldn't stop. There was one last anomaly to investigate and I figured that the last anomaly, had to be our shipwreck. I left Pancho and Julieta to solve the division problem with the government and I returned to California to present our situation to the investors.

"We have one target left." I told my partners at the partnership meeting. We had all crammed into the living room at an investor's house. Chairs had been hastily arranged around the room but most people were standing at the back, squished shoulder to shoulder. "But I'm afraid we'll never know if that last target was the wreck or not, because we're out of money."

The murmuring started. The closely packed room seemed to come alive with movement as heads turned around, whispered conversations grew louder and hand signals were flashed back and forth. Behind me, on the dining room table, I had spread out all the data and readouts from our surveys. I had even displayed a third historical map that told of a shipwreck in Manta Bay.

I felt that familiar surge starting inside me again, a gust of energy lifting my spirits. It always happened when I got to talking about the shipwreck, trying to convince someone to invest. I kept giving them information about the target until someone uttered those wonderful words.

"So how much money do you need to check out that last target?"

By the end of February 1997 I had collected another ninety thousand dollars, and realized that treasure hunting was still like poker; you gotta ante-up if you want to see the last card.

It was a major effort to get the wheels of the expedition rolling again. The *Hooker* had to be drydocked. Permits, visas, boat registrations, all the paperwork had to be updated. A new anchor winch and life boat had to be shipped to Ecuador. I rounded up the crew again and even Zach returned to pilot the *Hooker* back to Manta one more time. When he arrived at the dock with his duffel bag and diving helmet, Zach handed me a plastic coated piece of paper that said:

Treasure Hunting in three easy steps;

1. Find hat

2. Insert hand

3. Pull out rabbit.

I spent almost a third of the money to rent a sophisticated Differential Global Positioning System (DGPS) to link up with our magnetometer by computer. The positioning system would keep our survey lines accurate to one meter, only a three foot error factor. Considering we were off as much as three hundred feet on previous surveys, it was worth the money.

The *Hooker* was still in drydock when the technicians and the DGPS arrived, so I took everybody to Manta by bus and we worked out of a hotel for four weeks. I kept the coordinates of our final target in my purse with me so I'd have them ready. Also so nobody could steal them from me. That purse was always slung around my neck, except when I slept with it under my pillow.

The DGPS had to be calibrated and a base station set up on land in a location where no obstacles were between it and the survey launch. The only safe place I could find, that was right on the beach, was the dump pile in the back of a fish packing plant. We had to enclose the unit in a plastic box to keep out the ants, beetles, cockroaches, mosquitoes, lizards, dragonflies and maggots.

Every morning at 6 AM we loaded all the gear onto our twenty-five foot fiberglass launch named *Grey Lightning*. Once the launch took off, I continued on to the fish packing plant, where an upside-down bucket was my chair and some rotten, smelly cardboard was my makeshift canopy to protect me from the blazing sun. All day long I sat beside the base station antenna while the technicians tried to tune in the system.

Day after day they fiddled with wires and computer programs, calling me on the hand-held radio to reset the base station every half hour or so. Finally the day came to hand over my coordinates to the technicians so we could survey the target site. Then it rained. A torrential downpour that flooded the Manta River and sent tons of mud all over the main streets, stopping traffic in every direction. We sat in the hotel.

"Maybe the universe is against us," I pondered as the five of us sat around the table at the hotel restaurant, an old rusty ceiling fan whirling slowly above our heads.

"No, Margee, this is just life." said one of the divers. "The universe is neither for us nor against us. It just generates the energy."

"Hey, the rain's letting up," sparked another diver. "Let's get out there and mag. I'm stoked."

With the sun streaking through breaks in the clouds, the launch headed out to sea and I took up my position at the dump pile alongside the base antenna. After five hours of magging, the radio crackled. They were calling me from the launch.

"Shore patrol, this is *Grey Lightning*, over."

"This is Shore Patrol, go ahead *Lightning*." I answered.

"Yeah Shore Patrol, we've got some sharks out here, over."

"Well check them out closer," I said excitedly. "I'll meet you at the dock in an hour."

Adrenaline raced through my body like an electrical shock as I hurried to cover up the base station and gather my bags and water jug. Oh, this is it, this is it, I kept hearing inside my head. Sharks, was our code word for some serious magnetometer readings. My fingers were tingling. A hundred thoughts at once were clamoring for attention in my brain, flashing like neon signs.

363

By the time I reached the dock the sun was sitting flat-bottom on the horizon, casting a burnt-orange luminescence on the thinning cirrus clouds that rippled across the sky. The divers and technicians looked as excited as I had been, so I knew it wasn't a false alarm.

"These readings look real good," One of the technicians said. "There's definitely something down there."

It took us two more weeks to find out what was actually down there. The *Hooker* had to be brought up from Guayaquil, the observer from the government had to be assigned to us and all the rigging had to be set up to support the dive operation. Hoses, couplings, safety lines, all the paraphernalia of a treasure hunt strung all over the boat so we could dig down through the sediment to the treasure.

When it was all ready and the first diver jumped into the ocean, his umbilical hose slinking into the water behind him, I grabbed Kevin's hand and we both stood at the railing watching the bubbles ascend in rhythmic bursts. Minutes ticked by as the air compressors revved up, the diver was engaging the air lift to suck up the sediment. Billows of mud and pebbles exploded on the surface of the ocean, churning and spiraling outward from the end of the air-lift tube in a brown stain carried east by the current.

It didn't take long, twenty minutes or so. The diver didn't say anything over the communication system, he just reported that he was coming back up. I squeezed Kevin's hand tighter. My gut was twisting with anticipation. I'd been waiting fifteen years for this moment.

When the diver was finally standing on the deck and his helmet was pulled off his head he looked at me squarely and said, "I'm sorry,

Margee. It's modern wreckage. Some chain and steel barrels and a big anchor with Danforth flukes. It's not the galleon."

I dropped my head to my chest. No tears, just exhaustion, a big emptiness welling up inside me like the vastness of space with nothing to grab onto. I didn't have to say anything. Everybody knew there were no more targets to dig on. Everybody knew this was the end.

We quit searching for the wreck on May 4, 1997, exactly 407 years to the day after the galleon had supposedly sunk in the Bay of Manta in 1590. There were still hundreds of things to be done before Kevin and I could actually shut down the operation and leave Ecuador for good, but on May fourth we officially admitted we couldn't find the wreck.

We pulled up all the dive hoses for the last time and headed the *Hooker's Holiday* back into the Manta harbor. It felt like a funeral. After several days of cleaning and packing the divers boarded the plane that took them back to the United States, leaving Kevin and me with the boat, and just enough money to make it home ourselves.

We were sad, and tired, and relieved. It was finally over, finished. All the years of searching had ended in frustration, the sour taste of defeat. I resigned myself to it. Most treasure hunts end this way; not finding the treasure. For me though it seemed like a double defeat. Kevin was scoffing at my experiment with thoughts creating reality, said he knew all along it wouldn't work, said he didn't believe the treasure was where we were looking anyway.

❦

Back in California I was faced with a mountain of paperwork. I formally closed the Partnership, said goodbye to all my partners and filed bankruptcy. A few months later Kevin and I were divorced. I passed through all of it in a bit of a haze, going through the motions, fulfilling my obligations. I didn't care anymore about success and I was certainly devoid of any attachment to the treasure. I'd lost everything.

A year later I returned to Ecuador to sell the boat. My Ecuadorian partners were still trying to get our half of the pottery from the government, saying it would be any day now. I busied myself with cleaning the boat and showing it to buyers until I got an all cash offer, less than half what the boat was worth.

On my last day in Ecuador, after I had gathered my few personal belongings from the boat and packed them in my suitcase, I was feeling free for the first time in years. I locked up the boat and flagged down a passing canoe to take me to the dock. I decided not to look back as I climbed the dock ramp and walked through the park along the waterfront street that had been my second home for so long. The firemen waved sadly adios. The beggars still tugged at my shirt for handouts and the iguanas still rustled in the trees above my head.

My plane ticket was sticking out the side pocket of my suitcase as I waited on the street corner for a taxi to take me to the airport. I was wondering what I would do next, now that my treasure hunting days were over, when an elderly, withered man approached me, asking politely if he could speak to me for a moment.

His Spanish was slurred. He was thin and bent, his chestnut colored skin stretched tight over the bones in his wrists. We walked to a park bench and sat down together facing the river, still in sight of the *Hooker* floating lazily beside her pilings. He made sure we were alone before he started talking.

"I have something to show you," he said as he opened the dirty cloth bag he was carrying and emptied its contents into my hands.

A dozen silver, Spanish coins toppled out of the bag, clinking into my palms as he told me his story. He said he knew where the galleon was at, that he'd found it when he was a boy diving in deep water, looking for octopus. He had seen a wooden head in the shape of a lion sticking out of the sand, but when he grabbed it, it broke off in his hands. He brought it to the surface and put it in his canoe. When he dove down again and scratched in the sediment, he found the few coins I held in my hands before his air pump stopped working and he had to surface and return home to fix it. There was a bad storm that night and when he tried to return to the place the next day he could find no trace of the broken-off, wooden masthead. The sediment had covered over everything. He had told no one of his find. He didn't trust the rich people of Manta or his friends or the government. But he did know how to get back to the spot.

Then he pulled something out of his pocket. He unfolded a worn, dog-eared map of Manta Bay and pointed his brown, weathered finger at a tiny "x" marked in pencil.

"Here it is." he whispered, checking around us to see if anyone was listening. "I've kept this secret all my life, until I saw you on television. You can dig up the treasure with your boat."

I wistfully glanced up at the *Hooker* knowing she was no longer mine. Then I glanced back at the old man's map, seeing that his "x" was about a quarter mile beyond where we had stopped searching for the wreck. Then I leaned back on the park bench, cupping the coins in my hands and realized that I'd created this reality, that my belief had actually manifested itself after all. Someone had finally shown me exactly where the treasure was.

A part of me knew I could pull all the pieces together again to go dig up the treasure. Another part of me knew all the problems that would besiege me if I did. Then a greater part of me took hold and I knew I didn't need the treasure. I didn't want it. I had proved to myself that thoughts create reality and that was more valuable to me than the treasure.

A deep sense of fulfillment swept over me with that realization. My insides felt the contentment of a journey's end. I could stop now. My search was over. I'd found what I was looking for.

"Señor," I said, hauling in a deep breath as I handed back his coins, "Thank you for trusting me, but you keep your secret. I want to do something else with my life now."

"Are you crazy?" he stared at me in wide-eyed disbelief. "What's more important than the treasure? Where are you going?"

"I'm going back to another dream I left many years ago." I said as I stood and waved at a taxi just rounding the corner. "I'm going back to my ranch!" Then I got in the taxi and drove away.

Epilogue

I got all the way to the airport before I realized I was a fool. No one would ever believe I had found the treasure unless I touched it with my own hands. The universe had handed me the location of the shipwreck, and like an idiot, I was walking away. Maybe I am crazy? No I'm not. I ordered the taxicab driver to take me back to the water front and as we turned the corner, I saw the old man still sitting on the park bench.

"I guess I'm not so crazy," I said to the old man as I sat down beside him on the bench. "Treasure is important. Are you still willing to take me to your spot?"

"Yes, yes señora," the old man beamed, his smile stretched from ear to ear. Then he cleared his throat and looked at me earnestly. "But I get ten percent."

"Of course you do," I laughed. "Everybody wants a percentage."

"Will you come to Manta with me now?"

"Sure. Just let me get some diving gear and a metal detector off the boat. What's your name, Señor?"

"Enrique," he said, puffing out his chest. "And you are La Bucanera."

"Evidently," I grinned, as I shook his weathered hand.

We took the bus to Manta and lugged my equipment down to the beach where Enrique had his own fiberglass fishing boat. It was exactly like the launch my crew had used for magnetometer surveys.

It was late afternoon when we motored out of the harbor. The wind had died down and the sea was as smooth as silk. I scrunched down in the boat so nobody could see me until we had cleared the harbor entrance and no other boats were around. Then I watched Enrique line up his land markings to return to his spot. It all seemed so magical, so unmistakably right.

We circled a few times, until Enrique nodded at me to drop the anchor, then he shut off the motor and the boat swung around into the current.

"The water is very clear today," Enrique said as he threw another line into the water with a heavy rock tied to the end. "It's about twenty meters deep here."

"I'm just going down to look around," I said as I struggled into my wetsuit. "I'll only be down for about fifteen minutes."

I didn't want to tell him that I was a little scared. I always had someone else with me, when I was diving off the *Hooker*. I tied a rope around my waist and told Enrique to pull me up if I was longer than thirty minutes. He nodded vigorously.

I was getting uncomfortably hot inside the wetsuit by the time I had all my gear on and I was sitting on the edge of the boat, ready to fall backwards into the water. My heart was thumping like a jackhammer. I put the regulator in my mouth and breathed deeply until I was calm enough to splash into the ocean. The shock of the cold water made me shiver as Enrique handed the metal detector to me and I let the air out of my safety vest. I grabbed the extra line and followed it down to the ocean floor, descending into darker green water.

When I touched bottom, I fumbled with the metal detector to get it turned on and adjusted the earphones on my head. Then I tied a small string to the line with the rock, so I had a center point. I swam circles around the rock, letting out more string each time I completed a circle. I could see about thirty feet ahead of me, but there was nothing to see. The bottom was just a flat surface of mud with some ripples in it.

I was just finishing my tenth circle when the detector blasted my ears with a high-pitched squeal. My hands were shaking as I swept the detector back and forth over a wide area and determined where the squeal was the loudest. Then I set the detector on the bottom and started digging.

Billowy clouds of murky water were forming all around me as I dug with my hands into the soft, sandy mud. A few inches down I rechecked the spot with the metal detector and heard the same high-pitched squeal. I dug down about a foot and checked again. Now I was pawing at the sediment with both hands like a dog digging up a bone. The only sound was my heavy breathing as the air bubbles rumbled past my head. Then I felt something... something hard.

"Please don't be a rock," I was praying to myself as I cleared away more mud and wedged my fingers around the thing, to scoop it out of the hole. Slowly the silt trickled off the object and I sat down on the ocean floor to gaze at it.

I stopped breathing.

I think my heart stopped too.

There, in the palm of my hand, was a solid gold figurine with intricate details. It had a tiny face and hands with jewelry and clothing carved on it like an Inca ruler. I stared at it for the longest time, thinking of all the treasure that was buried under the sediment around me. Then I heard myself giggling and my smile was so wide that sea water was seeping into the corners of my mouth. I shouted, "HALLELUJAH!" in my brain then I stood up and did a little dance, flapping my fins up and down like a drunken duck.

"I found it, I found it," I was yelling into my regulator. I was so happy I just wanted to float away. I'd found proof that the treasure existed. Fifteen years of my life hadn't been wasted. I slid the gold piece up the sleeve of my wetsuit and was picking up the detector when I felt Enrique's tug at the rope around my waist. I swam up to the surface and Enrique helped me climb into the boat.

I didn't say anything, I just pulled the gold piece out of my sleeve and handed it to him. He cradled it in his hands as if it was a delicate flower, then he hugged me profusely.

"I can't dig up the treasure," I told him as we sat on opposite sides of the boat, facing each other.

"Why not?" he pleaded.

"Because your current government doesn't honor its contracts. We'd never get any of the treasure."

"Let's steal it then," he smiled.

"You can," I smiled back. "I'll give you the metal detector and this diving equipment. I have to do some fine tuning on my mental processes before I dig up any more treasure. I have to think about keeping it, not just finding it."

"But if you can't dig up *this* treasure, what will you do?

With a wink I flashed him a buccaneer's grin and said, "I know where there's a wreck in the Azores."

NOTES

[1] God, <u>The Impersonal Life</u> (California: DiVross & Compnay, 1941), 61.

[2] Jane Roberts, <u>The Nature of Personal Reality</u> (New York: Bantam Books).

[3] John Randolph Price, <u>The Manifestation Process</u>
(Texas: Quartus Foundation, 1983), 1-4.

[4] <u>The Harvard Classics Vol. 7</u> (New York: Collier & Sons Corp.);
<u>The Crown Treasury of Relevent Quotations</u> (New York: Crown Publishers, Inc.);
<u>The Book of Unusual Quotations</u> (New York: Harper & Brothers.)

[5] James Allen, <u>As A Man Thinketh</u> (Pennsylvania: Runnin Press, 1989), 11.

[6] Murphy, Eddie, "Eddie Murphy Interview" (February 1990), <u>Playboy Magazine</u>.

[7] <u>Ocean Scenes</u> (New York: Leavitt & Allen Publishers, 1855), 71.

[8] Chopra, Deepak, <u>Creating Affluence</u>, excerpts read by the author.
California: Amber Allen Publishing and New World Library, 1993.

SOURCES CONSULTED

Allen, James. As A Man Thinketh. Pennsylvania: Runnin Press, 1989.

Chopra, Deepak. Creating Affluence. Excerpts read by the author.
California: Amber-Allen Publishing and New World Library, 1993.

Murphy, Eddie. "Eddie Murphy Interview." (February 1990). Playboy Magazine.

Price, John Randolph. The Manifestation Process
Texas: Quartus Foundation, 1983.

Roberts, Jane. The Nature of Personal Reality. New York: Bantam Books.

God. The Impersonal Life. California: DiVorss & Company, 1941.

Ocean Scenes. New York: Leavitt & Allen Publishers, 1855.

The Book of Unusual Quotations. New York: Harper & Brothers.

The Crown Treasury of Relevant Quotations. New York: Crown Publishers Inc.

The Harvard Classics Vol. 7. New York: Collier & Sons Corp.

Authentic Treasure Maps
of Ecuador

Through extensive research in the archives of Ecuador, Peru, England and Spain, many locations of shipwrecks off the coast of Ecuador were discovered. Here is your chance to own these maps for your own personal use and enjoyment.

Each map is $1000.00 and includes shipping charges.

Fill out the order form below and make your check payable to

Comet Shipping Corporation

Mail to:
Comet Shipping Corp.
P.O. Box 1351
Pleasanton, CA 94566
U.S.A.

Please allow 3-4 weeks for delivery - Do not send cash

Name _____

Address _____

City_____ State _____ Zip _____

Please send me the selected maps I have circled below. Enclosed is my (check or money order) — for $1000.00 per map.

Manta Bay   Island of Santa Clara

River Colanche   River Jama

Bay of San Matheo (Esmeralda)
